Offensive Films

Offensive Films

Mikita Brottman

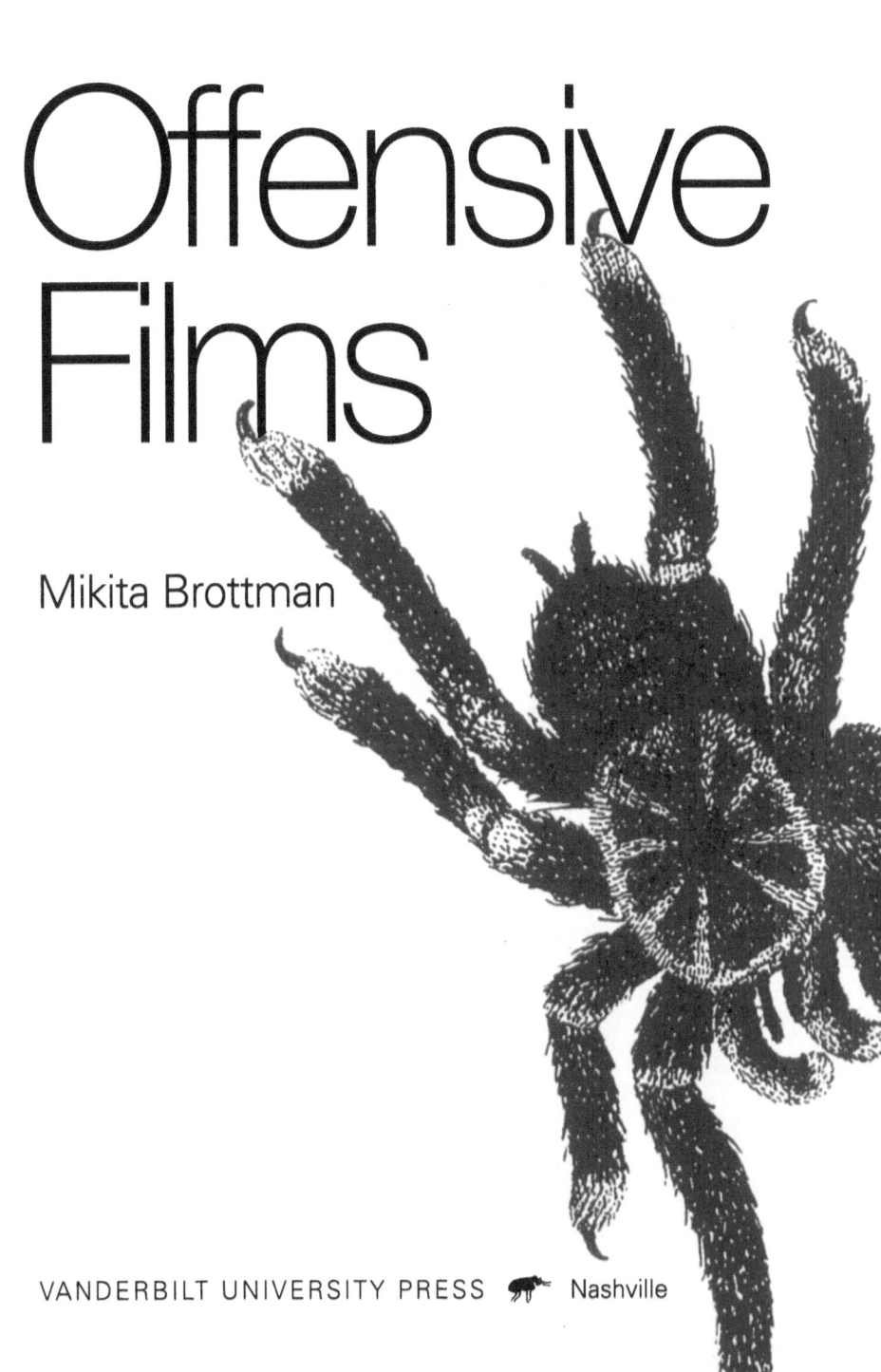

VANDERBILT UNIVERSITY PRESS Nashville

© 2005 Vanderbilt University Press
Originally published as Offensive Films: Toward an Anthropology of Cinéma Vomitif by Greenwood Press, © 1997 by Mikita Brottman. Published in revised paperback by arrangement with Greenwood Publishing Group, Inc., Westport, CT, USA. www.greenwood.com
All rights reserved

This book is printed on acid-free paper.

Designed by Gary Gore

Library of Congress Cataloging-in-Publication Data

Brottman, Mikita, 1966–
Offensive films / Mikita Brottman.
   p. cm.
   Includes bibliographical references.
   ISBN 0-8265-1491-X (pbk. : alk. paper)
   1. Horror films—History and criticism. 2. Sensationalism in motion pictures. I. Title.
PN1995.9.H6B67 2005
791.43'6164—dc22   2005005456

Contents

List of Illustrations   vii

Acknowledgments   ix

Introduction   1

1. *Freaks:* Carnivalizing the Taboo   15
2. Ritual, Tension, and Relief: The Terror of *The Tingler*   50
3. *Blood Feast:* There Never Was a Party Like This!   67
4. *Snuff:* "Where Life Is Cheap"   79
5. Once upon a Time in Texas   96
6. *Cannibal Holocaust:* The Last Road to Hell   113
7. Mondo Movies: Recarnivalizing the Taboo   133
8. An Experiment in Time: Gaspar Noé's *Irréversible*   160

Afterword to the Second Edition   170

Filmography   181

Bibliography   185

Notes   195

Index   203

List of Illustrations

Tod Browning with Schlitzie and other assorted freaks   23

The Bearded Lady gives birth   27

Judith Evelyn and Ghoul on the set of *The Tingler*   57

Judith Evelyn and Philip Coolidge, *The Tingler*   60

The bathtub scene, *The Tingler*   63

Behind the scenes at Exotic Egyptian Catering, *Blood Feast*   69

Fuad Ramses (Mal Arnold) removes the heart of his latest victim (Toni Calvert)   70

Marcy (Ashlyn Martin) is murdered on the beach   73

Suzette Fremont (Connie Mason) in a publicity still for *Blood Feast*   74

Sally (Marilyn Burns) escapes through the forest, *The Texas Chainsaw Massacre*   99

Director Tobe Hooper on set, *The Texas Chainsaw Massacre*   101

The Chainsaw Family, *The Texas Chainsaw Massacre*   104

Hitchhiker (Edwin Neal) and Sally (Marilyn Burns), *The Texas Chainsaw Massacre*   109

Alan Yates (Gabriel Yorke) in the "green inferno," *Cannibal Holocaust*   116

Professor Harold Monroe (Robert Kerman) and a TV company executive, *Cannibal Holocaust*   121

Video Cover for U.K. VHS Release of *Cannibal Holocaust* by Cult Epics   125

VHS cover for U.S. Release of *Faces of Death* by International Trading   144

Acknowledgments

The first edition of this book was published by Greenwood Press, Westport, Connecticut, in 1998. Parts of chapter 1 appeared in *Studies in Popular Culture* 18, no. 2 (1996): 89–107. Parts of chapter 2 appeared in *Trash Aesthetics: Popular Culture and its Audience*, edited by Deborah Cartmell, I. Q. Hunter, Heidi Kaye, and Imelda Whelehan (London: Pluto Press, 1997); *Film Quarterly* 50, no. 4 (1997): 2–10; and Barry Keith Grant and Christopher Sharrett, eds., *Planks of Reason*, revised edition (Lanham, MD: Scarecrow Press, 2004). Parts of chapter 3 appeared in *Continuum: The Australian Journal of Media and Culture* 9, no. 1 (1996): 24–36. Parts of chapter 5 appeared in *Cinefantastique* 27, no. 6 (1995): 26–28 (http://www.cfq.com), and *Necronomicon: The Journal of Horror and Erotic Cinema* 1 (1996): 45–59. Parts of chapters 5 and 6 were originally published in Mikita Brottman, *Meat is Murder! An Illustrated Guide to Cannibal Culture* (London: Creation Books, 1998; http://www.creationbooks.com). Parts of chapter 7 were published under the title "Mondo Movies: Recarnivalizing the Taboo" in *Cineaction!*, September 1995 (Special Issue: Murder in America), and in Stephen Prince, ed., *The Horror Film*, Depth of Field Series (Rutgers, NJ: Rutgers University Press, 2004). Parts of chapter 8 were published in *Film Quarterly* 50, no. 4, by permission of the University of California Press, ©1987 by The Regents of the University of California. Part of the afterword appeared in *Film and Television After 9/11*, edited by Wheeler Winston Dixon (Carbondale: Southern Illinois University Press, 2004). Acknowledgments to all concerned for copyright permissions. Stills from *Freaks* © Turner Entertainment Co.; stills from *The Texas Chainsaw Massacre* © Charles O. Grigson; stills from *Cannibal Holocaust* © Cult Epics. All Rights Reserved.

Introduction

THIS IS A BOOK ABOUT FILMS THAT HAVE been ignored, banned, censored, rejected, repressed, dismissed, and reviled. It is about films that have disgusted, appalled, offended and repelled people; films that have occasionally made their audiences physically faint or sick. The films discussed in this book have been cut, burned, outlawed, seized, confiscated, taken to court, and deleted. My own copies have been taken from me under the Obscene Publications Act. A taste for such films is deemed illegitimate, and aesthetic distaste brings with it the full force of moral excommunication and social rejection. Such tastes are considered aberrant, abnormal, and potentially contagious. The necessity of protecting audiences from such dangerous cultural forms is frequently invoked with the justification that these kinds of threatening depictions can trigger unspeakable acts and that society needs protection from the kind of people who might be led to commit such crimes. A taste for such films is generally described in terms of an addictive, infectious fan relationship sustained only by cinema zombies too attached to their media pleasures to be discerning consumers.

None of the films discussed in this book was made as a cultural statement or piece of political agitprop. All were made, first and foremost, as commercial ventures, designed to stir up cheap publicity by disgusting and exciting the gullible rubes, and each has generated its own wave of spectacle on the part of audiences, critics, reviewers, spectators, and film writers alike.

Some were succeses de scandales, others merely scandals, but all are generally considered too banal, trivial, or unsuitable to constitute part of any cinematic canon.

Sigmund Freud, in *Totem and Taboo* (1913), argues that things that are shunned frighten us because they manifest, in a terrifying or unfamiliar form, those parts of ourselves we are afraid to acknowledge: our repressed appetites, libidinal instincts, schadenfreude, fascination with flesh and death. Mikhail Bakhtin claims in *Rabelais and His World* (1968), along similar lines, that things are shunned when they reveal to us the inverse of all cultural forms, the upside down of tradition, the inside out of history, counterculture in a very literal sense. In this light, that which is eschewed can be understood as a kind of measuring rod to help us understand the nature of whatever is respected and revered. It is important to remember that eccentricity refers to the violation of the usual and the generally accepted. When life is drawn out of its usual rut, we are allowed to see the rut itself all the more clearly. As I go on to discuss in this book, what might at first appear to be eccentric, marginal, and offbeat is actually central to our understanding of the human experience, and those whom we tend to shun are, in fact, reflections of ourselves—and much, much more.

The particular films I have chosen to analyze in this book have been selected for a variety of reasons. Apart from being personal favorites, they present a wide range of different styles and techniques in the history of exploitation cinema over the last seven decades, their dates of release being 1932, 1959, 1963, 1973, 1974, 1983, 1989 to 1994, and 2002. Each film seems to have something important to show us about the cinematic forms and traditions of the particular decade of its release. This is a broad historical span and a wide area of study; almost by definition, these are cheap, quickly produced, "disposable" films, and there are lots of them. As a result, in searching out my selected examples, I have been careful to include only those movies that have been genuinely shunned from mainstream cinema—shunned because they are considered either offensive and obscene, or else too bizarre and strange to have any lasting effect. I am not interested in customary box-office blockbusters like Oliver Stone's *Natural Born Killers* (1994), nor in experimental art-house films such as the movies of Jörg Buttgereit, nor in cult "bad" movies like Ed Wood's *Plan 9 From Outer Space* (1959), nor in films that are deliberately resistant, knowingly radical in content or form, or self-consciously ironic, such as Kubrick's *A Clockwork Orange* (1971).

I am solely interested in those films that most people would consider undeserving of the same intellectual and critical treatment that is regularly applied to experimental and mainstream cinema. These films are neither exemplary, representative, nor benchmark texts. While the scope and categorization of exploitation cinema remains unexplored and unidentified—this being material that lies somewhere between conventional horror and genre categories, and thus a crucial area ripe for investigation—this book is neither a history of the exploitation film, nor an analysis of the relationship between mainstream and marginalized. The main point of writing this book is to show that those films that have been shunned, mocked, and rejected are, in fact—whether or not their directors and audiences are aware of it—of far more substance and interest than has previously been assumed. Most importantly, I am interested in films that can be understood as symptoms of a nervous disorder, revealing themselves to be part of the *unconscious* of mainstream cinema and thereby the locus of all its anxieties, problems, and frightening neurotic taboos.

Apart from being considered too trivial or too freakish to merit lasting attention, the films I have selected also provide, each in its own way, some kind of challenge to traditional culture's binarism of representation and participation, shattering those ideological boundaries that separate the presentation from the partaking. What distinguishes the films analyzed in this book from most other forms of exploitation cinema is that they do not acknowledge any distinction between actors and acts, between performers and performance. By displaying the nauseating, these movies induce nausea; they are both a spectacle to be witnessed and a part of our bodily lives. Everybody is a participant, because the very acts they involve embrace every body and every life. In the films studied in this book, relations of representation can be reconstituted as relations of participation, and the distanced screen is transformed into a public square where all human bodies are actors, as well as being the recipients and audience of the acts of others.

Some of the films analyzed in this book, such as *Blood Feast* (1963) and *Snuff* (1973), on first viewing, appear simple and foolish, or else seem to sport the mask of the rogue, consciously eschewing any lofty pretensions to meaning or significance, when what they are actually doing—albeit perhaps unconsciously—is appropriating such concepts and acknowledging them in a distorted way, wrong side out. In other words, their focus is on the experience of the human body and ideas about that experience, rather than on the realm of thought. This is an area of cinema that takes on a new significance when we approach it from the point of view of consumption, rather than production. It is also an exciting and stimulating subject in film teaching and research, as is the discussion of the body in cinema and culture—in pornography, graphic novels, soap operas, melodramas, and other "low" texts—which now forms a core element of many courses in the field of cultural studies.

Essentially, the kinds of films I am interested in studying in this book are the kind that produce physical effects on the body of the spectator. At their most successful, these "offensive" films present a frontal assault on the audience. They are total theater, in which all forces of expression and persuasion can be brought to bear, and this is what makes this kind of cinema so frightening to most people. Peter Stallybrass and Allon White (1986) have pointed out that middle-class resistance to "low" culture is rooted in the conception of a "proper" body, distanced physically and geographically from the grotesque "improper" body associated with "bad" tastes and "bad" places. The cultural prejudices of most critics, academics, and film reviewers have already paved the way for their strenuous disapproval of any "body genre" based on its presumed power to affect audiences physically, with pornography being the most obvious example. Offensive films are perhaps the most frightening example of this power, however, and are often regarded unambiguously as gratuitous sadism for entertainment's sake. Accordingly, the act of watching such films is often correlated with voyeurism or blood lust. For others, as the controversy surrounding the abject film *Snuff* (1973) made clear, the first taste of the forbidden is believed to initiate a terminal trajectory from bad to worse. Contact with such contagious films, some claim, can even lead to confusion or disregard for the distinction between "reality" and "representation."

Offensive films are a disreputable substream of the horror/exploitation hybrid, which is usually taken to include a number of underground cult movies and what were once known as "grindhouse" pictures. To me, these kinds of films have an active vitality about them that gives them a great deal of power, fueling the often radical connections they make between the real and the textual, discourse and desire, spectacle, gesture, and the body. Offensive films are neither presentations nor representations, but involve a series of real acts—both on-screen and inside the bodies of the audience—and include the participation of real human bodies: bodies in violence, bodies in sex, bodies in panic, bodies in distortion, and bodies in death.

Comprised of the fundamental and often gross realities of human flesh and the grotesque living body, this kind of cinema is an extremely radical force. It shows us personal, everyday forms of human life and all those coarse realities that are sublimated in traditional cultural forms: birth,

INTRODUCTION 5

death, sexuality, defecation, ejaculation, evisceration, and all our shared bodily functions that in other forms of cinema are made abstract or acknowledged only in the form of symbols. The pleasures offered up by offensive films are physical pleasures that split the body into fragments, fetishes, and other sites of libidinal playfulness. In this kind of cinema, the body loses its individual definition and is collectivized at a transindividual level. All things are degraded, materialized, brought down to earth, and turned into flesh. Offensive films display a bodily mirror world—the inverse of abstraction, philosophy, symbolism, tradition, and analysis. But only in the mirror can we see humankind as it really is: a grotesque and freakish parade of bodily deformities and perversions.

II

Since the movies analyzed in this book stand somewhere at the crossroads of the slasher movie and the exploitation film, it is worth examining both of these genres in some detail to acknowledge their own distinctive cinematic histories and to look at the ways in which they have been understood by film writers and critics.

The slasher movie, of course, is an offshoot of the traditional horror film, and has attracted a great deal of interest in the field of film studies ever since the publication of Ivan Butler's *The Horror Film* in 1967. Earlier writers on horror movies, like Butler, tended to concentrate on the horror "classics," such as *Frankenstein* (1931), *Dracula* (1931), and *King Kong* (1933), rather than more "downmarket" movies, which did not attract much critical focus until the publication in 1979 of Robin Wood's seminal essay, "An Introduction to the American Horror Film."

Since then, however, different kinds of horror films have attracted a flood of critical attention. Wood (1979), Carol J. Clover (1987), Noel Carroll (1990), and other academics are particularly interested in that once-neglected offshoot of mainstream horror known as the slasher movie. "At the very bottom, down in the cinematic underbrush lies—horror of horrors—the slasher (or splatter or shocker) film," writes Clover, "the immensely generative story of a psycho-killer who slashes to death a string of mostly female victims, one by one, until he himself is subdued or killed, usually by the one girl who has survived" (91). Clover describes the slasher film as "drenched in taboo and encroaching vigorously upon the pornographic," and lying "by and large beyond the purview of the respectable (middle-class, middle-aged) audience" (91) and of respectable criticism. She notes that slasher movies are "never written up," and Roger Dadoun (1989) agrees that, "like the 'mentally ill,' relegated to the sidelines of communities, societies and consciences, the horror film leads a marginal existence" (44).

Clover's *Men, Women, and Chainsaws* (1992) is a dramatic and convincing exploration of gender boundary-crossings in the slasher movie. She argues that important ideas in the history of horror move through a trajectory of increasing influence as they travel from low-budget films to the mainstream. Barbara Creed's *The Monstrous-Feminine* (1993) closely examines the relationship between the contemporary horror film, psychoanalysis, and feminism, with special emphasis on Julia Kristeva's (1982) notion of "abjection." Wood's "An Introduction" (1979) uses Freud's interest in "the uncanny" and the "return of the repressed" to understand audience reactions to horror movies, especially to representations of bodily danger and threat. Other helpful work on the slasher movie within the last twenty years includes Carroll's exploration of interstitial imagery (a variant of Kristeva's theory of abjection) in *The Philosophy of Horror* (1990), Vera Dika's readings of "stalker" film cycles (1990), Louise Krasniewicz's exploration of John Carpenter's *Halloween* in terms of cultural anthropology (1992), and David Hogan's analysis of sexuality in the horror film (1986).

This critical fascination seems to have arisen, somewhat ironically, because the slasher movie belongs to a subgenre that is almost universally dismissed as trivial, valueless, or "just entertainment." Krasniewicz argues that the "modern horror film offers the moviegoer a story whose seeming purpose is to offer entertainment and temporary refuge from the monotony and tensions of everyday social existence. American narrative films, especially those employing generic conventions, usually claim to demand no more than that the audience sit back and lose itself in the story" (33). Consequently, she argues, "these films' productive exchanges are worth considering, no matter what their silly plot or technical merit" (45).

Clover, debating the merits of using such a crude Freudian topography as the conscious/unconscious division upon which to map complex cultural artifacts, has argued that the slasher's low-horror qualities are the very qualities that make it such a transparent source for subcultural attitudes toward sex and gender in particular. "One is deeply reluctant to make progressive claims for a body of cinema as spectacularly nasty toward women as the slasher film is," she writes, "but the fact is that the slasher does, in its own perverse way... constitute a visible adjustment in terms of gender representation" (126).

V. Vale and Andrea Juno (1986) argue that "low-budget slasher movies can often present unpopular or even radical addresses to social, political and racial inequities in hypocrisy, in religion, and government" (84). Wood

(1979) claims that the popular dismissal of the slasher movie as "just entertainment" allows it to present repressed material, as do jokes and dreams, in such a way as to appeal directly to our unconscious, without having to bypass the psychic censor. Wood believes that low-budget horror, for him the by-product of cultural crisis and degeneration, is "currently the most important of all American [film] genres and perhaps the most progressive, even in its overt nihilism" (203). Tania Modleski (1986) has argued that the slasher film "does *not* promote the 'specious good' (but indeed often exposes and attacks it)," and "does *not* ply the mechanisms of identification, narrative continuity and closure to provide the sort of narrative pleasure constitutive of the dominant ideology" (48).

The slasher movie has many functions. Its audience is predominantly teenage (or slightly older) and predominantly male. Clover points out that the maleness of the majority audience makes clear that the slasher film speaks deeply to male anxieties and desires (125). James Twitchell (1989), among others, has indicated that the contemporary slasher movie functions as a rite of passage for the adolescent male, warning of the consequences of socially inappropriate behavior. The over-determination of symbols and archaic references in the traditional slasher film foregrounds its relationship with folklore, early literature, and the oral story, as do its free exchange of themes and motifs, archetypal characters and situations, and the accumulation of sequels, remakes, and imitations.

Krasniewicz, analyzing the way bodies are used in slasher films—and in the societies compelled to make and watch them—believes that the anticipated and necessary failure of the slasher film's characters and viewers to learn the lessons encoded by the film results in an endless series of sequels and spin-offs that perpetuate the exchange of moral lessons and proper behavior needed to govern unruly bodies in human societies (46). Anthropologist Claude Lévi-Strauss (1984) has argued that the dominant myths of a society are the direct representation of a shared psychic problematic, shared not on the basis of any mysticism or telepathy, but on the basis of the dominant group's regulation of common obsessions through repeated representation. Similarly, film scholar Stephen Prince (1988) regards the slasher movie as a compulsive symbolic exchange in which members of a social order nervously affirm the importance of their cultural heritage. He believes that the slasher movie, like the films studied in this book, is concerned—albeit unconsciously—with the social aspects of both individual and group identity, since it addresses the persistent question of what must be done in order to remain human.

III

Exploitation film evolved just prior to the 1920s, when cinema publicity campaigns designed to tease and titillate first used promises of displaying the forbidden on screen, or the cinematic depiction of some vice. The assurances of such campaigns invariably implied that the audience would see far more on screen than was actually delivered. Eric Schaefer (1992) argues that exploitation film existed since 1920 as a distinct form that paralleled the rise of classical Hollywood cinema until roughly 1960 (34). According to Schaefer, there were a number of genres defined by their disreputable subjects—nudity, childbirth, venereal disease, drug use—within a form that, contrary to classical Hollywood cinema, emphasized spectacle at the expense of narrative coherence and spatial and temporal continuity. The earliest exploitation films were theatrical movies that broke with the film industry's Production Code and were shown in marginal, grindhouse theaters in large cities, as well as independent theaters in small towns.

Under the broad heading of "exploitation film"—a term that was used at least as early as the mid-thirties—fall a number of subcategories, usually defined by the forbidden topic they exploited. These early films initiated exploitation as a promotional practice involving such stunts and displays as elaborately decorated marquees, lurid lobby displays, and "adults only" showings. The subcategory most often produced was the sex hygiene film. Movies with titles like *Damaged Goods* (1913), *A Victim of Sin* (1915), and *The Scarlet Trail* (1918), dealing with subjects generally considered too delicate for public discussion (including syphilis and gonorrhea), were considered harmful and dangerous in their appeal to curious and morbid minds. Nevertheless, in the 1920s, cinema distributors grew even more willing to capitalize on the taboo topic of sex hygiene, using exploitation techniques by allowing only men over the age of sixteen into the cinema and promoting the films with prologues boasting of their "actual views" of diseased men and women with ugly sores open to view, and of nauseating close-ups showing the ravages of venereal disease on the human body.

Exploitation films continued to find commercial success in marginal venues until the 1950s, when the fall of the Hollywood studio system, the wane of the Production Code, and the relaxation of state censorship laws meant that "classical" exploitation disappeared as its subjects were reintegrated into mainstream motion pictures. Those exploitation filmmakers who continued to make a living outside the mainstream began to film more burlesque shows and increased their output of nudist movies.

Perhaps the most influential exploitation movie ever made was Herschell Gordon Lewis's notorious *Blood Feast,* which in 1963 ushered in a second

INTRODUCTION

cycle, the "new wave" of exploitation cinema. Lewis's emphasis on grotesque, outrageous special effects in the depiction of grisly mutilations—although mocked and reviled by the mainstream Hollywood press—initiated a flood of sex-and-violence, blood-and-guts exploitation films arriving at the country's grindhouse, drive-in, and B-movie venues. These were generally divided into three categories: "ghoulies," "roughies," and "kinkies." Lewis, the self-styled "Wizard of Gore," was king of the ghoulies: low-budget horror like *Blood Feast* (1963) and *The Gruesome Twosome* (1967). The roughies were ruled by Lewis's partner in crime, the celebrated lowbrow pornographer David F. Friedman, director of boisterous erotica like *The Defilers* (1963). And the kinkies—or soft-core skin flicks—were directed by the likes of Russ Meyer, whose film *Lorna* was released in 1965, and Michael and Roberta Findlay—best known for the infamous *Snuff* (1973)—who made a trilogy of kinkies, starting with *The Touch of Her Flesh* in 1967. Of course, these categories were sometimes very difficult to separate, and certain films would often be referred to in the trade as a "roughie-kinky," or a "kinky-ghoulie," or even a "roughie-ghoulie-kinky."

In the late sixties and early seventies, the designation "exploitation film" began to be modified to indicate what in particular was being exploited, which led to the "sexploitation" cinema of the late sixties, the "blaxploitation" films of the seventies, and so on. Today, the term has broadened dramatically in its implications and is now used to refer to almost any low-budget genre movie, from vampire films, to soft-core porn, to martial arts. In this book, the term "exploitation film" is being used in its original, "classical" sense and maintains its earlier undertones and implications. The films analyzed here not only involve a strong element of exploitation in their respective narratives, but all were originally promoted in highly exploitative ways, including elaborate stunts and displays, well-publicized court cases, elaborately decked-out cinema marquees, or luridly graphic video covers, as well as such ploys as self-imposed "R" ratings and staged "protests" outside selected theaters.

IV

The ultimate aim of offensive films is the arousal of strong emotions in the lower body—nausea, repulsion, weakness, faintness, and a loosening of bowel and bladder control—normally by way of graphic scenes featuring the by-products of bodily detritus: vomit, excrement, viscera, brain tissue, and so on.

Some of the films analyzed in this book, such as the *Death Scenes* series (1989, 1992), are explicitly devoted to the display of the real, opened human body. Others, such as *The Texas Chainsaw Massacre* (1974), rely more heavily on the buildup and release of tension, as well as shock and graphic exhibitions. Yet others, such as *The Tingler* (1959), rely on off-screen mechanical apparatuses to produce the desired effect. These films all utilize a variety of different modes of representation, from entirely fictive, to pseudo-verité, to depictions of the "real." Whatever their individual perspective and direction, however, all the films analyzed in this book are explorations and extrapolations of the human body, its waste products, effusions, and debris.

Tod Browning's *Freaks* (1932), the first film analyzed in this book, involves a cast of human oddities, including amputees, midgets, "pinheads," dwarfs, and Siamese twins, all of whom played a requisite part in the film's promotional tactics.[1] Although Browning does not exploit these human anomalies within the film's narrative and had no intention of inducing fear, weakness, and nausea by selecting this curious cast, these were clearly sensations that the film initially provoked, resulting in a ban of almost thirty years. Next, William Castle's *The Tingler* (1959), though not especially offensive in narrative terms, is included in this study for two reasons. First, it is remarkable for the exploitative strategies surrounding its cinematic presentation, including the wiring up of selected theater seats to administer an electric shock to certain unfortunate members of the audience at strategic moments in the plot. Second, *The Tingler* is all about the sound of the human scream—a sound that, as displaced deflatus, stands for excrement in its abstract, conceptual, or spirit form.

Lewis's *Blood Feast* (1963) is perhaps the most disreputable of all offensive films, notorious for the stomach-churning horror of its low-budget special effects. Michael and Roberta Findlay and Allan Shackleton's *Snuff* (1973) was a scandalous piece of perverted filmmaking, whose ostensible presentation of an on-screen murder in the context of the Tate-LaBianca slayings five years earlier initiated the rumor-panic about "snuff" movies still doing the rounds today.

Tobe Hooper's *The Texas Chainsaw Massacre* (1974) is one of the best-known and most commercially successful horror films of the last thirty years, with its sensational fusion of dramatic tension, a slasher-style plot, fairy-tale imagery, and grisly special effects. Ruggero Deodato's jungle saga *Cannibal Holocaust* (1981) caused a similar stir, with its reckless promotional campaign and inventive use of on-screen animal mutilations, heralding the new mondo cycle of the late eighties and early nineties. Mondo movies like *The Killing of America* (1981) and *Death Scenes* (1989) exploit nauseous news outtakes of freak accidents, violent crime, and global unrest, predicting a strange new direction in the history of exploitation film.

Finally, Gaspar Noé's *Irréversible*, released in 2002, suggests a number of subtle and thoughtful connections between violent animal aggression and the tenderness of human emotions. Despite being dismissed by critics as a deliberate and sophomoric attempt to shock (*Village Voice* critic J. Hoberman commented after watching the movie that he felt less like taking a shower than wiping his shoe), Noé's film is perhaps the most radical understanding of the way human relationships are involved and intertwined with rape, violence, and murder. *Irréversible* is exploitative in the way in which human relationships are exploitative—by definition. Indeed, what is being exploited in all these films is not only the taboos surrounding the imaging of bodily evisceration and death, but obsessive tendencies in our culture as a whole.

The films selected for analysis in this book deal almost exclusively with issues of the opened human body. Just as the most explicit hard-core porn reveals as much as possible of the labial area and the vaginal opening (in the "split beaver" or "open box" shot), so the most sought-after examples of horror films are those that show the most vivid evidence of the "real" opened body (spilt blood, brains, intestines, and bodily fluids). This connection between horror and porn is quite significant. It is interesting to note that Freud linked the female genital organs to the *unheimlich*, the uncanny (1919). "It often happens," writes Freud, "that neurotic men declare that they feel there is something uncanny about the female genital organs. This *unheimlich* place, however, is the entrance to the former *heim* (home) of all human beings, to the place where each of us has lived, once upon a time and in the beginning" (275). Clover (1992) has noted that "it is no surprise that the rise of the slasher film is concomitant with the development of special effects that let us see with our own eyes the 'opened' body" (110). Jacques Lacan (1970) believed that the primal scene is always conducive to trauma, and it has been argued that the horror text's consistent release is in the displacement of the violence of the primal scene into the violence of death.

One of the conclusions reached by Carroll (1990) in *The Philosophy of Horror* is that what creates fear is evidence of "things out of place," things that defy categorization. Carroll goes on to enumerate various classifications of what he describes as the "interstitial," from massivication and magnification (giant apes, ogres) to horrific metonymy (bats, rats, spiders), to the bodily (blood, saliva, feces) and the morally interstitial (psychopaths, necrophiles, pedophiles, and so on). Carroll's theory of the interstitial—essentially a broader version of what Kristeva (1982) terms "abjection"—has its difficulties, not least of which being that the horrific nature of the interstitial depends largely on cultural context (there is little of terror, for example, about blood on a steak, shellfish in a seafood restaurant, or manure on a freshly plowed field), but Carroll's theory is essentially a useful one.

Kristeva (1982) points out that the critically impure is that which is based on a natural "loathing." Anthropology suggests that there is nothing "loathsome" in itself, since the loathsome is that which disobeys classification rules particular to the given symbolic system. It has long been testified that what causes fear and horror—and also, in a somewhat different context, what causes humor and laughter—is evidence of an absence of bodily control, witnessed most vividly by the collapse of bodily boundaries and the external appearance of things that should properly be kept inside the body. Anything that protrudes from the body, or leaves the body's confines, is considered distasteful and grotesque. This is partly why taboos have developed around bodily processes of elimination, such as defecation, menstruation, childbirth, urination, sweating, blowing the nose, sneezing, bleeding, and ejaculation, as these are all acts that are performed on the threshold between the body and the outer world. Freud (1919) supported, and elaborated upon, Friedrich W. J. von Schelling's (1848) definition of the uncanny as something that ought to have remained hidden but has come to light.

The kinds of horror films analyzed in this book are more frightening and abhorrent than the traditional slasher movie or other styles of exploitation film, as their lack of narrative commitment or, just as often, structural cohesion means that the entire movie, if necessary, can be devoted to displays of the ex-liminal body. Many of the films analyzed in this book contain grisly catalogs—both real and fictional—of blood spilling out of wounds, brains emerging from open skulls, dismembered torsos, broken joints, eviscerations, and the discharge from tissue fluids. All the films analyzed in this book involve a network of fantasies relating to the body—the body dismembered or divided into pieces, the display of organs and viscera, the transformation and alteration of internal objects: a relentless depiction of the abject. These films, rather than slasher movies, deserve to be understood as the covert taboo films of Western culture, ignored by critics of the traditional horror film and regarded by most people with that uneasy combination of loathing and compulsive curiosity by which, in this culture at least, we have come to identify the taboo.

The conjunction of imagery shared by all the movies analyzed in this book has motivated my choice of critical and analytical perspectives. Without exception, all ten films are centered around images of the opened human body and its associated detritus. These films are all topographical narratives of the human body split open, infested, rendered asunder, pene-

INTRODUCTION 13

trated, truncated, cleft, sliced, suspended, and devoured. They all deal with bodies inverted, reduced, transmogrified, assailed, out of control, and thereby made ridiculous. These depictions, all of them elemental, cultic, and uncanny, are representations of bodily transgressions and broken taboos. They stand for the inside out of civilization, culture, and the human body; they depict the unconscious nightmare of mainstream cinema.

Since all the films in this book deal with archetypal, folkloric images of bodily infraction, most of them are studied in the light of Freudian psychoanalysis, especially Freud's work on the uncanny (1919), the repetition-compulsion, and the death drive (1923). In other places, and partly because of its compatibility with Freudian psychoanalysis, I have also elected to use some traditional anthropological texts, especially the work of René Girard (1977) and Mary Douglas (1966, 1978, 1992). But while psychoanalysis and anthropology create a useful gateway to understanding the transgressive nature of most of these films, each film demands its own individual "take," and, in many of the chapters, I also rely heavily on the writings of that most demonstrative philosopher of the human bodily carnival, Mikhail Bakhtin (1968, 1981, 1984). Rather than using these textual readings to stage a debate between different cultural epistemologies, I am simply aiming to adopt an eclectic critical method that enables different discourses to be deployed regardless of their occasional discrepancies.

Finally, it is important to mention that this is a study of a set of movies that seems to form a particular pattern in the history of horror/exploitation cinema, not a particular group of film directors. Many of these films were constructed in remarkably brief lengths of time—less than a month, in some cases—and on exceptionally low budgets. None of them was manufactured for any reason other than commercial profit. This is very important. As Wood (1979) and other writers have suggested, it is only these kinds of films that—due to our disregard for them—are allowed privileged access to a level of the unconscious that other, more serious, more acceptable films are not. The unprofessional production values, clumsy narratives, and hastily conceived structures of such films, as well as their wide commercial appeal, give them the same kind of value that free association has in psychoanalysis, making them important vehicles for helping us to understand the bodily nightmares of the culture that gives rise to them.

Each chapter in this study should be considered not simply as an exposition or interpretation of a particular film. Instead, I am using each of these movies as a springboard for analysis and inquiry into various aspects of the human condition, whether this be the uncontrollable, terrifying nature of the physical body or the epistemological questions raised by the contemporary urban legend. In other words, this is not simply a study of selected films, but an investigation into what these films have to teach us about the predicament of existing in a human body. For example, although it begins with an in-depth analysis of Tod Browning's 1932 film *Freaks,* chapter 1 goes on to examine the history of ethnographic showcasing, the demise of the traditional "freak show," and the way in which what Philip Rieff has described as "the triumph of the therapeutic" has led to a narrowing of the distinction between physical and "psychological" freaks. Similarly, in chapter 4, analysis of the Findlay/Shackleton film *Snuff* gives way to a study of the urban legend and its relationship with specific personal acts, temporal structures, and physical incarnations. In short, this book is not simply a study of some loosely connected movies, but an exposition of what films like this have to teach us about the human condition and its bodily incarnations and infractions.

When discussing the nature and significance of the films themselves, my main concern is to understand the unconscious of each cinematic narrative, not any directorial strategy or intent. I make no apologies for going beyond what any of these films' directors may have consciously intended their movies to express. The fact that most of these films have been dismissed by the majority of critics as schlock, kitsch, or cheap commercial trash simply makes them all the more interesting to me. The movies studied in this book—trash cinema par excellence—open up and reveal the inside-out mirror world concealed and betrayed by traditional cinematic forms, presenting a filmic epiphany, where the king is stripped of his regal vestments to reveal the jester beneath.

Just as the hysteric's symptoms show a continuity with the past through repetition as symbol, so certain kinds of narrative—like the films in this book—can live on in the unconscious in pantomime form. Like the story that fuels nightmares long after it has been obliterated from conscious memory, the movies studied in this book contain the kind of revelation that has a profound unconscious effect, however quickly and thoroughly its brutal displays are seemingly ignored, outlawed, or forgotten.

1 *Freaks:* Carnivalizing the Taboo

DIRECTOR TOD BROWNING WAS NO STRANGER TO the darkness of carnival, vaudeville, and circus. At the age of six, he ran away from home to join a carnival troupe, and, during 1913 and 1914, he made several world tours in various circuses in the roles of barker, clown, and then comedian. His early films often had their source in the circus underworld; most notable is *The Unholy Three* (1925), which featured Lon Chaney as a circus ventriloquist who teams up with two other sideshow exhibits, a strongman and a midget, to use their carnival skills against society. Even darker in its theme is *The Unknown* (1927), for which Browning also wrote the screenplay—the macabre story of a knife-thrower who performs his act with his nimble toes. *Freaks* (1932) was inspired by Todd Robbins's short story "Spurs," which appeared in *Munsey's Magazine* in 1923 and concerned a sadistic dwarf who exacts punishment on his faithless wife by riding her piggyback from one end of the country to the other.[1] In his cinematic rendering of this strange tale, Browning employed Ringling Brothers and Barnum and Bailey circus sideshow exhibits to act as the perpetrators of symbolic violence.

Freaks begins with a written warning, scrolled up the screen and decorated by marginal drawings of human oddities and misfits:

> Before proceeding with the showing of this HIGHLY UNUSUAL ATTRACTION, a few words should be said about the amazing subject matter.

BELIEVE IT OR NOT ... STRANGE AS IT SEEMS, in ancient times anything that deviated from the normal was considered an omen of ill-luck or representation of evil. ... **FOR THE LOVE OF BEAUTY** is a deep-seated urge which dates back to the beginning of civilization. The revulsion with which we view the abnormal, the malformed and the mutilated is the result of long conditioning by our forefathers. The majority of freaks, themselves, are endowed with normal thoughts and emotions. Their lot is truly a heartbreaking one. They are forced to live the most unnatural of lives. Therefore, they have built up among themselves a code of ethics to protect them from the barbs of normal people. Their rules are rigidly adhered to, and the hurt of one is the hurt of all, the joy of one is the joy of all. The story about to be revealed is a story based on the effect of this code on their lives. Never again will such a story be filmed, as modern science and teratology is rapidly eliminating such blunders from the world. With humility for the many injustices done to such people (they have no power to control their lot), we present the most startling horror story of the **ABNORMAL** and the **UNWANTED**.

Suddenly, this "scroll" is crumpled up by a freak-show impresario encouraging a large crowd to recoil and shudder at "the most amazing, the most astounding living monstrosity of the time." "Friends," the showman explains, "She was once a beautiful woman. A royal prince shot himself for love of her. She was known as the peacock of the air." Browning then cuts to the main body of the film, which is shown in the form of a flashback. The beautiful aerial artiste Cleopatra (Olga Baclova) performs her circus act on the trapeze, watched adoringly by the German midget Hans (Harry Earles, who also played the midget in *The Unholy Three*) and his jealous midget fiancée, Frida (played by Earles's sister, Daisy). Out of the ring, Cleopatra teases Hans, flirts with him, and invites him back to her caravan for a glass of wine.

The film's perspective then widens to a shot of local landowner, M. Duval, strolling through the forest with his gamekeeper, who is attempting to describe to Duval the "horrible twisting things—crawling, laughing, *whining*" that he has spotted in the forest. Just then, in a clearing, the two men stumble upon Madame Tetralini, "keeper" of the circus freaks, exercising her docile "children" among the trees: a writhing torso with no arms or legs, four or five dancing pinheads, a twisted pygmy playing the mouth organ, and a frolicking half-boy balancing on a tree stump—our first sight of the unsettling freaks.

Back in the circus, Cleopatra inadvertently learns from Frida that Hans is heir to an enormous fortune, and with the help of her lover, the strongman Hercules (Henry Victor), she plans to seduce him away from his diminutive fiancée, marry him, and then poison him for his money. She readily manages to get Hans to fall in love with her, but not without arousing the suspicions of the freaks and their cohorts—the clowns Phroso, Roscoe, and the Rollo Brothers (Wallace Ford, Rosco Ates, Edward Brophy and Matt McHugh respectively); showgirl Venus (Leila Hyams); and the freaks' "nanny," Madame Tetralini (Rose Dione). Cleopatra's seduction of Hans culminates in a terrifying wedding banquet, during which the writhing freaks, elated with champagne and festivity, work themselves into a frenzy, resulting in a lurid chant directed at Cleopatra ("we accept you, one of us ... gooble gobble, gooble gobble, one of us, one of us"), to which she responds by hurling their "loving cup" back into their grinning faces and shrieking abuse at them.

Soon after the wedding, Hans becomes ill, and it is generally accepted among the freaks that he is being poisoned by Cleopatra. Little by little, they begin to congregate around her caravan, refusing to leave Hans alone with her, watching silently through the trailer windows, hiding between its wheels and peering out furtively through the gaps between its steps. Eventually, even Hans comes to understand the hoax that has made a victim of him, and he ceases to swallow Cleopatra's "medicine." The opportunity for the freaks' revenge comes one turbulent night when the circus has just decamped on its journey to another town. Amid the darkness of the storm and the chaos of the crashing wagons, the freaks writhe their way through the dirt and mud to stalk Cleopatra and Hercules. Hercules is attacked at knifepoint—possibly slaughtered by a dwarf—and Cleopatra suffers an even more terrible fate: She is transformed into a freak.

At this point, we return to the opening sequence of the impresario's showcase, to witness his "living, breathing monstrosity." It is, of course, none other than Cleopatra herself, ravaged by the freaks and turned into a lame, scarred, clucking misfit—half woman and half chicken, a macabre oddity crouched on a bed of straw. "How she got that way will never be known," proclaims the showman. "Some say a jealous lover. Others, that it was the code of the freaks. Others, the storm. Believe it or not, there she is."

Freaks was recut (or mutilated, as some would have it) and reissued in 1962, by which time the original negative had been destroyed, which explains the mediocre quality of the copies shown today. Versions of the film in general circulation omit the final "lost" scene of Hercules' punishment. He is stabbed in the groin by a dwarf while the other freaks are writhing toward him in the mud, armed with knives and other cutting implements. The reissued version of *Freaks* includes no further reference to Hercules, suggesting that the freaks have killed him. In fact, Hercules is not killed but castrated—a punishment far more appropriate to the logic of the film because, after all, Hercules is only the tentative accomplice of an assassin and does not thereby necessarily deserve death. Having dispossessed Hans of his virility by cuckolding him, the logic of the narrative demands that Hercules should then lose his own organ of generation. The original footage includes a brief return to Hercules at the end of the scene in the sideshow. Here, Cleopatra is shown in her pit, transformed into a chicken-woman, and Hercules is seen standing on a nearby podium, exhibited as a castrato, singing in a falsetto voice.

The pre-1963 footage also included a palliative sequence gesturing toward the reconciliation of the main protagonists. Hans, rich and lonely, refuses to see or speak to anyone at all until Phroso, forcing himself on Hans's domestic solitude, enters with Venus and Frida. While Venus and Phroso conceal themselves behind the bedroom door, Hans and Frida melt into a syrupy embrace.

II

A 1932 *New York Times* film critic remarked of *Freaks* that "the difficulty is telling whether it should be shown at the Rialto, where it opened yesterday—or in, say, the medical center." The publicity for the film in this newspaper carried a special warning: "Children will not be permitted to see this picture! Adults not in normal health are urged not to!" The film's infamy was a result of public dismay at its use of genuine human misfits and sideshow oddities. *Harrison's Reports* (1932) commented, "Anyone who considers this entertainment should be placed in the psychological ward in some hospital. Terrible for children or for Sunday showing." Richard Hanser (1932) of the *Buffalo Times* claimed that "while the story may tax the credulity of the onlooker, it has the fascination of the horrible. It must surely be a nightmarish spectacle for children, and they had better be kept away." The reviewer for the *New Yorker* (1932) agreed: "I don't think that everyone on earth should see it. It's certainly not for susceptible young people."[2]

Richard Watts Jr., in the *New York Herald Tribune* (1932), noted that "it is obviously an unhealthy and generally disagreeable work, not only in its story and characterization, but also in its gay directorial touches."[3] Most other, similar objections to the film centered around its "unhealthy" subject matter and ethically questionable practice of displaying authentic human oddities on a cinema screen for public entertainment. Philippe Carcassonne

(1978), in *Cinematographe*, implies that a major reason for the negative reception of *Freaks* was the film's intolerable nature, which, he claimed, resided not in its parade of atrocities, but in the "thoroughly pre-Biblical" assumption of impunity that the able-bodied protagonists automatically assert over the freaks.[4]

Still others claimed formal or technical reasons for this public disaffection. Some felt that Browning had deliberately violated traditional narrative conventions by refusing the cinema audience an identifiable protagonist apart from the ranks of the deformed and disquieting freaks, thereby blocking the habitual process of audience identification. By refusing to supply a traditional narrative structure, Browning does not allow the audience to play its part in the game, and thus—some would say—the film was a lost cause even before it was banned (see, for example, Léger 1975, 89). Others argued that the film was *formally* monstrous—at fifty-some minutes, too long for a short feature and too short for a long one—thereby preventing it from finding a niche within the contemporary system of distribution. Similarly, the movie was very difficult to classify at the time of its release. Neither horror movie, nor documentary, nor feature film, it was very much a marginal oddity itself—and, as such, had grave problems finding its public (see Léger 1975, 89).

Ironically, because so many of the film's detractors cited the use of "living, breathing monstrosities" as the main reason for its public perception as a hideous and nightmarish spectacle, this atmosphere of general concern and disquietude did very little to help the freaks in their off-screen lives. Violet and Daisy Hilton, the Siamese twins, made their last public appearance in 1962 in Charlotte, North Carolina, at a drive-in movie theater where they had been brought by an unscrupulous agent to publicize the reissuing of *Freaks*. The agent took the money and ran, leaving the impoverished twins stranded at the drive-in. Through the kindness of a grocery store owner, they eventually found jobs in Charlotte as checkout clerks, though the store owner had to buy them dresses to wear on the job, since they only had their show clothes (see Bogdan 1988, 172–73).

Johnny Eck, billed in *Freaks* as "the boy with half a torso," continued to travel in a sideshow after the film's release. His "true-life" exhibition booklet claimed that he owned a twelve-piece orchestra in Baltimore, for which he was conductor and composer, although this seems to have been at best an exaggeration (see Bogdan 1988, 215–16).[5] Schlitzie, the central pinhead character, was forty years old when she appeared in *Freaks*. She had previously been exhibited as "Maggie, the Last of the Aztecs." In the end, she was forced off the sideshow platform to spend the rest of her days in large custodial institutions. The pinhead twins were played by Elvira and Jenny Snow, two sisters born in Georgia and exhibited by their brother as Pippo and Zippo, and as the brother and sister Zippo and Flippo, in a number of different circus sideshows (see Bogdan 1988, 142, 146). The bearded lady was Jane Barnell, first exhibited when she was four years old and still appearing in freak shows, dime museums, amusement parks, and circuses up until the early 1940s. She is billed in *Freaks* as "Olga Roderick" and was exhibited under a variety of different stage names, from "Princess Olga" and "Madame Olga" to "Lady Bluebeard" (see Bogdan 1988, 229).

III

Freaks was rereleased in Paris in 1963 into a very different cultural climate from that of its initial appearance, and it inspired a number of highly sympathetic articles in the French film press. The movie was consequently revived in the United States, England, and New Zealand, mainly on the arthouse circuit, where it has played for extended seasons ever since, especially throughout the 1970s and 1980s, sometimes breaking box-office records. It has been shown on television in Europe and the United States, and it is now widely available on videotape and DVD.

French critics and reviewers of the 1960s and 1970s found the documentary aspect of Browning's project both daring and authentic, especially the conflation of the real and the monstrous in the spectacular bodies of the freaks. Most agreed that the death of Lon Chaney (in 1930) had allowed Browning—pressured in part by the demands for realism made by the sudden success of the talkies—to move into a superior register. It was noted that the inherent questions of Browning's Chaney cycle were taken even further in *Freaks:* namely, what marks the border between human and animal, and—more pertinently perhaps—between exhibition, exploitation, and cinematic spectacle?[6]

Paul Gilson, one of the first French critics to rediscover the film, referred in 1951 to "the splendid force of this forgotten melodrama" and went on to claim that "this violence belongs nowhere else than amid the grandeur and terror of certain 'tales of the extraordinary,' notably Edgar Poe's 'Hop-Frog'" (160–61). Others singled out the scenes of the wedding feast and of the freaks' majestic revenge as consummate set pieces of the *cinéma fantastique.* Critic Jacques Pinturault (1957) was especially impressed by what he described as "the dark wedding scene, lit only by the glow emanating from a large white tablecloth . . . where the montage, moving faster and·faster, exasperates the nervous tension until the ultimate paroxysm which separates two worlds from one another: that of the normal, and that of the marginal" (20). Another French critic, Raymond Lefèvre (1965), referred to the menacing vengeance scene as "a hallucinatory sequence which reminds one of the summits of the fantastic in cinema" (227).

Critic Claude Michel Cluny (1978) praised the same sequence for its impressionistic juxtaposition of "white shadows in the night . . . rampant monsters in the mud and the rain . . . lilliputian avengers among the seemingly gigantic furniture of their apartments" (29). Other critics praised Browning for his daring subject matter. Jean A. Gigli (1969) described *Freaks* as "neither a horror film, nor a documentary, but a film of love among men, for whom the camera seeks to hide their monstrosity, and show signs only of their humanity" (135). And Jean-Marie Sabatier claimed in 1973 that *Freaks* was a masterpiece because "the director took for his heroes characters 'apart,' physically abnormal, but the spectator, overcoming his repulsion, is led to prefer them to the physically normal but psychologically monstrous" (160–61).

Later, throughout the 1970s, high praise for the film's tenderness and authenticity became the order of the day in French criticism of *les films fantastiques*. Claude Beylie (1973), in *Ecran*, insisted upon the audience imperative to "'understand' the monsters . . . to discover in their piercing eyes another, much greater monstrosity—that of mankind, and this discovery has something joyous about it, something healthy. . . . *Freaks* is pure metaphysical tragedy . . . composed in the light of that somewhat neglected philosophical doctrine: phenomenology" (17). And in *Cinéma 78*, Claude Michel Cluny (1978) described the film as "a monstrous parade reflecting back the soul of the spectator . . . a baroque universe marked by an intense poesy" (29).

In the United States, the rerelease of *Freaks* was welcomed by an equally receptive public, though one with rather different motivations. Browning's film was strenuously embraced by the counterculture of the 1960s and 1970s, for whom the term "freak" suggested a radically democratic embracing of self-designated individuality and diversity.[7] The radical politics of the 1960s, in the United States at least, was characterized by a new articulation of heterogeneous social groups and by a mixing of political and psychological demands for dramatic visibility. Leslie Fiedler (1978), writing in the 1970s, saw in the new reception of *Freaks* a latter-day tribute to lost monsters by the enchanted youth of the counterculture, rejecting a political conservatism that preached division and secularization. To Fiedler and other of the film's exponents, the film's vengeful parade of oppressed and rejected misfits suggested the radical potential of a violent and revolutionary counterculture against the gigantic, "normalizing" hegemony of exploitative capitalism.

In fact, *Freaks* has never lacked a sympathetic public on the art house circuit since its rerelease and reclassification (as restricted to those over sixteen) in the 1960s and 1970s.[8] The current ideological climate of openness to the most diverse and individualistic appropriations of class, race, ethnicity, gender, and sexuality is a highly appropriate one for the film's public acceptance, especially in the light of the current countercultural popularity of body decoration and modification (including tattoos, body piercing, and head shaving). But the film's newfound popularity was not wholly uncritical. Some, especially the French, were disturbed by Browning's unsophisticated device for attempting to reassure his public that *Freaks* was not necessarily a reflection of American ideology. The film is set in a highly generic France, loosely signified by some of the characters speaking in "European" accents (Hans, Frida, Cleopatra) or being assigned vaguely "foreign" sounding names (Monsieur Duval, Madame Tetralini).

Others refuted the assumption that Browning made no concessions to voyeurism by drawing attention to two scenes in particular: the familiar sequence in which the "living torso" is exhibited accomplishing the prodigious task of rolling and lighting his own cigarette, and the scene in which Frances, the armless woman, uses her feet to convey food and drink to her mouth. In an article written in 1975, French critic Jean-Marie Léger claimed that what was happening in these scenes had no significance as far as the film's narrative was concerned, and therefore these scenes represented unique concessions to voyeurism (160–61). One might equally argue, however, that the narrative function of such sequences is made clear in the final scene—which involves the "living torso" writhing toward Hercules with a knife between his teeth. In this scene, the audience is reminded that, however deformed and mutilated they may appear to be, all these characters have been seen to overcome their handicaps in other circumstances.

A far more serious criticism of the film, and the source of much commentary, is its potentially ludicrous ending. Not only is it impossible to imagine these polite and docile freaks as torturers and murderers, even under the most extreme circumstances, but it also makes no sense to suggest that they have managed to transform a normal, healthy woman into a scarred and feathered chicken. The film's ending is a sore point even among its strongest sympathizers, and some have claimed that this scene debases an otherwise commanding piece of cinema. Critic Werner Adrian (1976), for example, argues that the final presentation of Cleopatra is Browning's sole mistake in the film. "He has misused an old gag invented with Lon Chaney," writes Adrian, "whom he transformed into a giant chicken, so that the final shot of Cleopatra is not horrendous, but comical. She looks like a half-plucked oversize fowl" (59).[9]

It is not difficult, however, to acknowledge this final image of Cleopatra as that of a mutilated woman who has been dressed up by the showman in a feathered costume to give her the appearance of a bizarre "chicken-woman," just as all the other freaks in the sideshow are outfitted in accordance with their exotic roles. The "living torso" wears a knitted swimsuit, Frida sports a miniature tutu, and Schlitzie and the Snow twins display beribboned top-knots. Our knowledge of the laws of the circus make it entirely conceivable that the chicken-woman is no more than a "half-woman"—something like the female equivalent of Johnny Eck—costumed and disguised as a "gaffe," to appear as shocking and bizarre as the "real" freaks in the sideshow.

Tod Browning with Schlitzie and other assorted freaks. © 1932 Turner Entertainment Limited. All Rights Reserved. Courtesy of BFI stills, posters & designs

In a 1973 review of the film in *Photon*, critic Eli Savada suggested an even more intriguing possibility, and one that recasts the entire cinematic narrative in a rather disquieting role. "It is entirely possible," wrote Savada, "to view the entire story the barker relates to his customers—from the flashback to the carnival up until the freaks' revenge—as a purely fictional account dreamed up by the showman to dupe the crowd from the film's offset" (34). If this suggestion bears weight and the tale of the misfits' revenge has been dreamed up by a boastful impresario to terrify the able-bodied voyeurs, then the film has a lot more to tell us about the human imagination than the human body.

IV

Cleopatra's final transformation into a chicken-woman is a highly significant part of the film's narrative, not an isolated and disjointed denouement. Chickens, and the idea of chickens, play a constant role in *Freaks*, from Koo Coo the bird-woman, costumed as a bespectacled fowl, doing a "chicken dance" on the dinner table, to the magic "chicken language" of the wedding banquet (*gooble gobble, gooble gobble*).

One of Phroso's gags, which Venus fails to find amusing, involves wearing an enormous clown suit with a huge collar. When hit on the head with a spade, his head disappears into the costume and he runs around the fairground squawking and flapping his arms like a chicken. At another point, Koo Coo the bird-woman, dancing on the table during the wedding banquet, crooks one of her spindly legs and lets out a squealing fart, much to the frenzied hilarity of the assembled freaks. The chicken, the totemic fetish of the freaks, is the visible, external sign of freakery, as is clear to those fairway geeks and heavy-metal singers who specialized in biting off their heads. The chicken stands for the boundary condition of the freak, whose hybrid identity, bestial speech, incoherent gestures, and inhuman body all suggest a border condition between human and animal. Author Mary Russo (1995) argues that it is highly appropriate, according to the symbolic economy of the narrative, that Cleopatra's body—which was first exhibited to us in the air, as an idealization of womanhood—is cut down to size in order to fit the sacrificial requirements of freak justice (91–92).[10]

Interestingly, the hybrid speech code of the freaks and their cohorts, of which the "chicken language" is just a single example, is highly multivocal, full of linguistic anomalies and diversions in the form of puns, stutters, jokes, name-calling, and nonsense. Examples include the speech of the stuttering Roscoe (married to Daisy, one of the Siamese twins), who seems to mimic Violet and Daisy's bodily redundancies by his own compulsive repetitions. His recurring accusation, whenever his wife has to leave with her sister, is that it is her "excu... excu... excu... alibb-bb-bbi." While on the one hand, *alibi* is the right word (her "other place," her *alius ibi*), on the other hand, by the time Roscoe has spluttered out the whole word, its final double syllable has become effective (*bye bye*), for Violet and Daisy are long gone.[11]

A similar reference to bodily ambivalence and redundance is Joseph/Josephine's crush on Hercules. The first time Hercules discovers the hermaphrodite staring at him, the scene is comic ("shh... shh... shh... she likes you," splutters Roscoe, "but *he... he... he* doesn't!"). But the second time is more sinister. Hercules chases Joseph/Josephine away from Cleopatra's trailer, but by the time he has caught up with him/her to feign a punch at Joseph (with the words "here's one for your eye!"), Josephine is demurely applying her mascara. The implicit message in Hercules' threat is that it is Joseph/Josephine's ambiguous gaze that deserves punishment. This is made explicit by a later sequence that shows Daisy's face lighting up when her twin sister Violet is being kissed, suggesting that Josephine's other half—that is, Joseph—is equally aroused by the excitement of his female counterpart and that Hercules unconsciously recognizes this possibility.[12]

A number of other sequences in the movie reinforce the same point. Roscoe warns his Siamese sister-in-law that he doesn't want his wife "mixing with the tramps *you* hang round with," or (with a double irony, since he is himself a clown) "getting familiar with that cheap clown," or "lying in bed all day with *your* hangover." Later, he blames his fatigue on his sister-in-law because she "wants to stay up all night and read," and introduces himself to his sister-in-law's fiancé with the words "you must come to v... to v... to v... to see us sometime." Earlier, the unified susceptibilities of the Siamese twins are reinforced by a scene in which Violet, her eyes closed, is able to feel Phroso pinching Daisy's arm—a scene which, later on, is paralleled by one in which Hans quarrels with his fiancée, Frida, his real-life midget sister:

> *Frida:* To me, you're a man, but to her you're just something to laugh at. The whole circus is laughing at you.
> *Hans:* Let them laugh. They can't hurt me!
> *Frida:* But they hurt *me*, Hans!

Let us not forget, after all, the "code of the freaks," the sinister and symbolic unity of which we have twice been warned—once in the film's foreword, and once by the freak show impresario: "The hurt of one is the hurt of all; offend one, and you offend them all." The narrative of *Freaks*, we are advised, is "a story based on the effect of this code upon their lives," a code that is "a law unto themselves" and "rigidly adhered to."[13]

These kinds of linguistic oddities would have been amplified by the fact that talkies were still something of a novelty in 1932 and many of Browning's earlier films had been silent. Each segment of *Freaks* seems to have its own special magic word, which plays with all kinds of vocal and gestural metamorphoses, and these magic words are used to throw many of the film's unsettling scenarios into a state of psychic crisis. Some of these ritual words include *joke, laugh, monsters, poison, imagination,* and, most significantly, the word *freaks,* as in the scene of the wedding banquet, where Cleopatra—overexcited and drunk on champagne—screams the word repeatedly at her wedding guests.[14] Critic Jean-Claude Biette (1978) claims that these magic words, certain of which are notable only in relation to other words that oppose them, perform a substantial informative purpose in the narrative. "The keywords . . . reveal of each character how and in what way they are formed," writes Biette. "The physical presence of 'actors' experiencing trouble with doubled or mixed-up bodies . . . sends ambiguous messages and defies nomenclature. These words imply acceptance by the body on the one hand, and violent refusal on the other" (26).

A good example of this linguistic and bodily ambivalence comes with the birth of the bearded lady's baby, announced around the fairground in a whisper by the bird-woman (a "little bird" spreads the news), causing all the freaks to congregate in the bearded lady's caravan, where her bedsheets are drawn back with a dramatic flourish:

> *Phroso:* Oh, ain't that cute. What is it?
> *Mme.* Tetralini: A girl.
> *Phroso:* Oh boy, that's great. And it's going to have a beard.

Another nice scene of gender confusion occurs when Hercules is berating Roscoe, dressed as a classical matron, for ruining his comedy act with his unfeminine behavior. "A Roman lady! Scratching herself!" complains Hercules. "Well," whines Roscoe, "can't a Roman lady itch?" Later, Phroso makes a joke on the same theme when trying to comfort Venus, who has just walked out on her ex-lover, Hercules:

> *Venus:* Hey. You're a pretty good kid.
> *Phroso:* You're darn right I am. You should have caught me before my operation!

These puns, stutters, and verbal redundancies are emblematic of the film's obsession with otherness and duality in the symbolic form of mutilation, amputation, doubling, and renunciation. The film itself, moreover, suffers from a formal duality. While it is both a fictional narrative about Nature's revenge on herself as well as a documentary contribution to modern teratology, which comes first, and which is the incidental accompanying result of the other?

The film imposes a permanent relativism on the states of grandeur and proportion, thereby refusing to allow anyone to have the last word. When Cleopatra uses an infantile tone to speak to Hans (asking him, "Are you a man or a baby?"), Hans and Frida, in turn, imitate the cloying tones of the "big whore," Cleopatra. In the case of Schlitzie and the other pinheads, their beribboned topknots and pretty dresses both highlight and travesty the otherness of femininity that lies beneath their characteristic bodily performance as novelty heads, as Phroso's gentle teasing of the snickering Schlitzie makes clear. "Oh, Schlitzie, what a pretty dress!" he tells her. "Oh, how beautiful you look tonight. You're just a man's woman, know what I mean? . . . If you're a good girl, when I get to Paris I'm going to buy you a beautiful hat with a lo . . . o . . . oong feather on it."

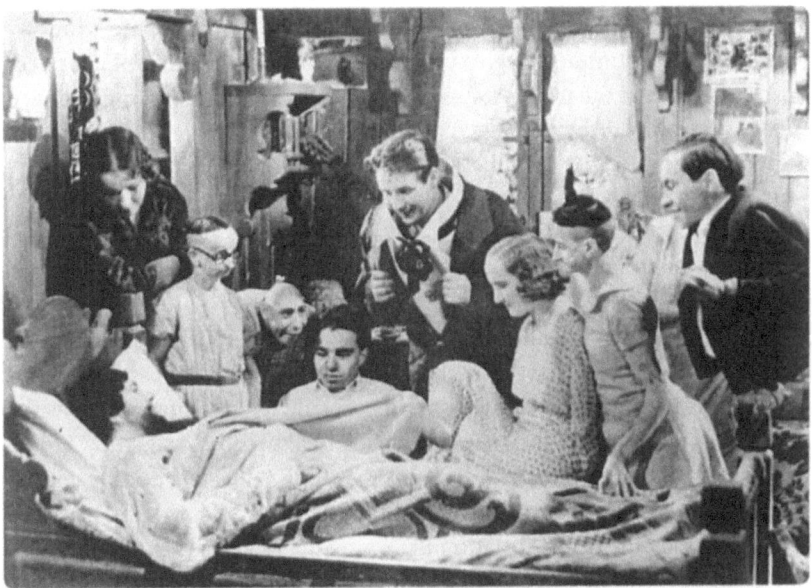

The Bearded Lady gives birth. © 1932 Turner Entertainment Limited. All Rights Reserved. Courtesy of BFI stills, posters & designs.

Much is made of the sinister codependence of the freaks themselves. Throughout most of the narrative they are noble and compassionate individuals, whose gentle respect for one another suggests an appreciation of the need for tolerance and privacy. On the other hand, it is difficult to forget the circus impresario's chilling words about "the law of the freaks," especially when the misfits themselves remind us of the symbiotic nature of their special lifestyle. One particular domestic moment between Frances the armless lady and her midget husband Angelo is an especially poignant example:

> *Frances* (sewing with her toes): Cleopatra ain't one of us. Why, we're just filthy things to her. She'd spit on Hans if he wasn't giving her presents!
> *Angelo* (placing a glass of wine between his wife's toes): Let her try it! Let her try to do anything to one of us!
> *Frances* (drinking from her glass): You're right. She don't know us. But she'll find out!

There are also a number of less comfortable sequences in which Browning exploits the freaks' chilling determination and single-mindedness in the execution of their "code." Like silent phantoms, the misfits begin to congregate around Cleopatra's wagon. A dwarf presses his nose against the windowpane; the "living torso" wriggles under the caravan's wheels; pinheads peer out from beneath the trailer steps—all embraced by stretches of prolonged silence. Later on, a dwarf, Angelo, and the "half-boy" meet in Cleopatra's wagon, waiting for her to return from her evening's performance. As they wait, Angelo plays ominously on his mouth organ as the storm builds outside. In these scenes, where the freaks wait calmly for some clandestine opportunity, the memory of "the code of the freaks" evokes a mood of imminent peril.

The film's system of allusion is similarly inventive. Philippe Carcassonne (1978) points out that not only does the physiological appearance of the freaks recall numerous creatures described in ancient writings (such as the men cut in two by Zeus and then stuck back together face-to-face by Apollo in Aristophenes' *The Banquet*), but also that their collective destiny constitutes a troubling illustration of some of the great Platonic myths. This point is reinforced by the transformation Browning operates on the mythical connotations of the names of the three principal characters. Cleopatra, the passionate lover of the gods, becomes a calculating bitch; Venus, the triumphant beauty, is a rejected showgirl; and the only labors performed by

Hercules are garish displays of brute strength, exploited for a credulous throng (43). And Nature, which has played such a destructive series of tricks on the freaks' bodies, is ironically in tune with their emotions all the way through the film. Edenic serenity welcomes the games of the dancing pinheads in the forest, and the punishment of the perfectly formed wrongdoers is accompanied by torrents of thundering rain.

The mise-en-scène of *Freaks* consists of the fleshly realization of an unconscious human obsession with atrophy, marginality, anomaly, mutilation, and redundancy. There is no simple axiom to explain the significance of this narrative. *Freaks* cannot be reduced to the opposition between "human monsters" and "monstrous humans" any more than it can be said of the film that "normality" disguises evil or that infirmity hides generosity. The gesture of Cleopatra, who refuses to become "one of them" by drinking from the freaks' "loving cup," embodies the rejection of the film by a public that found it decidedly impossible to identify with living atrocities. Banned, mutilated, and rejected, the film itself can be regarded as a freak, a mutation, a hall of mirrors that shows us finally that there is no "them," but only "us"—a set of deformed caricatures whose individual identity is no longer recognizable, bound forever to other strange bodies and misshapen, atrophied selves.

V

In order for us to fully understand the way in which Browning's film embodies humanity's obsession with anomaly, atrophy, mutilation, and abnormality, and thereby to acknowledge the complexities incarnate in the living form of the freak, it is necessary to take a somewhat wider perspective on the exhibition of human beings for pleasure and profit. The kind of circus freak show that forms the setting for Browning's film was common in the late nineteenth and early twentieth centuries, and was generally sustained by the exhibition of individuals with what we would now refer to as congenital handicaps, hormonal dysfunctions, and chronic disorders. Other circus freaks displayed major, minor, and (occasionally) fabricated physical, mental, or behavioral differences.

Yet others merely required cultural or phylogenetic differences. An interesting fact about the sideshow exhibits in *Freaks* is that, while all of them display acute bodily differences, many are also distinguished by cultural or racial otherness. The "living torso" is billed as "Randian" and was sometimes known as "Prince Randian of India," although his physiognomy is more negro than Indian, and he was in all probability of U.S. origin, like most of the freaks in Browning's film, despite their exotic names. Schlitzie and the Snow twins, for example, had previously been exhibited as the "Last of the Aztecs" or the "Lost Aztec Children," a hoax that was abetted by their oddly shaped heads, diminutive bodies, and mongoloid facial features. Other cultural distinctions are more subtle. The midgets Hans and Frida are plainly meant to be German, and the dwarf Angelo (Angelo Rossito) has a Mediterranean complexion, whereas all the able-bodied protagonists are, without exception, recognizably Caucasian.

These examples suggest that in the freak show, physical deformity was often equated with racial or cultural difference, highlighting the relationships between the freak show and other exhibitions of human difference. The nineteenth-century circus freak show was, in fact, a popular offshoot of a more sober attempt to come to terms with human otherness—the ethnographic showcase. Since the first days of European expansion, it was a matter for serious debate whether or not the humanoid creatures discovered in foreign lands were actually humans at all. The line dividing human from nonhuman has never been a particularly clear one, and even when foreigners have been granted the conventional attributes of humanity, the question remained as to whether or not they were *entirely* human and thereby entitled to full human treatment. In order to understand the many puzzling issues imprisoned in the body of the freak, it is important to appreciate the extent to which physical deformity and cultural otherness are connected in the history of human display.

Early travelers' tales repeatedly tell of the strange, misshapen creatures to be found in foreign lands, whether in the jungles of central Africa or in isolated European villages. Swiss physician and psychiatrist Felix Platter (1563–1614) has left us an account from 1602 of stumbling across cretinous infants in a village of the Valais, in France, which sounds strikingly similar to Duval's gamekeeper's shocked description of his first encounter with the misfits in *Freaks*. "They present an ugly sight," wrote Platter, "sitting in the streets and looking into the sun, and putting little sticks in between their fingers, twisting their bodies in various ways, with their mouths agape" (95–96). Some seventeenth-century scientists and physicians believed that those suffering from the accident of abnormal birth, such as albinos or cretins, were possibly new species of human beings. Others dismissed medical writers' descriptions of people suffering from ordinary diseases like goiter as being on a par with travelers' tales of fabulous animals and monsters.

Later, in the wake of European expansion, ethnographic showcases such as the Paris World's Fair regularly exhibited healthy, able-bodied people from non-Western cultures in specifically constructed pavilions and "native villages," such as the display of four hundred "natives" from the French colonies of Indochina, Senegal, and Tahiti at the Paris World's Fair of 1878. Sometimes these "natives" were encouraged to beg for money thrown into their showcases by visitors. Others were exhibited as part of the natural history of their colony, along with apes and baboons. Perhaps the best-known example of this latter practice is the case of Ota Benga, a pygmy boy displayed in a cage with a chimpanzee and later an orangutan at the Bronx Zoo, with a label informing zoo-goers of his age, height, weight, and provenance (the Kasai river in the Congo). The *New York Times* of September 9, 1906, reviewed the zoo's new exhibit and reported that "the pygmy was not much taller than the orang-outang, and one had a good opportunity to study their points of resemblance. Their heads are much alike, and both grin in the same way when pleased."[15]

As part of the showcase, Benga and similar exhibits were forced to stay within a precisely circumscribed part of the exhibition space, and the boundary between this space and that of the citizens visiting and inspecting them had to be respected unconditionally. This is also the case in *Freaks*. The entire narrative revolves around the "space" occupied by the able-bodied protagonists and that allotted to the freaks, into which Cleopatra calculatingly trespasses. In fact, the freaks are described very much in terms of their own "species," with its laws, practices, and jurisdictions, the transgression of which impels their ritualistic execution of sanctioned justice. As the showman says, they "have built up among themselves a code of ethics to protect them from the barbs of 'normal' people," "their rules are rigidly adhered to," and "their code is a law unto themselves."

Sometimes, as in the case of Ota Benga, these human exhibits were displayed virtually as animals—a common arrangement fed by contemporary scientific theory. Visitors were sometimes encouraged to approach them and touch them, as one might an animal in a zoo. At other times, they were displayed as ferocious cannibals who lived by bloodthirsty sacrificial rituals. A set of aborigines from Queensland on exhibit at the Frankfurt Zoo and elsewhere in May 1885 was described in the exhibition catalog as "the first and only obtained colony of these savage, savaged, disfigured and most brutal race ever lured from the remote interior wilds, where they in ceaseless bloody feuds and forays, to feast upon each other's flesh. The very lowest order of mankind, and beyond conception most curious to look upon."

This rhetoric of feral brutality was traditionally associated with all that was corrupt and unnatural, and there existed a whole body of publications theorizing on similarities of physical appearance between particular types of human insanity and particular animal species. As the foreword to Browning's *Freaks* reminds us, "anything that deviated from the normal was considered an omen of ill-luck and representation of evil." The vocabulary of taming and savagery employed to muster public excitement about captured circus animals was also used for the ethnographic showcasing of human beings, who were often, according to cultural anthropologist Raymond Corbey (1993), "commodified, labelled . . . scripted, objectified, essentialized, decontextualized, aestheticized and fetishized . . . thus becoming narrative characters in the citizen's articulation of identity—of Self and Other" (367–68).

The reverse situation—the exhibition of Westerners by non-Western peoples—is far rarer, but not altogether unknown. A British party was at first kept in cages by the Senegalese while it was debated whether or not the strange creatures were actually human, and, according to Corbey (1993), similar reports came in from time to time from other parts of the world (363–64). Devotees of Melanesian cargo cults have been reported to sit around tables with bottles of flowers in front of them, dressed in European-style clothes, waiting for a cargo place to materialize. Other cults use magic pieces of paper inscribed with kabbalistic writing. Europeanness, or Americanness, is transformed into a theatrical display that plays an eloquent part in the cultists' traditions. Anthropologist Peter Worsley (1959) points out that when the Melanesians first saw American blacks living lives of luxury, or on equal terms with GIs, it seemed that the old prophecies of the cargo cult leaders had been fulfilled at last (159).

The distinction between "us" and "not us" has always been a troublesome one to make, mainly because—while such distinctions tend to be based chiefly on the physical manifestations of racial characteristics—there is still no reliable way of distinguishing one race from another. While it is certainly possible to classify a great number of people on the basis of their physical features alone, there is still no known feature, or group of features, that applies in all cases. To confuse matters even more, many of the differences between races are invisible, ranging from the shapes of bones, to the consistency of ear wax, to slight variations in body chemistry. Some can be as subtle and discrete as the sensitivity of the eye to various strengths of light. It is known, for example, that certain races have more pigmentation in the iris and at the back of the eye, where the image falls.[16]

The main difference between the nineteenth century's reaction toward ethnographic showcases and the modern audience's reevaluation of *Freaks* is one of ideology. While visitors to Ota Benga's cage at the Bronx Zoo may have found the display touching and poignant, as many journalists of the time did, there was never any real sense of acknowledgment that the strangeness of the exotic other was something "we" shared and that only "our" repression of "our" atavistic impulses gave this kind of display its power to shock. To the postmodern unconscious, however, the modern myth of the primitive as essential human stripped of all civilized niceties has become an ideological commonplace and something we all take from granted.

The notion of depth employed by this myth is a significant element of the postmodern condition and has had an unbroken hold over our imagination ever since Freud's (1913) use of archeological imagery to describe the conscious and the unconscious. Freud implied that whatever is unearthed is the treasure, and the deeper it is hidden, the more valuable it must be. As Frances Mascia-Lees and Patricia Sharpe (1992) point out, "We expect to discover in other cultures, as Dorian Gray did in his portrait, only hideous manifestations of the truth of who we are, manifestations we can use equally well to criticize or sustain our social order. We look to other cultures as little more than veiled images of our own unconscious drives" (654).

VI

If the freak show generated confusion between physical deformity and "otherness," it generated even further confusion between the individual's identity and his or her role as a freak. As *Freaks* testifies, in the nineteenth- and early twentieth-century circus freak show, dwarfs, hunchbacks, giants, amputees, hermaphrodites, and Siamese twins as well as people suffering from obesity, hirsuteness, and primary microcephaly were all put on display and "sold" in much the same way that today's promotion agencies advertise film actors, personality vehicles, star "packages," and so on. Often, the appeal of this promotion relied on generally unsuccessful attempts to fake a generic merchandising of the individual and his or her role as a freak, as in the common "franchising" of fat ladies as Dolly Dimples, Bunny, Jolly, or Baby, just as, for example, there is more than one set of excessively tall basketball players traveling under the name of the "Harlem Globetrotters."

In *Freaks*, Schlitzie and Koo Coo are both billed as "herself," the Snow twins as "Zip and Pip," and the hermaphrodite as "Joseph/Josephine." Other sideshows used the same technique. The famous Henry Johnson, a microcephalic African American man, more commonly known as Zip or What Is It?, apparently colluded with his manager in a number of exotic frauds surrounding his billing as "Wild Man" or "Man Monkey," as testified in his well-publicized "last words" apparently spoken to his manager, "Well, we fooled 'em for a long time" (Fiedler 1978, 130). General consensus among freak-show entrepreneurs and their rubes seemed to be that public curiosity about unique physical abnormalities was related to common human anxieties about the body. "When I look at freaks it makes me content by comparison to be less than perfect," claimed Clyde Ingalls, boss of the sideshow for Ringling Brothers (Drimmer 1973, 10).

As we learn from *Freaks*, the original circus sideshows exhibited their human oddities in a variety of modes apart from that of the horrifying and monstrous. Attempts to confuse the "real" person with the constructed freak often led to the individual being exhibited in the aggrandized mode, which endowed the freak with status-enhancing characteristics. The aggrandized mode was particularly appropriate for giant and fat ladies, as in the case of Celestia Geyer, also known as Jolly Dolly or Dolly Dimples, billed as "The It Girl of Fat Ladies" and "The World's Most Beautiful Fat Lady" (Fiedler 1978, 180). It was, however, also used for midgets like Violet and Daisy Hilton in *Freaks*. Presented as "wonders," "marvels," or "prodigies," the aggrandized exhibit's elevated status was—theoretically at least—based on his or her ability to overcome disadvantages, which was considered to be a sign of moral worth: "The 'wonder' was not merely physical, it was the work of steadfast courage and perseverance" (Bogdan 1988, 217).

In time, some of the freak-show managers who used the straight aggrandized mode of presentation for their exhibits occasionally began inserting humorous twists into their pamphlets and performances. For example, a parodic wedding might be arranged between a dwarf and a giant, or a fat lady and a skeleton man, such as the widely reported 1924 wedding between Peter Robinson, the Living Skeleton, and Fat Lady Bunny Smith. In *Freaks*, the Bearded Lady is the mother of the Skeleton Man's (bearded) baby, and the dwarf Angelino is married to the armless lady. These kinds of publicity stunts had the apparent function of easing the tension some of the rubes may have felt in the presence of the freaks, or of poking imaginative fun at other people's domestic tranquility, or else comically amplifying the suppressed or merely tacit mismatched qualities and dispositions of "normal" couples. At its most base, this comic mode of presentation descended into straightforward mockery. Toward the last decade of the nineteenth century, the exhibition of fat people (usually dressed in skimpy costumes) increasingly contained elements of farce and ridicule, especially when a particular freak's career needed perking up with a touch of novelty.

Over time, developments in medicine and anthropological knowledge undermined some of the wild stories about the origins and capture of mentally retarded people, so the exhibition of (for example) primary microcephalics, such as Schlitzie and the Snow twins, moved from straight presentations emphasizing the attraction's scientific merit, to mockery and farcical displays. In such cases, the exhibit might be dressed as a child with his or her head shaved, perhaps (like Schlitzie) with a beribboned topknot emphasizing the oddly slanting features, or dressed in some bizarre and ridiculous outfit, like Koo Coo, the bespectacled bird woman in *Freaks* (see Bogdan 1988, 415).

In the early twentieth century, a common ignorance about other races, coupled with a belief in racial hierarchy and the undisputed superiority of Western culture, made this exotic mode of presentation highly popular until well into the 1930s—as with the Wild Aztec Children, the Wild Man of Borneo, or the Missing Link—until developments in science, medicine, and geographical knowledge rendered this style of exhibition no longer feasible. The best recorded examples include Hiram and Barney Davies, a pair of midgets from Long Island billed as "The Wild Men of Borneo," and the celebrated twins Maximo and Bartola, a pair of half-mulatto, half-Indian midgets exhibited from 1851 until well into the present century and billed as "The Wild Aztec Children," due to their strangely shaped heads, diminutive bodies, and mongoloid features (see Fiedler 1978, 45; Bogdan 1988, 177).

Further into the twentieth century, the exhibition of people with physical and mental differences came to be seen as increasingly offensive and degrading. This growing tide of popular opinion transformed the circus sideshow into the cultural form we recognize today, where self-made freaks such as tattooed people, fire-eaters, and sword-swallowers fill out the list of exhibits. But the presentation of self-made freaks was not always considered more acceptable and less degrading than the exhibition of "natural" freaks. Bogdan (1988) draws our attention to the "geek" or "gloaming geek," a wild man who, as part of his presentation, would bite the heads off rats, chickens, and snakes. Often, the geek was a down-and-out alcoholic, who performed in exchange for booze and a place to stay. "It was this type of coarse exhibitionism," writes Bogdan, "that helped earn carnivals reputations for being sleazy and morally reprehensible" (Bogdan 1988, 262; Fiedler 1978, 130).

Historical writing about freak shows has occasionally glorified the role of the freak as a saintly creature with a marvelously stoical disposition, considerate to those in trouble and miraculous or angelic in spirit. Others have suggested that the freak claimed an elevated position in the carnival status system, having nothing to do but exhibit himself or herself in order to make a sometimes quite substantial living. In distinguishing between "natural" and "self-made" freaks, for example, it has been claimed that "natural" freaks had higher status in the sideshow than "self-made" freaks (see Mannix 1990). However, ethnographic research into the carnival social system has proved otherwise, suggesting that while freaks are appreciated and often well-liked in the carnival, they are seldom envied, occupying a status similar to that of showgirls who perform in dance shows, magicians, illusion performers, and so on (Easto and Truzzi 1972, 551).

In the age of mass media, most people would agree that it is ethically wrong and morally degrading to display deformed human bodies for curiosity and profit; and numerous cities, states, and even countries (the former Soviet Union, for example) have passed laws prohibiting it (see Drimmer 1973, 15). The social acceptance of a large number of minority groups has widely extended popular notions of "nature" and "the natural," while, at the same time, structuralist readings of the body commonly reinforce the dichotomy between consciousness and the corporal, between representation and its *representatum*, upon which Western logic has been based since antiquity. More materially, perhaps, post-Saussurean anthropology has no need to refer the development of culture to any natural (extracultural) demands (see Sáez 1992, 135). It is commonly held that how the West views human otherness has less to do with the physiological characteristics of certain individuals than with our own cultural identity and our tendency to confuse the role a person plays with that person's "true self."

Today, physical or mental abnormalities are more likely to be considered—in Western culture, at least—in terms that are scientific, psychoanalytic, ethnographic, or anthropological, rather than moral ("anything that deviated from the normal was considered an omen of ill-luck") or spiritual ("gods of misfortune and adversity were invariably cast in the form of monstrosities"). Perhaps a pertinent example of contemporary ethnographic showcasing is the phenomenon of "cannibal tours," packaged vacations in which Western tourists are taken into areas of Africa and South America to encounter "primitive" (or ex-"primitive") peoples who have been encouraged to act out their "uncivilized" role to the tourists in a mutually exploitative encounter (see MacCannell 1990, 14).

Although much of anthropology and ethnography defines itself in opposition to the sensationalism and pseudoscience of the freak show, still, ethnographic showcases in the original sense can be observed where tribal peoples are isolated in the "zoos" of research papers. Medicine and psychology are still highly theoretical modes of "presentation," carefully constructed frameworks that emphasize particular aspects of the individual at the expense of others and that are directed—like the anthropological research paper—toward fostering a particular impression in a certain audience (Bogdan 1988, 276). The same kind of showcasing is to be found in "mondo" documentaries such as *Mondo Cane* (1963) and *Shocking Asia* (1974) (see chapter 7), with their "realistic" depictions of unusual human behavior and strange cultural practices from around the globe (see Staples 1994, 661).

As the disciplines of anthropology and ethnography have turned increasingly toward self-critique, it has become a recognized commonplace that differences between ethnographer and exhibitor, between anthropologist and missionary, between fieldworker and tourist have not been so absolute as was once supposed. Ethnographic and anthropological narratives that include the researcher in the story have opened the way for other, more personal narratives that acknowledge more closely the personal, unconscious, and emotive aspects of the ethnographic encounter (see Mascia-Lees and Sharpe 1994, 660). The main difference in our contemporary versions of ethnographic showcases and public freakfests is that these displays are now considered, however implicitly, to reveal not so much about the lives, feelings, and traditions of other people, but, more and more obsessively, to reveal layer upon hidden layer of ourselves.

VII

The freak show has not vanished completely from twenty-first-century culture: It has merely found other, possibly more subversive, cultural forms. The daytime talk shows hosted by such impresarios as Jerry Springer, Maury Povich, Montel Williams, and Sally Jessy Raphael often feature the special appearance of freaks. People suffering from morbid obesity, little people like Harry and Daisy Earles, people dying from AIDS, people whose plastic surgery has gone horribly wrong, hermaphrodites like Joseph/Josephine, thalidomide victims, transsexuals, deaf-mutes, and people with cerebral palsy have all appeared on daytime talk shows. Most of these freaks are exhibited in the mode of "sensitive appreciation" (an alternative to the "exotic," "comic," or "aggrandized" mode), with host and audience asking "sympathetic," "understanding" questions in an apparent attempt to acknowledge and understand the difficulties society puts in the way of the physically deformed human body. The "guests" are generally treated as respectable, intelligent human beings, and the television impresarios usually choose to adopt the currently fashionable style of "sensitive and thoughtful display."

No amount of "sensitive awareness," however, can disguise the fact that the exhibits on display in the contemporary mass-media freak show are being exhibited (and occasionally—though not often—paid substantial sums of money) to display their abnormal physical conditions: hence their prime-time curiosity value. While the audience of freak shows like Madame Tetralini's might have been motivated, at least partly, by provincial inexperience and a naive curiosity about Wild Men from Borneo or Children of Lost Aztec Civilizations, the cable television audience can have no such motivation. Access to different races or cultures, by way of cheap travel, media depictions, or racial integration has meant that the exotic is no longer a plausible mode of representation, on the talk show at least. And while freak shows like Madame Tetralini's might have been visited by (at the very most) a thousand rubes a day, one single episode of a daytime talk show is sent out by cable and satellite to an international network of viewers. Where Madame Tetralini's freak show would have pandered to the naive curiosity of a small, highly impressionable minority, the contemporary television freak show appeals, seemingly, to a far more disturbing nexus of emotions: perverse voyeurism in the guise of thoughtful and understanding sensitivity.

Today's freak show has moved out into the mass media and beyond, onto the streets. A glance over the display of any shopping mall card and poster outlet will reveal a garish collection of freak postcards and greeting cards featuring photographs of "comic" fat ladies in tutus and ballet slippers or bikinis, or a light-hearted selection of self-made freaks, from tattooed men and "gurners" (bizarre face-twisters) to punks and other fashion victims. Others are presented in the exotic or aggrandized mode as catwalk "supermodels." Unnaturally emaciated mannequins like Jodie Kidd and Kate Moss would have rivaled the Skeleton Man for top billing in the original form of freak show. Those other fashion models who are valued for their Slavonic or African features (such as Alek Wek, Naomi Campbell, and Nadja Auermann) have been turned into aggrandized curiosities appealing to exactly the same impulse as that which sent crowds of impressionable rubes to gaze at the Wild Aztec Children or the Missing Link. And the "gloaming geek" of the fairground who repulsed so many people by biting the heads off rats, chickens, and snakes has his contemporary counterpart in stars of heavy metal such as Alice Cooper and Ozzy Osbourne, whose cultic reputations are founded on similar abilities. The self-made freak in the form of the "human dustbin" is another form of geek. Outrageous showmen who have taught themselves the ability to swallow broken glass, to eat metal, and to vomit up live fish have for the last seven or eight years been a staple entertainment at campus parties and magic shows, both in live performance and on television. A few years ago I attended an event at the student bar at the

University of East London, which featured Steve Brown, the "human dustbin," who could not only swallow live goldfish in a variety of different colors but could also regurgitate them—still living—in the color sequence requested by a member of the audience.

Freaks are also at large in the pornography industry. There has always been a large market for pornography featuring obese women, especially if their obesity is concentrated in the areas of the breasts and buttocks. Many magazines and websites (and a number of movies) are devoted to pornographic displays of obese women, and there is an equally thriving market for photographs of women with colossal breasts, both natural and artificial. Hard-core porn is well-known for its male studs with their abnormally large genitalia—such as the legendary John Holmes, or "Johnny Wadd"—but may also feature occasional "guest" freaks of different varieties, such as dwarfs, monorchids (men with only one testicle), and triorchids (men with three testicles). This kind of material is a none-too-distant cousin of "specialist" magazines, websites, and movies for connoisseurs of "golden showers" and "water sports" (women urinating, usually on men), scatology (women defecating), and pedophilia. Publications such as the *Fetish Times* and the *Amputee Times* cater to the tastes of those erotically fascinated by the aesthetics of amputation and surgery (see Parfrey 1977, 94–95), though these kind of publications use sketches and pen-and-ink artwork more than actual photographs.

The freak show has also gone tabloid. Newspapers like the *Weekly World News*, while claiming—however ironically—the status of "family newspapers," regularly feature as curiosity pieces stories about people suffering from congenital malformations, hormonal dysfunctions, and other kinds of chronic disorders, both natural and self-made. Garish photographs are often accompanied by "true-life" stories, sometimes employing the aggrandized and at other times the comic mode of display. A British tabloid called the *Sunday Sport,* when it was first published, included a feature entitled "Freak of the Week," exhibiting photographs of human oddities, with comic-parodic stories attached. One of these was the tale of a child suffering from progeria, a rapid aging syndrome, who was christened by the newspaper with the name "Jimmy Wrinkle." Another set of freak photographs, this time of an enormously obese woman known only as "Gert Bucket," was accompanied by a mocking, Swiftian tale about how she was responsible for the collapse of the Berlin Wall, single-handedly bringing peace to a divided Germany. This kind of tongue-in-cheek, voyeuristic, schlock-horror reporting can also be found, although in a more sober form, in women's magazines such as *For*

Woman and *Women's Own*, whose popularity is often a direct result of story headlines like "My Twin Sons Were Joined at the Hip," "I Counted My Ten Toes for the Last Time," or "I've Got Two Wombs and Two Vaginas!"

Less candidly sensational displays of freaks in the media also include "human interest" documentary television programs, such as those often broadcast on The Learning Channel, which deal with some of the social issues surrounding disability, such as experiments with centers for independent living; charity advertising campaigns, marriage, social and sexual prejudice, and so on. Although seldom overtly voyeuristic and sensational in the style of *Jerry Springer* or the *Weekly World News*, such programs often involve extensive footage of people with various kinds of bodily deformities, the most frequently exhibited being hydrocephalics, thalidomide victims, amputees, deaf-mutes, and people suffering from cerebral palsy. Programs such as these are made by and for the able-bodied community, ostensibly to promote social awareness of disability issues. Yet it is often the case that the more disabled the interviewee, the more such programs become a "spectacle" rather than a source of social information. While clearly there will be a certain minority who will watch such programs for the same reasons they buy the *Amputee Times*, for the rest of the audience—and, indeed, for the show's producers and directors—it is ultimately impossible to separate altruistic social concern from voyeuristic self-satisfaction. No able-bodied person can watch such programs without a sense of appalled relief, however unconscious or vestigial, not to have been born a freak.

In fact, the contemporary mass media exhibit so many different forms and manifestations of the malformed human body that it is not overstating the case to claim that the freak show has gone prime-time, both reflecting and impelling current obsessions with body piercings, tattoos, dreadlocks, and so on. Cultural anthropologists Mascia-Less and Sharpe (1994) relate Western culture's obsession with the deformation of the human body to "expressions of hysteria at the loss of the primitive," (662) which can take a whole variety of forms, from a fascination with exotic tourism to dabblings in body piercing, self-mutilation, and auto-trepanning. Another example is the debate surrounding the so-called "Roswell footage," the obviously faked autopsy of what is supposed to be an alien body recovered from the wreckage of an extraterrestrial spacecraft that crashed at Roswell, New Mexico, in July 1947. According to UFO lore, military personnel kept the unfamiliar bodies alive (for as long as two years, according to some sources) for the purposes of anatomical research. Those involved in the incident, including the "autopsy" cameraman who sold the footage, refused to contemplate the possible existence of alien life forms, referring to the captured bodies simply as "freaks."

VIII

Despite the sanguine prediction in the foreword to *Freaks* that "modern science and teratology is rapidly eliminating such blunders from the world," Western society today contains more bodies that meet one or another of the requirements of the freak show than ever before. Today, the exhibition and presentation of deformed, mentally handicapped, and non-Western people for curiosity and profit seems wholly incongruous with our current social and political perspective, our sense of privacy, propriety, and the dignity of the individual. The freak show, in its original circus format at least, no longer exists. "The concept of *freak* no longer sustains careers" (Bogdan 1988, 267). Most people understand that the freak show was founded on prejudice and discrimination toward the bodily abnormal and deformed, and the contemporary notion of "handicapism"—a set of assumptions and practices that promote the differential treatment of people because of apparent or assumed physical, mental, or behavioral differences (Bogdan and Biklen 1977, 14)—is as useful a term as "racism" and "sexism" for understanding prejudice as something that is taken for granted, ideologically, in our culture.

Today's political climate makes it very easy to find the circus freak show reprehensible because its mode of spectacle centered wholly on the physical. Exhibits in the nineteenth- and early twentieth-century freak shows were presented for one very clear and simple reason: There was something odd, exceptional, or prodigious about their physical bodies. Although the aggrandized and comic modes of presentation might have attempted to promote some kind of association between the physical abnormality and the individual's character, such considerations were always "extras": The main attraction was always the physical deformity of the freak's body. It was generally acknowledged that the attraction of the exhibit was a visual, physical, and occasionally even tangible anomaly that had very little to do with character, personality, or "true" self, as many case histories testify. The most famous of the exhibits in *Freaks*, for example, were well-known partly because of the contrast between their monstrous physical appearance and their morally superior characters. Harry Earles, the midget, was known for his intelligence and acting abilities; Siamese twins Violet and Daisy Hilton were famously clever and graceful, attracting a number of suitors in their younger days. Schlitzie the pinhead, although severely retarded, was renowned on set for her affection and playfulness, and Johnny Eck, the "half-boy," was bright, funny, and talented. The film endorses a clear dichotomy between consciousness and the physical body.

It is difficult to appreciate how the contemporary mass-media freak show is very similar to its circus counterpart, and therefore difficult to find it as reprehensible, mainly because of its almost randomly interchangeable exhibition of freaks of the body and freaks of the consciousness—or, as one journalist put it, "divorced transvestites, overweight claustrophobics, schizophrenic stepchildren of hearing-impaired Satan worshipers" (Grossberger 1986, 26). Episodes of *Jerry Springer*, for example, have featured members of a family who all claim to be homosexuals, and mothers who want their children to have plastic surgery (against the child's wishes). Single episodes of the daytime *Oprah!* have, in the past, included debates on ethical dilemmas (Would You Donate an Organ to Save Your Child?") alongside moral oddities (a professor of anthropology who believes that arranged marriages should become universalized) and people with medical afflictions (an interview with "Magic" Johnson, discussing, in front of his wife, the sexual promiscuity that led to his contraction of the AIDS virus).

Geraldo Rivera, a show that was at one time more carnivalesque than most of its daytime counterparts, tended to focus on moral and psychological (rather than physical) freaks and the aftermath of their actions. One show, for example, featured the widow of David Linsford, a forty-seven-year-old police officer murdered by three men during a vehicle check. The murder was recorded by an in-car television camera and the footage was shown on *Geraldo*, with the widow's face inset so that viewers could witness her distraught reaction as she witnessed the murder of her husband for the first time (see Kerekes and Slater 1993, 121). In a similar (though slightly less voyeuristic) vein, *Donahue* of January 5, 1993, featured Mary Jo Buttafuoco, the wife whose shooting was the focus of the Amy Fisher case[17], just after Fisher's trial and sentencing, inviting the reactions of the audience along with those of celebrity lawyer Alan Dershowitz.

Oprah Winfrey, on the other hand, used to specialize in the exhibition of emotional freaks. Debbie DiMaio, spokeswoman for AM Chicago, which used to syndicate Oprah's show, admitted that "Oprah does best with controversial guests that have some kind of passion, and emotion, and a story to tell, something that happened to a person and they've made it through" (see Waldron 1991, 121). Oprah herself agreed. "I'm best at combinations," she claimed. "A sexual surrogate one day, Donny and Marie Osmond the next day, and then the Klan" (Waldron 1991, 109). Other past guests on

Oprah! have included stars of child pornography, a group of nudists, men with abnormally large sexual organs, and a fifteen-year-old boy who had been part of a Satanic cult for ten years, who claimed to have witnessed human sacrifices and who knew that one day he would have to sacrifice himself. "People make fun of talk shows because we do transsexuals and their parents," claimed Oprah. "But if I feel something is going on in the world and it's happening to somebody, maybe someone else is interested in it. I really think you can do anything with good taste" (Waldron 1991, 190).

This taste becomes more questionable, perhaps, when the boundaries between exhibited and exhibitor are broken, and the freak show's impresario joins the freaks on stage. This happened to Oprah when the topic of her show was incest. After listening to a middle-aged woman painfully recount to her audience the circumstances behind her autistic son's birth (that he was also her father's child), Oprah, exclaiming that she had also been the victim of sexual abuse, embraced the woman and broke down and wept. Scenes like this one substantiated the claim of Steve Edwards, the host of AM Chicago, that there is something bizarre and freakish about the talk-show impresarios themselves. "We are all strange people. We are all highly neurotic people," claims Edwards. "All of us have interviewed Siamese twins. All of us have had animals poop on us. This is a strange category of people" (see Waldron 1991, 105). Spectators have been absorbed in the past by Oprah's ongoing battle with her shape and weight, and how it might or might not affect her marriage prospects. These quirks seem to be essential to the current generation of talk-show hosts, particularly the rangy, smooth-pated, and laconic Montel Williams and the formerly 250-pound, ex-cult-movie actress Rikki Lake, the TV talk-show version of Madame Tetralini, tender and vulnerable nursemaid to her own young brood of freaks.

There is something particularly compulsive about the contemporary freak show's breaking of boundaries, whether these be boundaries between exhibits, keepers, and rubes, or the boundaries between physical, emotional, and psychological freaks. This seemingly random merging of physical and psychological oddities may have some pressing connection with what Philip Rieff (1966) has termed "the triumph of the therapeutic." U.S. culture, especially, has become increasingly secularized, with a popularized version of quasi-analyical psychotherapy—a therapeutic vocabulary—almost entirely replacing moral concerns. This symptom of the current political and ideological climate often creates a freakish, two-headed psycho-homiletics with "diagnoses" like "lack of self esteem" or "low sense of human dignity." The convicted rapist or child-killer once condemned as "evil" and "villainous" will now be referred to as "repressed," "psychotic," or "schizoid," their crimes the manifestation of "incomplete socialization," their character the result of "inadequate parenting."

It is this popularization of various styles of counseling and different kinds of therapy—processes that Freud, incidentally, would barely recognize—that opens the gate to the exhibition of psychic freaks. Unlike its circus progenitor, the contemporary mass-media freak show exhibits both freaks of the body and freaks of the consciousness in the same public arena. Both are considered to be victims of crippling circumstances beyond their own control: the first a sufferer from congenital malformations or hormonal dysfunction, the second a helpless victim of inappropriate acculturation or an emotionally deprived upbringing. The contemporary freak show's chosen mode of display, in line with the current ideological climate, does not always focus (except for prying camera work) on the physical, the visible, or the tangible, although physical manifestations of distressed formation, such as copious tears or uncontrollable twitching, are always to be hoped for. This demonstrative boundary-crossing makes the modern freak show very difficult to locate, and even more difficult to condemn.

IX

Freaks allows us to access some of the sociocultural dimensions of the freak show. A brief study of anthropological showcases reveals that the origins of such thoughts and questions are rooted in deep-seated historical anxieties about the nature of the human being. Both lines of research must begin with the same issue of phenomenological inquiry. What, in a human being, constitutes freakishness? Where does it begin, and when does it end?

Browning's freaks are pathologized because of their interstitial nature. Neither adults nor children, neither men nor women, neither humans nor beasts, these freaks fall outside all long-established cultural categories. What should properly be kept inside the body hangs out for all to see, and what should be part of the bodily insides is either obtrusive, truncated, mutilated, or absent. Ontologically, these freaks are abject because they embody both the sight and the site of pollution and taboo.[18]

Clearly, however, what might at first appear to be disturbingly marginal is often central to our self-understanding, and those that fascinate—that we at the same time both shun and pay to see—are in fact reflections of our own condition. Fiedler's mythological, psychoanalytic approach to the freak posits the notion that human beings have a deep, psychic fear of "pollutant" people with specific abnormalities. Dwarfs, for example, confront us with the fear that we will never grown up; hermaphrodites, with our own ambivalent sexual feelings; giants, with our own bodily monstrosity; and pinheads with the farcical knot that is the human cerebellum.

More profoundly, Bakhtin's reading of the bodily grotesque in medieval carnival can help us come to terms with our own obsessions with the deformed human body, both in the freak shows of nineteenth and twentieth-century circuses and in contemporary mass-media representations. Bakhtin points out that circus and carnival forms, as special phenomena, have survived up to our time, when other manifestations of popular-festive life, related to it in style and character (as well as in origin) have either died out long ago, or else degenerated so far as to become indistinguishable (Bakhtin 1968: 217). Displays of bodily deformity and the grotesque, according to Bakhtin, were a central motif of medieval carnivalesque, and have retained their significance in the contemporary version of the carnival. The revolution of medieval carnivalesque was driven by freakish images of bodily members, organs, and parts of the body, especially dismembered and mutilated parts. Typical motifs might have included distended bodily members, areas of the body exaggerated to gigantic dimensions: monstrous bellies and noses, gigantic ears, breasts, and testes together with an array of carnival figures, including giants, hunchbacks, and dwarfs (see Bakhtin 1968, 328).

Most of these carnivalesque motifs can be found in the works of Rabelais, whose sources include medieval "wonder" texts like "Great Chronicles," "Wonders of the World," and, especially, "Indian Wonders," brochures and pamphlets describing all kinds of esoteric marvels, including marginal human beings with a distinctly grotesque character. Freaks described in "Indian Wonders" include—in addition to your dime-a-dozen dwarfs, giants, and pygmies—satyrs, onocentaurs, cyclops, half-human, half-animal "hippopods" with hoofs instead of feet, sirens with fish tails, "sinucephalics" who bark like dogs, "scipedes" with only one leg, "leumans" with faces on their chests, monsters with eyes on their shoulders or their backs, and others who feed through their noses (see Bakhtin 1968, 344).

According to Bakhtin, medieval carnivalesque was full of all kinds of freakish anatomical fantasies and bizarre bodily dimensions and features. The medieval imagination would have been accustomed to grotesque images of anatomical topographies. For the medieval man, "both in literature and pictorial art, the body of mixed parts and the strangest anatomical fantasies, the free play with the human limbs and interior organs was unfolded before him. The transgression of the limits dividing the body from the world also became customary" (Bakhtin 1968, 347). Certain bodily deformities, moreover, have a particular carnivalesque importance. Writing about Rabelais's descriptions of Napoleon and the exaggeration of the size of his nose, Bakhtin cites Schegans's claim that the grotesque begins where exaggeration reaches fantastic dimensions, the human nose, for example, being transformed into a snout or a beak. The grotesque nose (symbolizing the phallus) and the grotesque mouth (a wide-open bodily abyss) recur in nearly every form of the carnivalesque, as well as in abusive and degrading gesticulations. Of all features of the human face, the nose and mouth play the most important part in carnivalized versions of the body, especially when they become inanimate.

The peculiar and strained laughter provoked by comic presentations of the ex-liminal body (whether in carnival or the tabloid press) is an index to the anxiety that all of us feel about the freakish physical conditions attached to the state of human consciousness. Carnival laughter releases a rictus of repressed otherness and allows it to return. Our anxious, hysteric reaction to the half-boy or the living torso, the grotesque carnival devil, is a direct expression of human ambivalence about the material bodily stratum, helping us to understand (if not come to terms with) precisely what it means to be human. This, I believe, is the key to why, in carnival, so much emphasis is placed by culture on the freakishly inverted human body. Additionally, the exhibition of the freakish human body in carnival, or at the circus, or on the talk show, might well be linked to fantasies about merging and fusion. Emphasis on bodily functions such as consumption, defecation, and reproduction (as in the wedding feast or the birth of the bearded lady's baby in *Freaks*) creates a dense atmosphere of material fusion in which all dividing links between man and beast, between the consuming and the consumed body, are intentionally erased. At carnival time, the distinctive character of the body is its open, unfinished nature, its intersection with the world (as in the case of the living torso or the half-boy). In fact, *Freaks* presents us with a whole series of bodies that transgress the limits between animal and human flesh, culminating in the bizarre final image of Cleopatra transformed into a chicken. All known cultural and bodily categories are very nearly eradicated, as bodies, such as those of the Siamese twins or Joseph/Josephine, are fused into an abject and abjecting image of one dense, self-devouring body (see Bakhtin 1968, 122). This, at any rate, is one way of making sense of the grotesque image of multiple barking heads, yapping all at once like Cerberus, that such modern-day impresarios as Jerry Springer and Rikki Lake seem to strive so hard to produce in their on-stage antagonists.

X

A little more needs to be said, by way of conclusion, about the ambiguous carnivalesque laughter provoked by the freak show, in whatever form it might take. If we look closely at those moments of apparent humor that arise in *Freaks*, for example, it becomes clear that these jokes and their responses are of a nervous, neurotic, hysterical nature. Scenes and characters whose function is to provide "official" laughter always fail: The clowns, for example, are either aggressive and arrogant like the Rollo Brothers, or else anxious and insecure like Phroso and Roscoe. Phroso's headless chicken gag does not amuse Venus, who regards the trick as outdated and pathetic ("Oh, that's how it is," complains Phroso. "You don't think it's funny. You think it's sad, do you?"). A very similar exchange occurs when Phroso, who has forgotten to keep his date with Venus, tries to appease her by demonstrating a new trick. "Funny gag, ain't it?" asks Phroso. "Yeah," replies Venus, sarcastically. "I'm laughing myself sick."

Although the "official" humor may fail, there is plenty of spontaneous, "unofficial" humor in *Freaks*, yet it is always of the neurotic and hysterical variety. The film's first reference to the freaks describes them as "horrible twisting things, crawling, laughing, whining," and of all the freaks it is Hans, in his indignity, who—quite unintentionally—provokes the most laughter. Cleopatra and Hercules both chortle together desperately as Cleopatra flirts with the midget through the closed door of her trailer, and the sideshow stagehands ridicule him in public as he stands on a box to massage Cleopatra's shoulders.

Later, the same stagehands slap their thighs and roar with laughter at the proud Skeleton Man's pigeon-toed walk. Schlitzie snickers at Phroso's mock-flirtation with her, but when she tries to speak, her words are incoherent, and we cannot help but wonder just how much of his joke she is able to understand and how much of her laughter is nervous hysterics. And the laughter of the wedding party is interrupted by Cleopatra's drunken shrieks ("No! No! Stop it! Freaks! Freaks! Freaks!"), producing a concrete realization of the bacchanalian ceremony's essentially tragic nature. For Hans, the tragedy is understood only when it is too late and Cleopatra's poison is already taking effect in his system. "But my darling," explains his new wife, "it was only a joke." "Our wedding. A joke," moans Hans, collapsing to the floor, drugged. "Now I know how funny it is. Everyone laughing, laughing, laughing...").

Browning's film functions as a useful case study to illustrate the ambiguous, neurotic nature of laughter and humor, about which much has been written, by Freud, among others. The manifold jokes, tricks, clowns' gags, and moments of hysteria in *Freaks* are all symptoms of the unconscious fear and anxiety provoked by any manifestation of the human body distorted, twisted, truncated, out of control, and thereby made abject and ex-liminal. This bodily abandonment to convulsions and paroxysms of anxiety testifies to a neurotic disease of which *Freaks* is a telling symptom. Its laughter is not the laughter of relief, but a terrifying rictus of horror invoked by the symbolic, physical manifestation of the state of being human and of having a human body.

As a version of Bakhtinian carnival, the freak show provides a time and a space where the expected traditions and reactions of humanity are reversed. Anthropology catalogs a number of tribes and peoples (such as the Ik of the Kidepo Valley in Africa or the Kaiadilt of Bentick Island in the South Pacific) who, due to some social or cultural trauma, have reverted to a state where symbolic laughter was the common reaction to the death of loved ones and family members, to danger and pain, to trauma and violence, and finally to the rape of children, to famine, starvation, and death. For the Ik and the Kaiadilt peoples, pathological laughter was the main symptom of a mass reversal of humanity, incorporating the complete dissolution of family life, total valuelessness, apathy, and collapse. Laughter among both these peoples was a manifest reaction to spiritual decay, withdrawal, depression, and suicide; it served as an accompaniment to such rites of self-mutilation as ripping out one's testes or chopping off one's nose (see Calhoun 1972, 215–20). *Freaks* helps us to understand how part of the function of laughter is to vivify the manifest incongruity between human social organization and the uncontrollable nature of the polluting human body, an understanding that ironically—like the carnival itself—serves only to reinforce the strictures of human culture. According to Mary Douglas, the laughter provided by jokes is an anti-rite:

> The rite imposes order and harmony, while the joke disorganizes. From the physical, to the personal, to the social, to the cosmic, great rituals claim unity in experience. They assert hierarchy and order. In doing so, they affirm the value of the symbolic patterning of the universe. Each level of patterning is validated and enriched by association with the rest. But jokes have the opposite effect. They do not affirm the dominant values, but denigrate and devalue. (Douglas 1978, 102)

The failure of the "official" gags in *Freaks* suggests the devaluation of the social structure. Spontaneous, "unofficial" laughter provoked by the indignity of the distorted human body mimics a leveling, a dissolution of hierarchies, a collapse of values. A horror of undifferentiated, disorganized, uncontrolled relations is echoed in the pathological laughter inspired by visions of human bodies that are mutilated, truncated, interwoven, crossed over, etiolated, doubled, and incomplete.

XI

It has often been asserted that the integral and harmonized body provides an experiential basis for the ego. But the ego might as well be the basis for our ambivalence toward the freak. As a vivid index of all manner of ontological transgressions, of deformations and distentions suggesting demarcations blurred, the freak that fascinates and appalls may well objectify the fearful desire to dissolve the contours of the self. Be that as it may (and this is not the place to explore the possibility further), the decline of the nineteenth- and early twentieth-century freak show does not mean that the obsession with the freak no longer remains with us; rather, it has either been (unhealthily) repressed or else been channeled into popular cultural outlets that are more in tune with our current climate and pseudotherapeutic vocabulary. For others, the fascination with freaks finds its release in the clandestine outlets of subculture, such as hard-core porn.

Either way, the freaks are still with us and will remain objects of compulsive fascination and curiosity as long as we have a human consciousness and a human body. As *Freaks* can teach us, our voyeuristic drive to seek out and sometimes to laugh at the freak is compelled by the nervous disease of the human condition, whose symptoms include a neurotic fear of the human body and its terrifyingly incomprehensible autonomous functions. Our unending need to seek out, display, and mock the deformed physical body is essentially a compulsive repetition of an ancient story—a story that tells us, over and over again, that as far as the condition of being human is concerned, we're all freaks together.

2 Ritual, Tension, and Relief: The Terror of *The Tingler*

IT HAS LONG BEEN A COMMONPLACE OF HORROR film criticism—ever since the publication of Robin Wood's "An Introduction to the American Horror Film" in 1979—to acknowledge that the experience of watching a "trashy" low-budget B movie can be far more profound than that available to the spectators of more "serious" cinema. Those critics and scholars interested in nuanced acting, narrative elegance, and thematic complexity unhesitatingly write off the exploitation films of William Castle as unadulterated schlock—a brand of suspense that is thoroughly unsubtle, relying on a surface facetiousness and tongue-in-cheek aplomb, enlivened by moments of sudden, shrill shock. And yet at the same time, Castle's movie *The Tingler* has been mentioned by a number of important critics, directors, and scholars—including John Waters (1983)—as one of the most memorable moviegoing experiences of their youth. An investigation of this paradox will reveal there is more to *The Tingler* than hokum-laden jolts and low-cost gimmicks.

One of the most important aims of film scholarship is to vivify the symbolic nature of the half-thoughts and semi-awarenesses that the plot of the film makes manifest, however superficial, sporadic, or facetious they may be. Interestingly enough, in an interview with *Cinéfantastique* (1984) less than two years before his death, Castle remarked on his fascination with contemporary theoretical analysis of his 1950s and 1960s horror films, which, as Castle points out with some pleasure, "are being treated with increasing respect, and taken very seriously today at the universities where they study them." He goes on to make some other observations:

> It's a very strange thing. I definitely feel that possibly in my unconscious I was trying to say something. . . . I never expected that they would put under a microscope pictures that I had made in the fifties and sixties and look for hidden meanings. Nevertheless, that is what is happening. . . . And I think about inner meaning, truly, it is possible that deeply buried within my unconscious was the feeling of trying to say something. . . . And I get this from *The Tingler*.[1]

The tendency to take Castle's films seriously is clearly not widespread enough for movie director John Waters, whose retrospective of Castle's work in *American Film* is in part an attack on critics for being slow to elevate "this ultimate eccentric director-producer" to cult status.[2] But in fact, Waters was behind the times. *Cahiers du Cinéma* had published a brief but serious article about Castle's work by way of obituary in 1977, remarking on some of the ways in which films like *The Tingler* stand as realizations of the spectacular "happening-cinema" conceived by the Futurist movement: a system of traumatization, "where the spectacle unfolds not only on the screen, but also in the room, with special effects that allowed the audience to be played with like puppets."[3] Comparing Castle's work to that of Italian horror auteur Dario Argento, *Cahiers du Cinéma* praised *The Tingler* for its radical use of color in an otherwise black-and-white film, describing the film as "unfolding at the limits of psychodrama" and "in the popular psychoanalytic style of Tennessee Williams." "For Castle," *Cahiers* rightly concludes, "only the spectacle counts" (Garel 1977). Although it was obviously intended as no more than a bravura commercial ploy, *The Tingler* is, in fact, a deeply complex and interesting film, and in wiring up his cinema seats with electrical cables, Castle was actually—albeit unknowingly—extending the principles of experimentation with theater, audience, and spectacle initiated by Fillippo Marinetti and his Futurist followers in the late 1920s.

II

Born in New York City in 1914, William Castle broke into show business at the age of fifteen, getting a small part in a Broadway show by falsely representing himself as a nephew of Samuel Goldwyn. He went through a wide spectrum of acting, producing, and writing jobs before going to Hollywood at the age of twenty-three. After a transitional period as a dialogue director, he began directing on his own. The first picture he directed was *The Chance of a Lifetime,* which, when it first appeared in 1942, was hailed by *Variety* as "probably the worst directed picture in the history of motion pictures." But Harry Cohn at Columbia gave the twenty-nine-year-old Castle another chance. *The Whistler* (1944), a thriller, was a commercial success, and the respect Castle earned as the film's director enabled him to pursue a successful career. He directed dozens of low-budget films, showing some flair for crime and action situations.

It was not until the late 1950s, however, that Castle really came into his own by setting himself up as an independent producer, director, and—most importantly—showman. He specialized in chillers and schlock-horror films, most of which were panned by critics for "poor taste" but still fared handsomely at the box office. His most ambitious and best-known film was his 1968 adaptation of Ira Levin's *Rosemary's Baby,* which he produced, but wisely left Roman Polanski to direct. Later in his career, Castle also produced a number of television shows and portrayed a producer in Hal Ashby's *Shampoo* and a director in John Schlesinger's *Day of the Locust* (both 1975); he finally died of a heart attack in 1977 on the set of the film he was producing for MGM.

But the Abominable Showman, or the King of the Bs—as Castle came to be known at Columbia—is probably best remembered for the series of low-budget horror films he made between 1958 and 1962, for it was in these successful but exploitative chillers that the director formed a personal bond with his audience through a wide series of feisty, carnival-style gimmicks. Early experiments with wide-screen 3-D features and on-camera appearances (to introduce himself and to prepare the audience for the forthcoming cinematic experience) encouraged Castle to play around with various promotional ploys and exploitation devices that guaranteed his films their box-office success. "I've modeled my career on P. T. Barnum," he once boasted, and his influence on the subsequent history of exploitation cinema is undeniable. John Waters, himself the proud inventor of Odorama, has referred to Castle as King of the Gimmicks (1983), confessing that "William Castle was my idol."

Castle's most bizarre and ambitious experiment in audience participation was without a doubt the device of Percepto. During all first-release screenings of *The Tingler,* Castle instructed movie theater managers to wire up small electric motors, similar to handshake buzzers, to a certain number of seats. At a specific point in the movie, a specially planted female stooge in the audience would burst into hysterics and have to be carried out by a (fake) nurse in uniform. Moments later, the projectionist would push a button activating the electrical charges on the wired-up seats, allowing certain unfortunate movie spectators to be hit at the base of the spine by a brief electrical jolt.

Like many of Castle's other gimmicks, Percepto did not always function as the director might have anticipated. The most common anecdote, recounted by Castle in his autobiography *Step Right Up!* (1976), involved a cinema whose management, having dutifully installed the Percepto equipment the night before *The Tingler* was supposed to be shown, decided to test the device on a group of older ladies who were watching *The Nun's Story* on the last night of its run, with predictably hysterical results. Waters tells an anecdote about a showing in Philadelphia where one beefy truck driver was so incensed by the Percepto buzzer underneath his chair that he ripped his entire seat from the floor and had to be subdued by five ushers (1983, 57). Other Castle fans remember their suspense being broken by the broadcast announcement that "the Tingler is wanted in the lobby." John Waters describes his experience of *The Tingler* as "the fondest movie-going memory of my youth":

> I went to see it every day. Since, by the time it came to my neighborhood, only about ten random seats were wired, I would run through the theater searching for the magic buzzers. As I sat there experiencing the miracle of Percepto, I realized there could be such a thing as Art in the cinema (1983, 57).

III

First released in 1959, *The Tingler* features a suave Vincent Price as Dr. Warren Chapin, a research scientist deeply involved in experimentation on the cause and often lethal effects of human fear. Chapin suspects that many people who have died from extreme fear were killed by a parasite that takes shape within the vertebrae—"the Tingler"—which can be prevented from materializing only by the victim's screams. However, if the victim is not able to release the tension caused by this fear by screaming, the Tingler takes shape and cracks the human spine.

Chapin's lab assistant (and sister-in-law's fiancé) Dave Morris (played by Darryl Hickman) catches live dogs and cats for the doctor to use in his experiments on the pathology of human fear, but Chapin is more interested in human subjects. His first victim is his spiteful, cheating wife, Isabelle (Patricia Cutts), whom he frightens into unconsciousness at gunpoint.

Studying X-rays of her spine, he and Dave discover the bony shape of the Tingler emerging from Isabelle's vertebrae. Next, Chapin attempts to experiment on himself by locking himself in his laboratory and injecting himself with "100 micro-milligrams" of liquid LSD, recording his hallucinations, and trying desperately not to scream. Skulls and skeletons come to life; he has trouble breathing; the walls close in on him; his Tingler emerges . . . but the doctor finally gives in to his tension and destroys the creature with a scream.

Eventually, Chapin finds the perfect experimental subject: a paranoid deaf-mute woman (Judith Evelyn) with a morbid terror of blood. With a little unexpected help from her avaricious husband, Olly (Philip Coolidge), the deaf-mute is trapped in her apartment over a silent-movie theater and slowly frightened to death by a series of shocks: windows slam suddenly closed; a rocking chair starts rocking of its own accord; a hideously masked stranger appears to pursue her with a hatchet; a beckoning hand emerges from the depths of a blood-filled bathtub (bright red Technicolor in an otherwise black-and-white film); and the woman's death certificate appears on the door of the bathroom cabinet—*Cause of Death: FRIGHT.*

Upon determining the reason for the woman's death—that she had indeed died of fear—Chapin is granted permission from the seemingly innocent Olly to perform an important experiment. In the laboratory in his home, the doctor manages to remove the Tingler from the body's spine with a pair of forceps, and we are given our first glimpse of its solid, powerful form—in silhouette only, however: Chapin is operating behind a strategically placed screen. Almost immediately, the Tingler attacks Chapin's arm, falling off only when he screams. The Tingler (recaptured and picked up gingerly with a pair of forceps) is then placed in a special locked box while Chapin and his wife toast his success. But Isabelle (who wants him dead so she can marry her lover) has drugged his wine, and he falls unconscious on to the couch while his vengeful wife goes to release the Tingler, which then crawls onto the doctor's prone body, choking him around the neck with its spiny pincers until disempowered at the last moment by the screams of Isabelle's sister, Lucy (Pamela Lincoln).

Finally convinced that he has "violated the laws of nature," Chapin takes the Tingler over to Olly's house to place it back in the body of Olly's dead wife. However, during the process the Tingler escapes, slips down under the floorboards, and makes its way into the silent-movie theater below. On the loose, it attacks a girl in the audience, causing widespread hysterics. Dr. Chapin's voice is heard from the darkened screen informing the audience that the girl is being taken care of and that everything is under control.

Moments later, a second Tingler attack takes place, this time on the projectionist. The lights dim again, and the projected silhouette of the Tingler crawls across the screen. Chapin addresses the audience once more, this time to encourage everyone to "scream for your lives!" until the Tingler is thwarted, the danger has passed, and, claims Chapin, "We can now return to our picture."

The scientist replaces the lethal organism in the body of its host and leaves for the police station. Olly, left alone, finds himself sealed in the apartment with the corpse. But the dead woman, in a perfectly timed postmortem muscular spasm, sits up and directs an icy stare at her husband. In the film's final ironic twist, Olly falls dead to the floor. *Cause of Death: FRIGHT.*

While Castle's experiments with audience, theater, and spectacle in *The Tingler* were surprisingly radical, the film itself is rather typical of the direction of American horror movies in 1959. Universal Studios was beginning to exhaust its series of horror "classics," and the genre was gradually succumbing to the influence of the British Hammer style, which relied heavily on gore effects and placed less importance on plot. Horror was becoming more and more distinctly a B-movie genre, and the influence of Hammer would soon lead to Roger Corman's Poe cycle of the 1960s, many of which also starred Vincent Price. In addition, *The Tingler* is closely influenced by the horror-comedy tradition of the 1940s, typified by such Universal fare as *Abbot and Costello Meet Frankenstein* (1948).

The unapologetically ludicrous plot of *The Tingler* is held together only by the presence of Vincent Price, who also starred in another of Castle's gimmicky shockers, *The House on Haunted Hill* (1958); some might even go so far as to claim that the casting of Vincent Price was William Castle's most successful stunt. In both movies, the courtly Price plays a smarmy, effete sadist who nevertheless always manages to evoke audience sympathy as the wronged or injured party. Somehow, he remains urbane and avuncular while plotting an ingeniously violent revenge on his tormentors. The character played by Price in these two films has much in common with the prissy, effeminate gigolo—a playboy kept by an older woman—he plays in *Laura* (1944); it also looks forward to his elegantly sneering turns in Roger Corman's Poe cycle, the best of which is perhaps 1961's *The Pit and the Pendulum*. Indeed, one might argue that the barely suppressed male hysteria and homosexual panic of Price's Corman roles finally came to fruition in the 1973 movie *Theater of Blood*, in which he plays a number of roles, including that of a gleefully gay male hairdresser named Butch.

IV

The Tingler lays bare a shared fascination with the physiology and the workings of the human body—both the bodies on screen and the participating bodies of the cinema audience—and it is this fascination that allows the critic to access the film's conscious and unconscious implications. The terror of the Tingler relates to our own understanding of the ancient commonality of the human body, its failings, ruptures, and weaknesses.

The pattern that starts to emerge from a close analysis of *The Tingler* is one that demonstrates the close relationship between the symbolic order and the bodily order, disclosing how each gives form to the other in a dynamic intermingling of meanings that constitutes the basis for the history of human cultures and the symbolic importance of their narratives. To chart analogues between the symbol structure of contemporary narratives and the belief systems of earlier societies is not, as it first may seem, an attempt to cast a net further and wider for random connections, but rather it is an effort to look more deeply at the history of the human body, with its secret and disguised level of conscious understanding.

A number of primitive cultures also tell stories like that of *The Tingler*, involving versions of the animal-double motif. Some societies accept it as a matter of certainty that many people have secret animals like the Tingler living inside their bodies. These are either people with the power to temporarily assume the form of an animal or animals that can assume a human form. For example, animal doubles like the Tingler feature prominently in the Navajo skinwalker legends and also in stories told by the Mandari, as well as by neighboring communities of the Nile frontage.

The salient point here is not that either Castle or his scriptwriter, Robb White—who, incidentally, found the whole Tingler story quite ludicrous[4]—deliberately based the Tingler on an ancient tradition. White was simply fitting a screenplay to Castle's compulsive quest for a new gimmick. But the narrative that they evolved together, like many of the narratives of popular culture, happens to tread upon a very ancient and well-worn path through the cognitive map of the human psyche. Budget limitations, the need for an exploitative trick, and minimal concerns with the niceties of plot and characterization meant that the story of the Tingler could bypass the psychic censors habitually constructed by a cinema audience that had come to expect a certain level of realism and coherence of plot, and instead appeal directly to the audience's unconscious. Indeed, the first spectators of Castle's tricksy film, assailed directly by an ancient myth, were reportedly as ill-prepared and as violently disturbed as the victims of the vengeful parasite itself.

THE TERROR OF *THE TINGLER*

In Mandari culture, to take but one example from anthropology, man-into-beast transformations are held to be an example of witchcraft with a highly specific purpose. Beast-men are deliberately summoned by someone who, like Dr. Chapin in *The Tingler*, feels himself injured and denied a just hearing through the customary channels. In most of the societies that acknowledge them, beast-men are a recognized (if rarely used) ritual sanction that backs up traditional control; often they are considered to be a legitimate (but dangerous) way of drawing attention to wrongs. The danger lies in the fact that the user, employing the beast-man in the hope of gaining redress, runs a calculated risk if widespread harm is thought to have resulted.

A series of stylized domestic incidents in *The Tingler* makes it quite clear that Dr. Chapin's wife is continually unfaithful to him. She is absent when he returns home from the pathology lab, for example, and does not get back until the early hours of the morning, when Chapin spies her kissing her lover good-bye. In another scene, he enters the house only to hear the back

Judith Evelyn and Ghoul on the set of *The Tingler*. © 1959 Columbia Pictures. All Rights Reserved. Courtesy of BFI stills, posters & designs.

door slam, and finds two stained wine glasses and a gold tie clip on the hall table. Isabelle, in turn, complains that her husband spends so much time at his laboratory that she has no choice but to be unfaithful. "You know, Warren, you've lost contact with living people," she tells him. "There's a word for you . . ." "There's plenty for you," interrupts Chapin. Later, the Higgins's marriage is shown to be equally dysfunctional. "You know what it's like, doc," complains Olly. "*She'd* have killed *me* if she could."

In this respect, it is interesting that the only two Tinglers that are actually exposed to us in this film—the first in the silhouette of the X-ray machine, the second "in the flesh"—belong to the film's two main female characters, Isabelle Chapin and Martha Higgins. In cultures like the Mandari, the distance between people and animals is seen to be narrowed, directly and menacingly, whenever peril results from female sexual misbehavior. One result of this is the "animal accident"—mauling, trampling, snake and scorpion bites—which befalls the promiscuous woman's close male relatives. In *The Tingler*, Chapin is almost choked to death by the Tingler that his wife has let out of his cage and unleashed upon him. Our own culture charts associations between promiscuity through metaphor and analogy. Unregulated sex (promiscuity, adultery, incest) is regarded by most cultures to be animal-like and to lead to animal-related dangers. Similarly, sexual behavior metaphors in most cultures, including our own, are animal-based (goats, rabbits, monkeys). It is also important to note that such animal-double motifs are not exclusive to the myths and legends of primitive and tribal culture. Western culture has plenty of animal doubles of its own. Vampires and werewolves have long been a staple of horror movies, and, elsewhere, superheroes like Batman and Spiderman are extensions of the very same theme.

According to anthropology, the traditional animal double inhabits ambiguous areas of the social structure, habitually presiding at funerals and ghost sacrifices. It has been suggested that the animal double presides over areas of social and cultural life that are by nature ambiguous, unpredictable, and dangerous. In the same way, Castle's Tingler is associated with murders, autopsies, and funerals, as well as the netherworlds of neurosis, paranoia, and mistrust, and the ambiguous domains of death and sex. As the narrative unfolds, we come to learn that the Tingler presides over a night-world of psychosis, adultery, theft, bribery, corruption, broken promises, broken marriages, and wife-murder.

Significantly, the animal double does not always take the form of a mammal; it may equally take the form of an insect or fish. The Tingler is a kind of hybrid parasite—a cross between a worm, a lobster, and a centipede. Castle describes it in his autobiography as "sort of like a lobster, but flat, and instead of claws it has long, slimy feelers."[5] While there are plenty of examples of animal doubles that take the form of shellfish or insects, it is worth examining the fact that these categories of creatures are in themselves ambiguous or liminal. Shellfish, reptiles, and insects are the equivocal residue of the animal world, considered by some cultures to be the enemies of human beings (see, for example, Halverson 1976). Some anthropologists have suggested that insects are considered abject and interstitial because they are generally not rated as food (in most countries at least), whereas reptiles and shellfish are determined to be freakish and ambiguous because their cold-bloodedness distances them from our far greater affective closeness to warm-blooded animals. In this light, it is somewhat ironic that insects, reptiles, and shellfish are referenced metaphorically in many societies to describe the kind of witchcraft accusations that occur within a domestic situation, where people all live closely together, as in the Kwahu proverb "only the insect in your own cloth will bite you" (see Bleek 1976).

The Tibetan version of the animal double is an apparition, either unconsciously or voluntarily created, of a *tulpa*, the only difference being that African versions of the animal double generally depict the body from which it withdraws as remaining inanimate. Alexandra David-Neel's description of the *tulpa* in her 1967 book *Magic and Mystery in Tibet* suggests that it can be "either alike or different from its creator" (217–18), it does not need to be specifically invited to appear, and the author of the phenomenon generates it unconsciously and is not necessarily in the least aware of the apparition being seen by others. Like Castle's Tingler, the *tulpa* is perhaps best described as a spontaneously materialized "thought-form creation," a "magic formation generated by a powerful concentration of thoughts" (218). Unlike the animal double, the *tulpa* can actually take any shape at all, however nebulous, and has tangible properties discernible to others. David-Neel describes one *tulpa* she came into contact with as a "foggy form," "a soft object whose substance gave way under [a] slight push" (218).[6]

In fact, Castle's Tingler has perhaps more in common with the Tibetan *tulpa* than with the more traditional African forms of animal double. Like the Tingler, the *tulpa* is induced to appear by various powerful emotions or by a powerful concentration of thoughts, and, also like the tingler, the phenomenon is almost always produced without the conscious cooperation of its author. Even more significantly, once the *tulpa* is endowed with enough vitality to be capable of playing the part of a living creature, it tends to free itself from the body of its maker and from its maker's control. Tibetan occultists claim that this happens nearly mechanically, just as a child, when its body is fully formed and able to live apart, leaves its mother's womb. "Sometimes," remarks David-Neel, "the phantom becomes a rebellious son and one hears of uncanny struggles that have taken place between magicians and their creatures, the former being severely hurt or even killed by the latter" (218).

In the narrative unconscious, the tale of the Tingler matches legends recounted by Tibetan magicians about the particular kind of *tulpa* that is expressly intended to survive its creator and is induced specifically for that very purpose. Magicians and occultists relate many cases similar to Chapin's,

Judith Evelyn and Philip Coolidge, *The Tingler*. © 1959 Columbia Pictures. All Rights Reserved. Courtesy of BFI stills, posters & designs.

in which the *tulpa* is brought forth in order to fulfill a mission, but escapes and does not come back, "pursuing its peregrinations," as David-Neel explains, "as a half-conscious, dangerously mischievous puppet" (200). And because it is the materialized form of such violent and overpowering emotions, once the *tulpa* has been visualized and animated, it is extremely difficult to dissolve. As part of an experiment in meditation, David-Neel summoned up a tangible illusion of her own, whose form grew gradually fixed and lifelike and became a kind of guest, living in her apartment (221).[7] Her *tulpa* eventually escaped her control and took on a life of its own, even to the extent of materializing to others, who took it for a real being. According to David-Neel, the *tulpa* was not easily destroyed. "I ought to have let the phenomenon follow its course," she writes, "but the presence of that unwanted companion began to prove trying to my nerves; it turned into a 'day-nightmare' . . . so I decided to dissolve the phantom. I succeeded, but only after six months of hard struggle. My mind-creature was tenacious of life" (220).

An interesting twist in the links between the Tingler myth and the *tulpa* narrative is that, although the tingler is evidently an embodiment—rendered sensible to others—of Martha's mortal fear, the *author* and *master* of the tingler is not Martha, but Dr. Chapin. It is Chapin who discovers, summons, induces, and extracts the tingler, simply using Martha's body and emotions as the vehicle for his experiment. Some magicians argue that the discord and uproar wreaked by the unruly *tulpa* is a result of its performance of the unconscious aggression of its creator in the conscious, physical world. If this is true, then whose unconscious aggression does the escaped Tingler embody? Is it Martha, the neurotic deaf-mute, projecting her bitterness and envy onto the able-bodied teenagers in the audience by forcing them to scream and scream again, rending and tormenting their vocal chords? Or is it Dr. Warren Chapin, the cuckolded husband, obsessed with his wife's infidelity, wreaking vengeance on the dating teenage couples in the movie theater by crawling up the girls' skirts, making them cry out in abhorrence and disgust?

V

Interestingly, a number of primitive and tribal cultures conceive of the animal double as fecal in form and consistency. If the province of this creation is to negotiate those ambiguous areas of culture, society, and the body, it is wholly befitting that the animal double should emerge from the indistinct boundaries of the human body. In direct opposition to everything we consider human, the animal is a category inhabiting all those dark, shadowy cracks and crevices of human culture and the human body: not inside but outside, not the womb but the anus, not birth but defecation—and sometimes neither here nor there but *in between,* which inevitably connects it to the interstitiality of the horror genre itself. Noel Carroll, in his book *The Philosophy of Horror* (1990), describes the horror genre as interstitial in nature. Its monsters are frequently neither man nor beast, neither living nor dead, or else are a result of such otherworldly processes as magnification (*King Kong, Night of the Lepus*) or reduction (*The Fly, The Incredible Shrinking Man*). Others belong to the category of the psychologically or morally interstitial (such as the psychopath, serial killer, or child murderer), sharing the category of those frightening bodily products (blood, excrement, tissue fluid) that, when appearing outside the bodily confines, are by necessity interstitial and thereby out of place, corrupt, and taboo.

It is surely not stretching the imagination too much to acknowledge that there is something rather fecal about the Tingler. After all, it is a wormlike protuberance that gradually emerges from the anal inner space, and its arrival is heralded by a range of physical perceptions and sensations both pleasant and disturbing. The emergence of the Tingler involves agonized writhings, expressions of pain and relief, groans and wrenching sounds, followed by the sudden expulsion of a solid object from the space at the bottom of the spine. In fact, *The Tingler* is perhaps the most extreme of a whole subgenre of horror movies whose threats are fecal in nature, from the oleaginous slime of Chuck Russell's *The Blob* (1998), the body-burrowing parasite of the *Alien* series (1979, 1986, 1992, 1997), and the drain-dwelling leeches of David Cronenberg's *Shivers* (1975) to the amorphous entity of Frank Henenlotter's *Basket Case* movies (1982, 1990, 1992).

Vincent Price's Dr. Warren Chapin is both shaman and conjurer, producing from behind a screen—as though by sleight of hand—a living fecal animal from the body of a dead person. Speaking symbolically, the Tingler is not just feces, but feces from a corpse—a product that occupies the highly marginal and ambiguous character of the rotten, provoking the same feelings of revulsion as other dirty matter, such as sweat and urine, but impelling, at the same time, a strong element of fascination. Interest in feces is usual in animals and is a familiar part of the development of the child's psychological life. Feces is the first substance that the child can give or refuse to the outside world—an attribute that is soon shared by substances of far more interest to the child, including gifts, money, and genital compulsions. Feces, like other liminal substances such as sweat, saliva, urine, menstrual blood, and sexual excreta, have long been associated symbolically with magic,

The bathtub scene, *The Tingler*. © 1959 Columbia Pictures. All Rights Reserved. Courtesy of BFI stills, posters & designs.

bewitchment, and the defilement and castration of both body and soul; hence, in most cultures at least, the careful rituals of cleansing after defecation, urination, coitus, menstruation, and childbirth.

Given this powerful preoccupation with bodily cleanliness and the careful avoidance of contact with impure matter, it seems ironic that the only living Tingler in the film emerges from the body of a deaf-mute woman with an acute obsessive-compulsive cleanliness complex. Mrs. Higgins is terrified by fears of contamination: She refuses to shake Chapin's proffered hand on the grounds that she's just finished washing her own. Olly complains that his wife is afraid of the germs on people's hands, and, consequently, their bill for towels comes to five dollars a week. As the fecal attributions of the Tingler imply, despite our revulsion from feces and from dirty matter in general, much of our cultural symbolism and narrative mythology revolves around this theme. A dirty fecal animal with "the strength of a hydraulic press" and the power to kill any human being it encounters, the Tingler embodies our ambivalent attitude toward fecal power and contamination, toward the terrifying involuntary processes our bodies undergo, and toward the nightmarish emissions they produce.

In *The Tingler*, the ability to produce a human scream prevents the emergence of this fecal creature from the anal space. The fecal animal, "the force that makes your spine tingle when you're scared," has somehow transformed itself into a human voice. The metapsychology of the inner space of the human body image is so complex and multifaceted that it allows for plenty of cathexes, both concrete and symbolic, between different bodily openings, inner spaces, and the contents hidden behind these openings. In fact, the entire structural foundation for the inner body image is created by the cathexis of various sensations and actual functions of the body simultaneously with phase-specific images and figures of speech that are connected with the body (see Hägglund and Piha 1980, 256–83). So, for instance, the sound of the human voice can easily be imaginatively experienced as feces, flatus, or urination—especially in cases of psychosis where the image of the body, especially its inner space, is disturbed. In relation to the top half of the inner body image, the lungs, larynx, and ears compose an inner space entity, the "excrement" or product of which is the human voice, words, and sounds—we react to important experiences by taking a deep breath, as though to internalize the auditory experience better, and our reaction to experiences we dislike or despise often involves expiration. Thus, in relation to the metapsychology of the human body image, it seems quite natural that a fecal image from the anus should be cathected into the inner space of the human voice.

THE TERROR OF *THE TINGLER*

According to Dr. Chapin, the Tingler is a parasite that feeds off the stress and tension experienced in the spinal column at moments of intense fear. This tension can be released only by screaming, which, in turn, cuts off the Tingler from its source of strength and renders it powerless. Scream, and you are safe. Fail to scream, and your body is lost to the Tingler. When Dr. Chapin exhorts the on-screen audience to "scream for your lives!" to disempower the escaped Tingler, he is also encouraging the screams of the *actual* cinema audience—by now hysterical—whose panic-stricken reaction to random jolts of electrical energy should ideally, at least according to Castle's plan, serve as a promotional device to excite and encourage the crowds waiting in the lobby for the next showing.

The escaped Tingler embodies not only the link between oral and anal expulsiveness, but also the basic notion that there are anal feelings at the movies and that these feelings are specifically activated by this film. Put in its most simple terms, the human fear of losing control of one's defecatory functions—embodied by the sight of an enormous, swollen fecal animal, alive and on the loose—is cathected into the socially legitimate chaos of ritual screaming (itself inspired by the screams of the on-screen cinema audience). As I suggested earlier, uncontrolled defecation and an ungovernable vocal spasm are essentially different manifestations of the same bodily impulse, the significant difference being that chaotic defecation is considered horrific and polluting, whereas ungovernable screaming—especially when participating in the public viewing of a horror movie—fits into a legitimate social category and has a communally accepted social function. To view *The Tingler* as it was originally screened is therefore to take part in a socially endorsed ritual of mass cathexis, where the threat of contamination is faced head-on, displaced, and, at least temporarily, "overcome." And for those audience members fortunate enough to select seats rigged up with Perceptobuzzers directing an electrical jolt at the base of the spine, just at the top of the buttocks, the experience can only have been doubly exciting and doubly hysterical. Perhaps the dynamics of this socialization procedure make it easy to understand why watching *The Tingler* is recalled by so many film lovers as one of the most intense and exhilarating moviegoing experiences of their youth.

VI

The Tingler is a tale of warning. It is the story of assault by a fecal animal double that comes to life inside the body at the peak of terror, extending "from the coccyx to the sternum," and which, when released outside the body, takes on a life of its own and crawls around frantically, causing a violent anal jolt when it attacks. This fecal creation is the product of massive unreleased tension and can be calmed only by the cathexis of this defecatory neurosis into the vocal release of the scream. On one level then, this is a film about what Philip Rieff (1966) has described as "the triumph of the therapeutic," a trait of which is the widely held belief—almost a commonplace, by 1959—that emotions we fail to get "out" somehow remain repressed "within" us until they find their own way "out," possibly of their own accord, and possibly in a rather frightening and dangerous way. The popularization of Freudian psychoanalysis allows for the expression of certain kinds of so-called repressed desires and urges to become increasingly acceptable in the name of psychic cleansing. As it has become increasingly common over the last thirty years to attribute such repressed complexes to triggering childhood events (usually sexually or emotionally abusive parenting), the disclosure and display of such drives has met with increasing approval.

But *The Tingler* is a more involved film than a reading based on this very simplified therapeutic model might suggest. This is not a film about the expression of repressed fears in a tension-breaking psychic catharsis. Because it cannot be "attributed" to a single triggering event, because it will never become socially acceptable, and because its effect is universal, the defecatory obsession is not really a neurosis we can "get in touch" with or "come to terms" with, as other unconscious urges have come to be characterized. Horror at the perverseness of our bodily emissions is not just a repressed impulse waiting to return, but part of the neurological disease of being human. *The Tingler* is a bodily nightmare in which a fecal animal, swollen to frightening proportions, is given a life of its own and let loose upon the unsuspecting world of consciousness. The plight of an unfortunate neurotic deaf-mute whose unreleased tensions grow so great they overcome her is simply the signal impelling the process of cathexis in the cinema audience from anal neurosis to oral expulsion and back again. Contrary to therapeutic fashion, however, this cathexis neither alleviates nor endures. The relief expressed in the scream of the spectator is nothing more than a socially admissible ritual of momentary release. In Castle's fantasy, the scream destroys the neurosis. But in the waking reality of our bodily lives, the fecal process, like all the best monsters, is totally indestructible.

3 *Blood Feast:* There Never Was a Party Like This!

MADE FOR A MERE $24,000 IN 1963, HERSCHEL Gordon Lewis's infamous *Blood Feast* is regarded—when it is regarded at all—as the absolute nadir of exploitation cinema. Original publicity posters, declaring the film "More Grisly Than Ever, in *Blood Color*," promised its audience they would "Recoil and Shudder" when witnessing "the Slaughter and Mutilation of Nubile Young Girls—in a weird and horrendous Ancient Rite!" The extravagant advertising worked. The film was shot in four days of principal photography, without a single rehearsal, using crew left over from Lewis and Friedman's soft-core nudie flick, *Bell, Bare and Beautiful* (1963); the script was written on a few sheets of paper and some napkins; the pyramid and sphinx that appear during the film's credits was the logo of the Suez motel in north Miami, where Lewis just happened to be staying at the time. Despite all this, *Blood Feast* was Lewis's biggest and most profitable hit in a twelve-year filmmaking career devoted to the making of almost forty money-spinning exploitation films.

Academic film theory erects a number of barriers to protect and defend itself from the threat of films like *Blood Feast*, including laughter, ridicule, contemptuous dismissal, the phenomenon of the late-night horror show on television, terms like *schlock* and *splatter*, and the treatment of the horror movie as camp. While it is true that audiences respond to *Blood Feast* with laughter and disdain because it is, by classical Hollywood standards, a wretchedly made movie—even Lewis has talked about the limitations of the actors' abilities and the fact that the script stresses gore at the expense of plausibility and coherence—there is something to be said for the film's transgression of classical cinema's barriers and limitations. Carol Clover (1992) makes the point that exploitation cinema displays quite openly and spectacularly before us images and meanings that most other kinds of films merely suggest or imply (236), and while there is a place in cinema for suggestion and implication, there is also a place for transparency and display. By operating at the "bottom line," argues Clover, "'low' or exploitation horror reminds us that every movie *has* a bottom line, no matter how covert, disguised, or sublimated it might be" (236). Although clumsily produced and low in budget, films in the tradition of *Blood Feast* are deeply frank and energetic; they repress nothing, speaking to unconscious fears and anxieties in the flattest of terms.

According to its director, *Blood Feast* is a film that works in the tradition of "the crude power of a play by Aeschylus, as opposed to a play by Sophocles." Lewis, an exploitation filmmaker who would do anything to publicize his films, clearly enjoyed these games of extravagant self-promotion. But this is not to say he is wrong: *Blood Feast* is an integrally primal and powerful movie, both in its role as the urtext for the slasher genre's treatment of violence and spectacle and in its confrontation with the ancient taboo of cannibalism.

II

The narrative of *Blood Feast* centers around the character of Fuad Ramses (memorably played by Mal Arnold), a mysterious lame Egyptian chef with "wild eyes" and a dragging left (and sometimes right) leg. Ramses is the proprietor of a catering company that specializes in "exotic feasts," a cover-up for his worship of the blood goddess Ishtar, whose altar is hidden in the back room of his shop. The beginning of spring heralds Ramses' preparations for the Blood Feast, a traditional Egyptian ritual whose observance requires the consumption of a bloody stew made of certain organs and limbs removed from the bodies of beautiful young virgins. On the seventh day of the feast, the goddess Ishtar will rise from the tomb and show herself in flesh and blood, a part of the people.

In order to gather together the ingredients for the sacred feast, Ramses commits a series of grisly ritualistic murders. The film opens with an attack on a young girl in the bath. Ramses pokes her eye out with a sword, then hacks off her legs and wraps them in newspaper. His second victim, Marcie

(Ashlyn Martin, Playboy Playmate of April 1964), is making love to her boyfriend on the beach when she is attacked and murdered; her brain is removed, still quivering. A third girl (Astrid Olsen[1]) is stalked to a motel where Ramses pulls her tongue out of her mouth with his bare hands. A fourth victim, whose murder we do not witness, has "the whole side of her face hacked away" but survives long enough to inform the police that her assailant was a "horrible old man" with "wild eyes," who said "it was for Eetar...."

Meanwhile, Mrs. Dorothy Fremont (Lyn Bolton) is planning a surprise birthday party for her daughter, Suzette (Connie Mason, Playboy Playmate of June 1963). When Mrs. Fremont visits Fuad Ramses' Exotic Catering Shop on the recommendation of a friend, she is hypnotized by Ramses into agreeing to host an authentic Egyptian feast for Suzette, a devotee of Egyptian history and culture. The day before the feast, one of Suzette's friends is stalked and captured by Ramses and taken to the altar of Ishtar where she is tied up and flayed to death, her blood gathered in a silver goblet. In the meantime, Suzette's boyfriend Pete Thornton (Thomas Wood), a detective on the case,

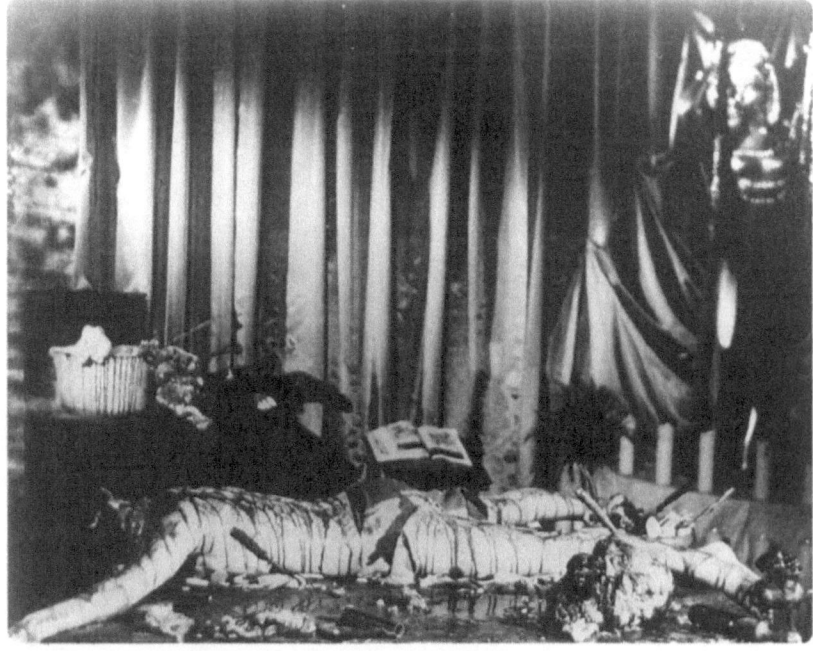

Behind the scenes at Exotic Egyptian Catering, *Blood Feast*. © 1963 Box Office Spectaculars. All Rights Reserved. Courtesy of Photofest.

has pieced together the word *Eetar* with the cult of Ishtar, something that he has recently learned about by attending a lecture on Egyptian history with Suzette. Pete and his men raid the catering shop, where they discover the body of the last victim and the preparations for the Blood Feast spread out on the altar of Ishtar. The police speed to the Fremont residence where Ramses, having lured Suzette into the kitchen, is on the verge of sacrificing her on the kitchen counter with a machete. The murder is averted; Ramses is chased out of town by the detectives and takes refuge by hiding in the back of a garbage truck where he is accidentally crushed to death, "like the garbage he was."

At the time of its first release, *Blood Feast* was reviewed extensively in *Time*, *Newsweek*, and *Variety*, to almost universal distaste. Ever since, it has attained the status of a cult classic, as "the infamous first gore film" and "the original splatter film." Critic Danny Peary (1981) describes the film as "one of the most inept pictures of all time. The acting is ghastly, casting abominable, scoring (by Lewis) miserable, camera-work clumsy" (25–27). James O'Neill (1994) comments that although the film is "technically inept" and

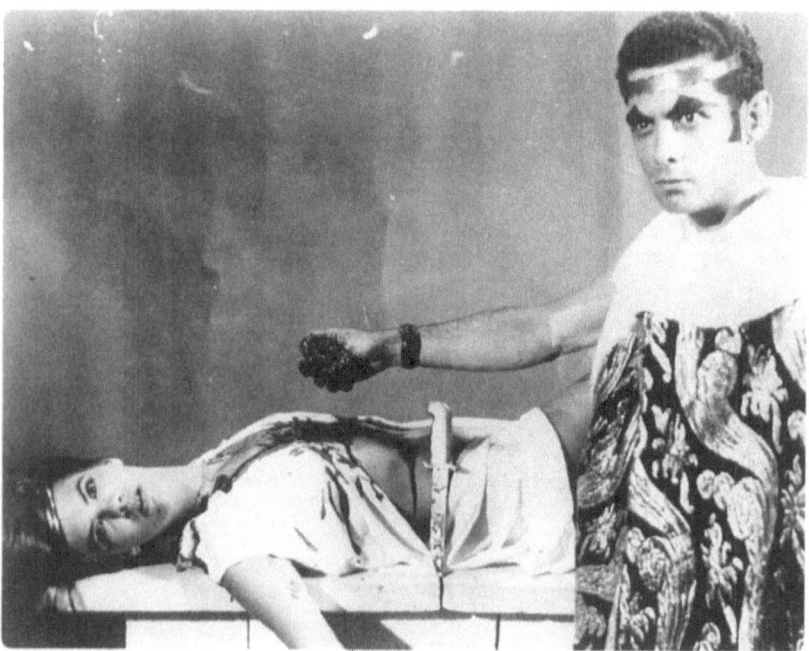

Fuad Ramses (Mal Arnold) removes the heart of his latest victim (Toni Calvert). © 1963 Box Office Spectaculars. All Rights Reserved. Courtesy of Photofest.

features "ludicrous acting," the "slash-happy bloodbath" is "sick fun, thanks to its ludicrously over-the-top gore effects" (68). Lewis went on to direct a whole string of similar exploitation films through the mid-1960s and early 1970s, including *Two Thousand Maniacs* (1964), *Color Me Blood Red* (1965), *The Gruesome Twosome* (1967) and *The Gore-Gore Girls* (1972). None of these luridly titled B movies was ever quite as successful as *Blood Feast*, but they were all financially lucrative.[2]

III

As its title clearly suggests, *Blood Feast* is a film all about cannibalism.[3] Fuad Ramses is a modern-day cannibal, who murders his victims so that he can eat their bodies—or, at least, parts of their bodies—in the worship of Ishtar. Ishtar herself, we learn, is a cannibalistic goddess, worshiped like Venus and Aphrodite of the Greek and Roman civilizations, except that "hers was an evil love that thrived on violence." Had the Blood Feast been successful, Mrs. Fremont, along with her guests, would have been dining on the flesh of her daughter. Instead of the birthday feast being held in honor of Suzette, Suzette would have become a part of the feast itself—along with the first victim's eye and legs, the second victim's brain, the third victim's tongue, the fourth victim's skin and face, and the last victim's heart. And then, of course, Ramses himself is symbolically ingested, ground up into a bloody pulp and swallowed by the crushing metal jaws of the garbage truck.

But what is crucial to the narrative of the film is that the Blood Feast itself never actually takes place. The meat is cooked, the stew prepared, the flavor added, and the table laid, but the sacrament never occurs. Fuad Ramses is caught (quite literally) red-handed at the very last moment and chased from the kitchen by police. The Blood Feast is prepared but uneaten. In fact, although this is a film all about cannibalism and cannibalistic rituals, no actual cannibalism ever takes place.

The recurrence of cannibalism as a theme in the myths and folklore of Western culture is commonly perceived in psychoanalytic terms, usually with reference to "the dread of being eaten"—a phrase used by Freud to describe fears connected with mothers and fathers. Actual instances of cannibalism in Western culture are invariably associated with a state of extreme mental derangement in which a person is driven to barbaric extremes: consider the cases of Ed Gein and Jeffrey Dahmer.[4] Cannibalism in Western culture is generally traced back to anxieties rooted in the reality of aggressive parental behavior, guilty fantasies projected onto fathers and mothers, the transformation of oral-aggressive tendencies or projected hostility toward the mother, who both nourishes the child and imposes a number of restrictions on him or her during the course of his or her development. These renditions of the cannibalistic taboo are for the most part psychoanalytic, usually Freudian, and are considered to relate to the world from the child's point of view—hence, the importance of food, the absence of food, consumption, privation, indulging in gluttonous urges, oral satisfaction, pleasure, survival (eating or being eaten), and good and bad behavior.

By the same token, mythic and fictive instances of cannibalism are usually interpreted as a disfigured form of parental aggression or a projection of the protagonist's oral greed. For example, "Hansel and Gretel"—a tale in which the gingerbread house attracts children for the witch to kill, cook, and eat—is usually interpreted psychoanalytically as a cautionary tale wherein the satisfaction of oral urges brings to life fiends whose voracious appetites outpace those of even the most famished children. Similarly, "Tom Thumb"—a story in which the giant plans to kill seven young boys and eat them with a good sauce—is most often considered to be a narrative that speaks to the child's guilty feelings about unrestrained oral greed and dependence.

Bruno Bettelheim (1976) argues that these tales about the victims and perpetrators of oral aggression function as rites of passage, serving to acculturate young children and help them to come to terms with loss, Oedipal conflicts, ambivalent emotions toward siblings and parent figures, and their own fears and anxieties about being a child and a human being. Freud remarked on the connection between murder, cannibalism, and incest, which seemed to him—as the most obvious and widespread cultural taboos—to be closely related (as psychoanalytic readings of other folk and fairy stories, such as "Jack and the Beanstalk" and the Eastern European tales of Baba Yaga, seem to testify). Freud suggests in his essay on "The Uncanny" (1919) that in most such stories, cannibalism becomes enmeshed with a complex array of matters touching on the dread of being devoured and on incestuous attachment.

IV

Blood Feast is a curious film with a substantial role in the subsequent history of exploitation cinema and slasher movies. It is curious because—like a number of archetypal folktales and mythological narratives—it is governed by the central metaphor of cannibalism *averted*. Although the entire film revolves around the murderous preparations for the Blood Feast of Ishtar, the only actual instance of human consumption in *Blood Feast* is Ramses' "filthy death" in the form of a symbolic disappearance into the grinding metal jaws of a garbage truck. Moreover, the historical standing of the film is also consequential, as it is regularly cited as the definitive urtext of the slasher movie genre. Both points deserve further explanation.

First of all, considering the governing narrative of *Blood Feast* as a metaphor can help us to understand and come to terms with the notion of the "primal deed." This concept is one of the most fundamental principles of psychoanalysis, whether it be—in Freudian terms—a reference to the incest and parricide of Oedipus, an infant's toilet-training trauma, or the patient's repressed recollections of parental sexual intercourse. Both Melanie Klein (1952) and Carl Jung (1936) also look back to the early experiences of childhood; and, to Jung, the conscious mind grows out of the unconscious psyche, which is much older than it and which goes on functioning together with it, or even in spite of it. The narrative of the primal horde[5] is usually considered to provide the basis for the two most essential taboos of totemism: incest and murder, which are permanently enshrined in psychoanalysis in this culture's version of the primal scene, the myth of Oedipus, and its eponymous psychological anxieties and neuroses. But what of our culture's third elementary taboo—that of cannibalism? Where does this taboo find its primal deed?

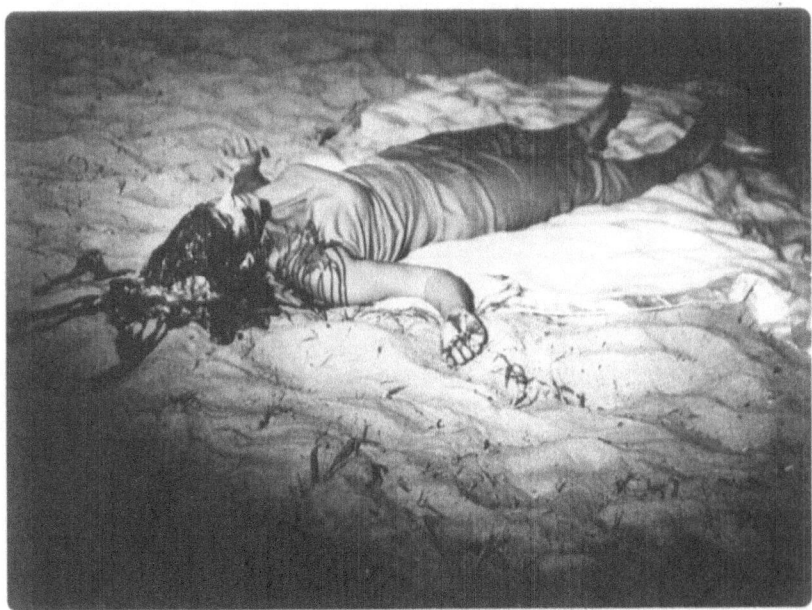

Marcy (Ashlyn Martin) is murdered on the beach. © Box Office Spectaculars. All Rights Reserved. Courtesy of Photofest.

The critical reaction of dismay and bewilderment at the release of *Blood Feast* to an unsuspecting public—widely declared in contemporary reviews, including unqualified aspersion from *Variety*—suggests that cannibalism is as strong a taboo, as capable of inflaming our imagination, as shocking to modern culture as incest or murder. Yet examples of the sacramental meal and sacrificial cannibalistic rituals in primitive or primitive-modern culture are fairly rare. Nor has the taboo of cannibalism become enshrined for Western culture in a narrative reformulation of the "primal deed" as palatable as the myth of Oedipus is for modern psychoanalysis. As anthropologist René Girard (1977) puts it, "We are perhaps more distracted by incest than by cannibalism, but only because cannibalism has not yet found its Freud and been promoted to the status of a major contemporary myth" (277). Murder and incest prohibitions are traceable, for the psychoanalyst, to contemporary manifestations of the Oedipus myth; yet—as the horrified public reaction to *Blood Feast* suggests—the prohibitions against cannibalism are intact, but still arcane in origin. We have no story to teach us of the primal deed of cannibalism: no one to tell us who ate, who was eaten, or whether it even happened at all.

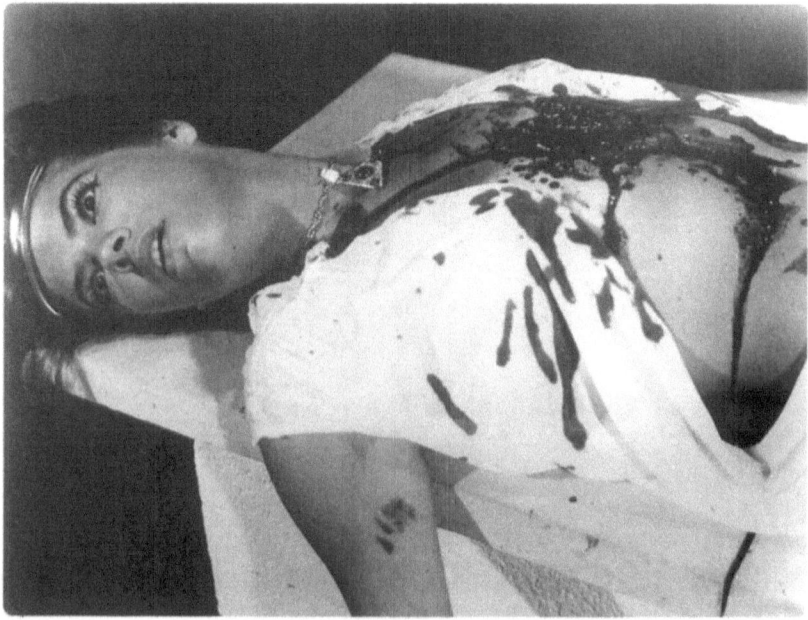

Suzette Fremont (Connie Mason) in a publicity still for *Blood Feast*. © Box Office Spectaculars. All Rights Reserved. Courtesy of Photofest.

But on another level—in another age and in other places—ritual cannibalism *does* happen; myths *are* based on true events, primal deeds *did* occur, and the feast of Ishtar *did* take place—as Ramses insists over and over again—"five thousand years ago." Understanding the narrative of *Blood Feast* as a metaphor can help us to come to terms with the way in which the manifest content of narratives can be regarded as a symbolic version of what is *not* told: the story that is lost. The governing narrative of *Blood Feast* is a metaphor for the psychoanalytic paradigm in which nothing is more significant than that which does not happen. For it is only by directing our attention to that which does *not* happen that we can start to pick up the clues to solving the puzzle of what *did* happen, once upon a time.

V

According to author Thomas D. Clagett (2003), director William Friedkin has suggested that an audience's emotional engagement with a horror movie begins while they are standing in line, a claim that acknowledges the profoundly formulaic nature of the horror film business (16). Innumerable critics of the traditional horror film have identified its original manifestation in the psychological trauma and suspense of Hitchcock's *Psycho* (1960). As for the less respectable face of horror—the slasher movie—the narrative foundations for this highly ritualized and formulaic tale are laid for the first time in 1963, in the story of Fuad Ramses and his Blood Feast.

The slasher plot is perhaps the most predictable narrative form in contemporary cinema. The audience of the slasher movie is generally highly "slasher-literate," competent in recognizing and anticipating its narrative conventions. Andrew Britton (1979) has described how watching a contemporary slasher film in a downtown cinema with a slasher-literate audience can be akin to participation in a kind of ritual: "The film's total predictability did not create boredom or disappointment. On the contrary, the predictability was clearly the main source of pleasure, and the only occasion for disappointment would have been a modulation of the formula, not the repetition of it" (2–3).

Blood Feast has been neglected in the slasher genre to which it belongs, just as (and partly because) it has been ignored by academic as well as popular film theory. But—at least in terms of narrative structure and symbolic form—the story of Fuad Ramses and his Blood Feast stands as the urtext for a long tradition of slasher and stalker films, from *Halloween* (1978) to *Scream 3* (2000).[6] To pick up once again on the psychoanalytic metaphor, *Blood Feast* is the "primal scene" of the slasher film genre.

Put in its simplest narrative terms, *Blood Feast* is the story of a bloodthirsty fiend who sets about killing and mutilating a series of sexually attractive, pubescent females one by one until only a single girl in the chain remains alive. This highly ritualized and formulaic narrative structure has been analyzed in all its potential variations by numerous critics of the slasher film, notably Carol Clover (1992). Despite countless possible thematic and structural variations, however, certain constraints remain in place. Virtually Aristotelian in structure,[7] the slasher narrative regularly adheres to the unity of time (usually taking place on one night), the unity of place (almost invariably small-town America), and the unity of action (each killing takes a unique but similar form). The terrible place in which all the victims sooner or later find themselves usually takes the form of a house (or similar building), from the Myers house in *Halloween*, to Freddy's boiler room in *Nightmare on Elm Street*, to Fuad Ramses's Exotic Catering Shop in *Blood Feast*, lit by candles and containing a number of menacing-looking cooking implements. Ramses' set of carving knives is an early version of the terrible weapons that play such a significant part in so many subsequent slasher movies: ice picks, chainsaws, hammers, axes, pitchforks, and crossbows.

Clover points out that the slasher film's harvest always reaps an inordinate number of victims. *Blood Feast* claims five (that we are aware of, at any rate), *The Texas Chainsaw Massacre* also claims five, there are four in *Halloween*, fourteen in *Friday the 13th Part 3*, and so on.[8] The archetypal slasher film victim is in her late teens and always "guilty"—at least in the terms set out by the filmic narrative—of some form of sexual aggression, or else she is depicted in a sexual context or drawn in overtly sexual terms. In *Blood Feast*, Ramses' first victim is murdered in the bath, the second while making love to her boyfriend on the beach, the third in a motel room rented by her boyfriend. Later slasher film cycles of the 1970s contain what Clover has described as the "final girl"—a masculinized tomboy who is resourceful in stopping the murderer and a character that allows male horror spectators to experience the thrill of identifying with a woman. But none of these traits is true of Suzette Fremont in *Blood Feast*, an attractive, feminine woman identified most clearly as Pete Thornton's girlfriend. In fact, it is Suzette's giggly ignorance that saves her life when Ramses tries to slaughter her in the kitchen.

Ultimately, the slasher film is characterized by its use of cinematic shock relating to body horror. Typically, the serial murders of the slasher film are distinguished by the opening up of the body and the shocking revelation of the taboo insides. In *Blood Feast,* this involves the removal of the brain and tongue, the "hacking away" of the face, flaying alive, the dicing up of body parts, and, in the memorable words of the newspaper headline following Ramses' initial murder, "Legs Cut Off!" This making vivid of our bodily reality through the revelation of internal organs and fluids evokes the trauma of the abject on display—or, in Joseph Conrad's words, "the fascination of the abomination."

VI

In her book *Men, Women, and Chainsaws,* Clover acknowledges the critical importance of the *Blood Feast* recipe. "It may be argued," she writes, "that *Blood Feast* (1963), in which a lame Egyptian caterer slaughters one woman after another for their bodily parts (all in the service of Ishtar) provides the serial-murderer model" (32). Other writers, including cult movie critics such as Michael Weldon (1983) and Joe Bob Briggs (2003), all agree that *Blood Feast* occupies the primary position in the narrative history of the slasher movie.

To participate (as audience) in the slasher-film narrative is to take part in a ritual ceremony, a public practice in which (as necessity arises, at the proper season or in certain circumstances) the communal magician—in his modern guise as filmmaker—is under an obligation to perform the magic, to keep the taboos intact, and to exert his control over the entire enterprise, just as Fuad Ramses, high priest of the murderous cult of Ishtar, is compelled to reenact the sacramental feast of the dark goddess.

Louise Krasniewicz (1992), in her anthropological reading of the slasher film, makes the argument that the failure of the film's protagonist to learn the lessons encoded by these narratives (don't go into the basement, don't answer the phone, don't leave your little sister alone, don't take the short cut through the woods) are paralleled by the slasher film's compulsive tendency toward remakes, sequels, and new chapters. The *Friday the 13th* series, for example, "finished" with Joseph Zito's *Friday the 13th Part 4—The Final Chapter* in 1984, which was rapidly followed by Danny Steinmann's *Friday the 13th Part 5—A New Beginning* in 1985, leading to many subsequent sequels. Wes Craven's original *Nightmare on Elm Street* in 1984 has spawned a whole array of offspring, from cinematic sequels to a television miniseries, from video spinoffs to Freddy Kruger gloves ("You too can be the bastard son of ten thousand maniacs!"). The slasher film's function as a rite of passage for adolescents of the media generation means that such sequels are a necessary accompaniment to the original ceremony. Each "new" manifestation of the slasher narrative has its own spin-offs, sequels, and by-products, leaving its audiences with the sense that Jason will always rise up from the swamp, Michael Myers will always return on Halloween night, and Freddy will never—really—be dead.

Like myths, fairy tales, and folklore, the slasher movie is a fixed tale type that has generated an endless stream of what are, in effect, variants. "Basically, sequels mean the same film," observed director John Carpenter in an interview with author Gilles Boulenger (2003). "That's what people want to see. They want to see the same movie again" (14). Carpenter makes the suggestion that, like the purveyors of folklore, the makers of slasher movies operate more on instinct for formula than conscious understanding. Clover (1992) agrees that the entire horror genre is structured around unconscious reenactment. "What makes horror 'crucial enough to pass along,'" writes Clover "is, for critics since Freud, what has made ghost stories and fairy tales crucial enough to pass along: its engagement of repressed fears and desires and its re-enactment of the residual conflict surrounding those feelings" (11).

Throughout cultural history—to turn once more to the metaphor of psychoanalysis—we are destined to repeat, from generation to generation, the primal deeds of our forefathers. This repetition-compulsion may serve the function of helping us to struggle through a cultural rite of passage (in the case of the Oedipus complex or the incest taboo) or a ceremonial performance of an ancient act (in the case of the Catholic communion, for example). In either case, the occasion of the original deed, and whether it happened in fact, myth, or fiction, has ceded its importance to the ritual retelling of the tale, from age to age, in its various cultural forms and manifestations.

Herschel Gordon Lewis's *Blood Feast* is, in psychoanalytic terms, the original narrative prototype impelling both the repetition-compulsion of the slasher genre in its endless litany of remakes, spin-offs, and sequels, as well as the horror film's obsessive interest in cannibalism—whether this be cannibalism averted, cannibalism as an act, or cannibalism as a metaphor (relating to the way in which films in the slasher genre "feed off" one another, helping themselves to "parts" and "pieces" of different narrative manifestations). But just as the original blood sacrament was never fulfilled, its various narrative reenactments, accordingly, are destined never to be completed or resolved.

4 *Snuff:* "Where Life is Cheap"

N 1976, A FILM DIRECTED BY MICHAEL AND ROBERTA Findlay entitled *Snuff* was released in cinemas in the United States. To most of those who watched it, *Snuff* was simply a badly made, loosely constructed, barely coherent film, dull in places, amateurish and unconvincing in others. A contemporary review in the *New York Post* (1976) declared that the film, despite its lurid publicity claims, contained "(a) less nudity than you see in an average issue of National Geographic, and (b) less torture than exists in most Saturday morning cartoons." Compared to most contemporary low-budget thrillers, *Snuff* was a rather lame imitation. Neither especially violent nor particularly explicit, *Snuff* seems an unremarkable, unexciting, fourth-rate B movie. Yet, because of various accidents of history, marketing strategies, and ethical debates in relation to the social conscience of the cinema audience, *Snuff* has attracted a notable amount of critical and academic attention. Not for the first time, a piece of low-budget, underground exploitation cinema has played a strange and conspicuous role in cinema history.

In 1970, husband-and-wife filmmaking team Michael and Roberta Findlay directed a cheap hippie-exploitation picture for less than $35,000, which they tentatively entitled *Slaughter*. The film was made in Argentina to avoid union costs; to save further money, it was filmed without sound, since most of the actors and actresses in the movie were native Argentinians and spoke no English. *Slaughter* was completed in very little time and sent to the United

States for audio-dubbing. When it was screened at Monarch Releasing Corporation in California, Allen Shackleton, the head of Monarch, recognized that the film, as it stood, made very little sense and was full of technical flaws. Shackleton decided to shelve the movie. As David Kerekes and David Slater (1996) explain, the original print of *Slaughter* was never shown theatrically (12–13).

Slaughter is basically the story of a South American hippie cult, consisting of four young, barefoot girls—Anna, Carmella, Suzannah, and Anjelika—and their unholy leader, Satán. Early sequences introduce us to the cult and its motiveless rituals: drug taking, motorbike riding, and tying one another up with ropes. The women are the lovers of Satán, to whom they are all bound in mental and spiritual bondage. One of them, Anjelika, is sent to the estate of local playboy Horst Frank in nearby Punta del Este in order to get pregnant by him, as Satán desires her to bear Frank's child. Anjelika promises to obey and also lets Satán know that she would also gladly kill for him.

The subplot, such as there is one, involves a low-budget porn movie being shot in South America by Max Marsh and his porn star fiancée, Terri London, an actress who'll "do anything to make a good picture." As Max and Terri are leaving for South America, an unnamed man is murdered in the airport toilets by an unknown assassin—a woman dressed in man's clothing. Upon landing, Terri is interviewed by photographers before being dropped off by Max at her rented apartment. The first thing she does, as soon as Max has left, is to call her lover, Horst Frank, and arrange to meet at the yacht club. Back at his estate, Frank informs Anjelika that Terri has returned and that their relationship must end.

Time passes. The porn film goes badly; Max is having a hard time with the co-production people. Terri gets pregnant—we assume by Frank. Max takes Terri to the carnival, and they lose one another in the crowds; Terri is taken aside and seduced by a masked stranger, who turns out to be Frank. Meanwhile, Anjelika seduces Max before stabbing him in the back—on whose command, it is not clear. Later, it turns out that six other people were also killed during the carnival, all of them with a similar knife embedded in their backs.

Terri is interviewed by the police, who find nothing suspicious. She moves into Frank's home with Frank and his father, a German arms dealer who has returned from Munich ten days earlier than expected. Anjelika comes over to pick up some of her things, bringing Satán with her. Satán and Herr Frank get into a quarrel and Satán is thrown out of the house. Back at the cult's headquarters in an abandoned factory, the other girls tie

Anjelika down and torture her lightly; they then stand around smoking pot while Satán and Anjelika have sex. Later, the hippie chicks rob a nearby general store, shooting the storekeeper, a female customer, and her daughter. In flashback, we are taught something of Anjelika's abusive childhood. Daughter of a shiftless drunk, she was raped and abused by the owner of the farm her father worked on. Finally, the farm owner, Louis, murdered Anjelika's drunken father and hung up his severed hands on the washing line. The following day, Louis was murdered by Anjelika's brother.

Back at Frank's estate, Horst and Terri are indulging in a little drunken petting with another couple, Antonio and his wife. The drunken Horst has sex with Antonio's wife while Antonio tries to watch. Elsewhere, Satán has resolved that "the time has come for slaughter." Anjelika and Anna ride up to the gates of the estate on their motorbike, and the gatekeeper, recognizing Anjelika, lets them in. Anna stabs the gatekeeper in the back while Anjelika goes up to the house. Suzannah and Carmella arrive, and the four women set about stabbing Antonio and his wife to death. Horst, in turn, is tied to a tree and whipped, castrated, and finally stabbed to death by Anjelika. The girls then enter Frank's house and creep upstairs to find the pregnant Terri in bed with Herr Frank, who is shot and killed by Anna. "Is that his?" asks Anjelika, meaning Terri's unborn baby. "Yes," confesses Terri. "Then you go and join him," says Anjelika, stabbing her in the stomach.

The Findlays' *Slaughter* ended here, and the film—as it was—spent five years on Allen Shackleton's shelf at Monarch. However, at some point in 1973, in the light of "snuff movie" rumors and contemporary anxieties precipitated by the murders of Sharon Tate and others on August 8, 1969,[1] Shackleton took *Slaughter* down from the shelf and started to think about some of the ways in which its technical flaws could be addressed, with a view to the film's possible rerelease. What he did, in the end, was to retain all the original footage of *Slaughter*—clumsy dubbing and technical flaws notwithstanding—and stick a final scene on the end, designed to make the film seem as much like an "authentic" snuff movie as was cinematically possible.

The final scene goes like this: After Anjelika has stabbed Terri in the stomach, the camera cuts back to a film studio where other cameramen are busy putting away their film equipment. The director, appraising an actress's performance, climbs onto a bed with her and they begin kissing, as a cameraman and sound man come into view. The director, a knife hidden in one hand, climbs on top of the actress and starts to fondle her breasts. When she begins to object to the fact that the scene is being filmed, the director calls on other members of the crew to help him hold her down. He then slices her arm with the knife, laughing like a maniac, then wrenches off one of her fingers with a pair of pliers. The actress begins to struggle, screaming, and, while crew members restrain her, the director saws through her wrist, amputating a hand, then stabs her in the stomach. Ripping open a prosthetic torso, he reaches inside, fishes about for a few moments, then, with a roar of joy, tears out a handful of steaming entrails. The soundtrack records heavy breathing and the beating of a heart. The screen flickers, then darkens. "Did you get it?" someone asks. "Yeah," comes the reply. "Let's get out of here."

II

Inspired by groundless rumors that snuff films from South America were currently being smuggled into the United States, Shackleton released his new version of *Slaughter* at the tail end of 1975 under the unambiguous title *Snuff*—although it later came to be known by a number of other, alternative titles, including *Big Snuff* and *American Cannibale*—and promoted the movie with the ad-line "Filmed in South America, where Life is CHEAP!" The film was consequently both a flop and a huge success, depending on the amount of publicity Shackleton managed to drum up to surround its release wherever it was shown. Peter Birge and Janet Maslin (1976) explain that it bombed in Boston after Al Goldstein, treating the film as a piece of pure "sexploitation," gave it an indignant zero on the "petermeter" in *Screw* (35). Birge and Maslin also report that in Gary, Indiana, a group of feminist activists and women in the media organized a publicity blackout, ensuring that the film averaged no better than a dozen customers at each screening (63).

Yet in New York, Philadelphia, Los Angeles, Buffalo, San Jose, San Diego, and other cities, the film attracted a tremendous amount of sensational attention. In a publicity coup worthy of William Castle, Shackleton advertised the film with teasingly misleading publicity slogans, including "The *Bloodiest* thing that *ever* happened in front of a camera!!" and "The picture they said could NEVER be shown." Shackleton's implication was that the badly constructed, inexpertly dubbed "fictive" footage was simply an unfinished, amateurish cover-up for the *real* point of the movie: the authentic, photographic recording of actual torture and murder, committed solely for the purposes of the film. Shackleton was also involved in a series of "leaks" to the press that insinuated the film had been produced in Buenos Aires and involved the murder of a "real woman." His innuendos were backed up by an incendiary poster campaign showing a woman's neck beneath the sharpened blade of a clapper board threatening to decapitate her. Shackleton also neglected to submit his film to the ratings board (in the fear, claimed some, that it would merit no more than an "R"), choosing instead to stamp his own product with the self-imposed "stigma" of an "X."

By early 1976, many critics and reviewers were beginning to recognize that they had been the victims of a painstaking hoax. Richard Eder, in the *New York Times,* remarked warily that "everything about the film is suspect: the contents, the promotion, and possibly even some of the protest that is conducted each evening outside the box office" (18). On March 18, 1976, the Adult Film Association of America published "An Open Letter to the Movie-Going Public of Southern California" in *Variety,* claiming that *Snuff* "was the greatest rip-off since Watergate" and that it would not be shown in any cinema associated with the AFAA. In New York, according to critic John Leonard (1976), the film was publicly investigated by Manhattan District Attorney Robert Morganthau at the behest of a group of prominent women involved in civil rights, led by Gloria Steinem, who objected to "the idea of murder as sexual entertainment." Morganthau (1976) concluded that the "murder" was "nothing more than conventional trick photography, as is evident to anyone who has seen the movie," adding that "the actress is alive and well and living in New York" (41). And in the *Los Angeles Times,* reviewer Kevin Thomas (1976) wrote that "*Snuff* can be quickly dismissed as the trash it is" (22).

But for most spectators and critics, these dismissals came too late. The film's release had been already caught up in a frenzy of publicity generated by feminist detractors, movie reviewers, the censorship board, local radio stations, civil rights activists and, not least, the collusion and intrigue of Allan Shackleton and his team at Monarch. When *Snuff* arrived in Monticello, New York, for example, members of the feminist movements NOW (National Organization of Women) and WAVAW (Women Against Violence Against Women) made complaints to the police against Rialto Theater owner Richard Dames on the grounds that the film's promotion "advertises and advocates murder of women as sexually stimulating." In San Diego, feminist activists picketed a local cinema screening *Snuff* by forming a circle in front of the theater half an hour before the film was due to begin and shouting "Stop *Snuff* now!" Apparently, several television crews arrived at the scene and the incident made prime-time news. The cinema manager decided that, as he was getting so much publicity, *Snuff* would be held over for another week.

Although it was often Shackleton himself who, through a series of anonymous tip-offs to press and government officials, brought the film so much attention in the first place, the involvement of the feminist movement, as Kerekes and Slater (1996) explain, led to a radical upward swing in the film's media profile (26). According to John Leonard (1976), at the National Theater on Broadway in New York a crowd of women protested at the film's premiere on February 5, 1976, carrying signs that read "We Mourn the Death of our Latin American Sister," even though the girl who is supposed to be "snuffed" in the film is quite clearly North American. As this irony suggests, those protesting against the film's release were rarely the same people as those who comprised its main audience—although, on occasion, even those who watched the film found its amateurish flaws and effects persuasive rather than implausible. St. Paul police officer Richard Morrill, for example, was disturbed by the film, remarking that "everything depicted in the final scene appeared to be in fact actually happening to the girl. The dismemberment of her body was so real it made me physically ill." Reviews like these provided Shackleton with the kind of publicity he could only have dreamed of. As a result, *Snuff* pulled in $155,000 in its first three weeks.

As many contemporary critics and reviewers noted, the film's audience consisted chiefly of those who had been made curious by all the attention—in other words, people who recognized the publicity to be a scam but who were interested in seeing the film anyway, mainly just to see how effective the scam really was. Columnist George Will (1976) commented that "the final murder, whether real or fake, is repulsive enough to convince the dismal viewers who want to believe it is real, which includes most of the people who shell out $4 to see it." Shackleton realized that the majority of the film's profits were generated by this kind of ambiguity. He admitted to a reporter from *Variety* ("Snuff Biz" 1976) that if the murder *were* real, he'd be "a damn fool to admit it," but added that "if it *isn't* real, I'd be a damn fool to admit it." Feminists picketing the film's release in Manhattan, according to Kerekes and Slater (1996), soon began to argue along similar lines, claiming that "whether or not the death depicted in the current film *Snuff* is real or simulated is not the issue" (27).

Most people involved in the film industry—and, indeed, most American cinemagoers—seemed to recognize that the publicity surrounding the film was a marketing hoax, an old-style exploitation technique. Most of the moviegoers who were excited by *Snuff* would have been used to the amateurish semi-incoherence of this kind of exploitation film from watching many others like it, from *Blood Feast* onward, at the grindhouse and drive-in cinemas that specialized in such films before the advent of the home VCR and DVD revolution. Any film as incoherent as *Snuff* released after 1980 would have gone straight to video. *Snuff* attracted the kind of publicity that it did attract, when many far more graphically violent and dubiously authored films are regularly advertised on the mail-order film market, because *Snuff* was not restricted to marginal venues. Shackleton's marketing techniques ensured that the film was released primarily in mainstream theaters, brought into the purview of people who would not normally have been familiar with movies of such poor quality, and reviewed almost wholly in the mainstream press. *Snuff* was a low-culture entertainment vehicle with no pretensions to art or creative intellectualism, made entirely for profit. But as Eithne Johnson and Eric Schaefer (1993) explain, through various accidents of circumstance and calculated publicity stunts, the film was brought before many of those critics, reviewers, and feminist activists who considered themselves arbiters of taste: hence, the vast outrage (49).

III

The phrase "to be snuffed out" (as a dysphemism for "to die" or "to be killed") has been around since the seventeenth century. The first time the term "snuff" was used in connection with filmmaking, however, as Kerekes and Slater (1996) point out, was almost definitely by Ed Sanders in *The Family* (1976), where it was used to describe "death movies" hinted to have been made by the Manson family (18).[2] It was not until the end of 1973, however, that the press began to grow excited about the possible existence of "so-called 'snuff films,'" a phrase that generally refers to amateur motion pictures involving an actual murder that is enacted solely for the purposes of the movie. Since then, the phrase has been used more and more loosely to refer to any film that includes the representation of on-screen deaths, such as mondo "shockumentaries" like *Death Scenes* (1989, 1992) and *Faces of Death* (1978, 1981, 1985, 1990) (see chapter 7).

However, since the "snuff movie crisis" of the 1970s, at least three major pieces of research have been conducted validating conclusively that no actual "snuff" movie has ever come to light. In 1976, the Adult Film Association of America offered a $25,000 reward, no questions asked, for a copy of a real "snuff" film; they were concerned that the possible existence of such movies would jeopardize their efforts to secure legitimate markets for pornographic films. No one ever submitted an authentic snuff movie, and the reward, as Johnson and Shaefer (1993) explain, was never claimed (65). Next, in 1984, Joseph W. Slade conducted an extensive piece of research on violence in the hard-core pornographic film, discovering conclusively that "to date, despite a thorough investigation by the FBI, despite a large reward posted by the publisher of the sex tabloid *Screw* and despite frenzied searches by collectors of the bizarre, no authentic snuff film has ever come to light" (163). Finally, in 1996, in the second edition of David Kerekes and David Slater's remarkably thorough survey of the death film, *Killing for Culture,* the authors conclude that an authentic snuff movie has yet to be discovered, although media crises about "films from South America" continue to recur on a regular basis.

Before taking a more detailed look at *Snuff,* it is important to consider some of the reasons why Shackleton's tagged-on ending to the Findlays's *Slaughter* led to the "validation" of all the rumors, myths, and legends about "snuff movies" that had been circulating in the media and elsewhere since the late 1960s. Contemporary folklorists, such as Jeffrey Victor (1993a, 1993b) and Bill Ellis (1990), have suggested that these kind of frightening rumors and urban legends can be understood as metaphors for social change. Rumor-panics, such as the crisis over "so-called 'snuff movies,'" work as cultural symbols, which a group of people can then use to give meaning to a social reality that is increasingly threatening and ambiguous—in this case, the impact of the Charles Manson/Sharon Tate murders. These rumor-panics then become "real" through the interactive process of the consensual validation of reality. For the women protesting against the exhibition of *Snuff,* for example, the film worked as a cultural index, validating a truth that they had long recognized but had been unable, as yet, to justify: that the fetishistic depiction of the female body—whether in pornography or automobile ads—leads the male spectator to demand further and further extremes of "perversion," which ultimately can drive him to seek out depictions of "real" female death for the sole purposes of sexual pleasure.

Snuff allowed complaints that had previously seemed trivial—about female frontal nudity in film, for example, or the use of the female body in television commercials—to appear far more legitimate and far more serious. In more ways than one, *Snuff* was a godsend for the feminist agenda. Whether the on-screen death of a woman was real or simulated was not the point, claimed the protesters. The fact that it had generated $155,000 in its first three weeks proved that there was a vast audience that *wanted* it to be "genuine" and would certainly turn up to see it if it *were* "genuine." As Kerekes and Slater (1996) point out, the urban legend about "snuff movies" suddenly developed an identity: Even if their existence had yet to be proved, this is what they looked like (28). There were now legitimate grounds for believing in the reality of an entire underground network in that cryptic place known as "out there"—the boiler room of Western culture—manufacturing snuff movies for the decadent gratification of a male audience finally jaded with the likes of *Insatiable* (1980).

Folklorist Jeffrey Victor (1993b) goes on to claim that "the symbolic pathways of some internalized legends function in personality, like archetype cognitive maps of social reality. Legends are not only 'out there' in our shared culture. They are also "in us,' psychologically" (59). In other words, the place where snuff movies are actually manufactured—the hidden boiler room—is, in fact, somewhere in our shared cultural unconscious. As Victor explains it, "legends create a perceptual set which can distort experience and cognitively arrange perceptions to fit into a pre-programmed cognitive map" (59).

Another way of understanding this idea is through the notion of *ostention*. Ostention allows us to recognize the urban myth as an interactive pattern of collective behavior, rather than a fixed and unchanging narrative. Folklorist Bill Ellis (1990), in an article entitled "Death by Folklore," examines how the often-unconscious acting-out of frightening collective narratives can take any form, from children going to a local graveyard on Halloween to the actual murder of human beings. A similar process seems to have been impelled by the many urban legends surrounding the manufacture of snuff movies—legends that were themselves precipitated by the moral and social impact of the Manson murders of August 1969.

The rumors of death films reported in Ed Sanders's biography of the Manson "family" were appropriated by the hysteria generated by the incomprehensible horrors of the Sharon Tate murders, and thereby given life. The rumor-panic surrounding snuff movies is perhaps best understood as a component of America's anxious reaction to collectively shared stories about immediately threatening circumstances in a highly ambiguous social situation. The rumor-panic was then "acted out" by Shackleton's splicing of additional footage onto an unremarkable low-budget B-movie and referring to it by the magic word: "snuff." The legacy of intimations, suggestions, and implications left over the course of the following twenty years by those who had either seen the film, or knew someone who had seen it, or remember the publicity surrounding it, or remember the controversy surrounding the publicity, have kept these narratives of snuff movies alive in the shared memory of our culture, sustaining the legitimacy of the snuff movie narrative as an index of social and moral hysteria. There were no snuff movies manufactured on the Spahn Ranch in California; nor any in Buenos Aires, Argentina; nor any elsewhere, not even "where life is cheap." But this is not to say that such narratives do not exist, nor that they are not manufactured on a regular basis in that frightening place that is the shared unconscious of a culture in crisis.

IV

Up until its spliced-on ending, *Snuff* is neither remotely sexually explicit nor particularly violent. Most of its murders are the result of unconvincing and long-distance shotgun wounds; the rest are unremarkable and bloodless. The sex scenes, such as they are, consist of soft-focus shots of the female face and breasts in sequences of loosely simulated heterosexual intercourse that is far less explicit than that contained in the average made-for-TV movie. For various reasons extraneous to the film itself, however, *Snuff* came to stand as a touchstone of cinematic pollution, falling as it does between traditional genre boundaries, blurring low-budget porno chic with grindhouse gore. *Snuff* was a movie that defied established cultural categories: neither horror movie nor porno flick; neither stag nor slasher; accordingly, it was doubly abject—unclassifiable, and thereby culturally contaminating. As a result, the film attracted twice as much hostility. Firstly, it encouraged the aversion of those critics of the horror film worried about both the influence of "low culture" on personal conduct and about society's responsibility for defining acceptable behavior. It also invited the antipathy of feminist critics worried that pornographic films could trigger misogynist or criminal impulses in their male viewers.

To feminists, *Snuff* the movie (and, subsequently, "snuff" the rumor-panic) was regarded as the ultimate sign of women's subordination in Western culture—the terminal event to which all fetishistic representations of women in the media (and elsewhere) ultimately lead. According to Gloria Steinem (1977), who led the feminist branch of the campaign against *Snuff*, "pornography's basic message is domination," therefore pornography contributes to a climate of "psychological degradation and physical danger" for women (55). *Snuff* was appropriated by the feminist movement as the ultimate event in hard-core pornography because—and for the first time—it seemed to justify many women's fear that it was a short leap from misogyny in representations to the actual murder of women for sexual thrills.

According to Carol Clover (1992), "the lower cinematic forms play by definition to male sadistic tastes" (225–26). *Snuff* galvanized feminist antipornography campaigners by validating their belief that increasingly violent misogynistic representations would, as Molly Haskell put it (1976), "create a demand for the real thing, towards which end women might indeed be murdered" (56). As Johnson and Shaefer (1993) explain, most antipornography feminists accept, with little hesitation, the belief that male patrons frequently attempt to act on what they see in pornography, that *Snuff* is a violently pornographic film, and that the snuff movie represents the archetypal sexualization of murder, toward which all pornography, whether soft or hard core, ultimately tends (54).

More recent feminist (and other) film critics have devised new categories for abject, subgeneric pictures like *Snuff*—movies that contaminate because we have no category to put them in. One such category is the "slasher cycle" (see chapter 3), which, as Clover (1992) observes, is notable for adhering to a strict progression in which "a killer methodically destroys sexually active females (and males) until he is subdued by a chaste tomboy wielding phallic weapons" (50). Clover (1992) and Linda Williams (1989) use the terms "body horror" and "body genres" to refer to such categories as the slasher movie, the stalker movie, and hard-core porn—categories that are often dismissed or suppressed, based on their presumed appeal to the lower parts of the body.

In fact, with virtually no sex, no nudity, and very little gore at all, *Snuff* is neither pornography nor horror but a disorienting, unconventional mixture of many different generic styles: low-budget thriller, female biker movie, Latin American carnival travelogue, "Manson-style cult" film, and sub-pornographic, hand-held-camera-style sexploitation feature. The fact that *Snuff* was a film that defied the boundaries of traditional systems of classification was precisely why it was appropriated by a variety of different pressure groups, cultural commentators, and civil rights activists as a metaphor for the archetypal extreme in violent, degenerate, exploitation cinema.

V

Although "snuff" (as a synonym for death) in connection with moviemaking was first popularized by reports of the Manson case, *Snuff* does not purport to be one of the infamous (and legendary) "snuff movies" made at the Spahn ranch. In fact, as the trial of the Manson followers brought to light, the existence of such films was one of the many myths surrounding the activities of Manson and his self-styled "family." However, despite its ostensible setting in Buenos Aires and Punta del Este, *Snuff* is unmistakably based quite artlessly on the Manson cult. The model for Manson is clearly the drug-addled Satán, with his mesmeric eyes, his sexual domination over his chosen female servants, his semitelepathic powers of mind control, and his gauche lines, such as, "You will feel the pain and you will not flinch from it," "You do not live for yourselves but for me—in me and through me," and—

somewhat cryptically and very badly dubbed—"I am who am." His barefoot, sexually liberated hippie-chick followers are plainly intended to resemble Susan Atkins, Lynette Fromme, Patricia Krenwinkel, and their friends. And the old abandoned factory where Satán and his band hang out is obviously based on the Spahn ranch, the abandoned movie set in Death Valley where Manson and his gathering lived. The pregnant movie actress Terri London is patently playing the role of Sharon Tate; Max March, her Polanski-style fiancé; and Horst Frank, Polanski's drug-dealing playboy friend Voyteck Frykowski.

Perhaps most striking in its similarity to real-life events is the final assault on Frank's mansion by the four hippie women under the orders of their absent master, Satán. In *Snuff*, Horst Frank is entertaining a decadent group of houseguests when the murders take place; on Cielo Drive, on August 8, 1969, Polanski was absent and his home occupied by his pregnant wife and her houseguests, Jay Sebring, Abigail Folger, and Voyteck Frykowski. Tate, Sebring, and Frykowski were attacked in the main room of the house; Folger was chased outside onto the lawn. In *Snuff*, Frank, Antonio, and Antonio's wife are stabbed to death on the patio and elsewhere in the house's grounds; Terri London is killed in the upstairs bedroom. The first victim at Cielo Drive was Steven Parent (a friend of the caretaker and gatekeeper, William Garretson), who was murdered as the "family" arrived at the estate. In *Snuff*, the first victim is the gatekeeper, Hymie, who recognizes Anjelika and lets the girls in, only to be stabbed in the back by Anna.

In addition, Horst Frank and his houseguests are seen to be somehow implicated in their own murders through their decadent behavior—not unlike Polanski's houseguests that night on Cielo Drive. Polanski's guests were determined by some factions of the press to be, if not an actual crew of cocaine-snorting, wife-swapping degenerates, then at least close enough to deserve a visit from the devil's punishing minions. In other words, the first set of Manson's victims lent themselves to their own slaughter. The unspeakable tragedy that befell Tate and her friends was enough to cause an anxious reversion to primitive thinking, where it is plausible to claim that victims have entered forbidden territory or breached an ancient taboo, and so brought their troubles upon themselves. There are only two real differences between this pair of cautionary tales—Manson and *Snuff*. Firstly, Satán's servants are shown to be the victims of abusive parenting, while Manson's women followers were mainly well-educated dropouts from stable middle-class families. Secondly, in *Snuff*, the killers and the victims have a tenuous link in the character of Horst Frank's ex-girlfriend Anjelika, while—despite much speculation to the contrary—Manson's followers had no idea whose house they were attacking on the night of August 8, 1969.

The Manson murders provided enough material for a wide range of similar cinematic "Manson-style cult"–based docudramas, mainstream movies, underground horror films, and made-for-TV pictures in the years immediately following the discovery of the bodies at Cielo Drive. Hippies, hippie leaders, drugs, communes, and murder became essential ingredients in every exploitation picture made between 1969 and 1975. Many of these films included highly subjective reenactments of the goings-on at the Spahn ranch, as well as their own bloodthirsty versions of the Tate-LaBianca murders. The year 1970 brought us *Love in the Commune* and *The Other Side of Madness*, both directed by Wade Williams; Al Adamson's biker picture *Satan's Sadists* ("The REAL story of the California Sadistic Tate Murder Hippie Cult!"); Robert Thom's *Cult of the Damned*; the Italian *I Demoni*; and, according to Kerekes and Slater (1996), Alexandro Joderowsky's *El Topo*—"conceived and scripted before the world had ever heard of Manson" (10–11).

Other versions included *Helter Skelter* (1976), based on Vincent Bugliosi and Curt Gentry's best-selling book of the same name, and Laurence Menick's *Manson* (1972), posters for which included the disclaimer that "we cannot disclose how some of these films were obtained, but you will hear the shocking FACTS told in their own words BY THE KILLERS THEMSELVES!" More recent offerings include Jim Van Bebber's *Charlie's Family* (2003) and Nicholas Shreck's *Charles Manson, Superstar* (1989). In fact, any use of the word "Manson" has provided a virtual stamped guarantee of depravity to all movies, television dramas, documentaries, and mondo pictures using the term, up to and including *Death Scenes 2* (1992), which boasts on its video cover of "uncensored scenes of the Manson family massacre," where "Sharon Tate and six others lost their lives during two nights of mindless savagery and slaughter" (see chapter 7). These "uncensored and graphic scenes of the crime" are, in fact, the recently released crime-scene stills and coroner's photographs of the bodies and their situation, taken by the Los Angeles Police Department homicide detectives on August 9 and 10, 1969.

The crisis in thinking surrounding the Manson murders, not unlike the snuff-movie crisis of the mid-1970s, seemed to be alarming and threatening enough to validate a primitive line of thinking: Instead of following a path of reasoning from effects back to their material causes, in the anxious quest for someone to blame for all the horror, the murders were attributed to a quasi-supernatural being—Manson. Manson was the cause of all this panic and mayhem. He was accused of wielding the powers of evil, of corrupting all our children, of ushering in the apocalypse. And yet—strange as it may seem to us now—Manson was present neither at Polanski's house on Cielo Drive, nor, the next night, at the home of Leno and Rosemary LaBianca a few miles away in Los Feliz (although he was present in the car that took the killers to the scene of their crime). Charles Watson, Patricia Krenwinkel, and Susan Atkins were all present at both crime scenes, but not Manson. Found guilty of no murder, it is Manson who remains, almost three decades later, in a high-security prison cell, and this clearly has important ramifications relating to the latent power of group identity. With the exception of Watson, most of the other members of Manson's "family" were released long ago.[3] There was, in fact, no such thing as the "Manson murders," just as there are no such things as "snuff movies."

This fact reveals some unusual aspects to the process of casting blame. According to anthropologists such as Mary Douglas (1992), the adversarial pattern of blame allocation is a construct of virtually every human society; "the communities that avoid casting blame are able to survive only according to an almost impossibly heroic program of reconciliation" (60–61). Blaming is a way of manning the gates, just as William Garretson manned the gates that night on Cielo Drive, the only difference being that this time the guard is armed. News that is going to be accepted as "true" information—that Manson is a psychopathic mass murderer, for example, or that there is a whole underground snuff movie network "out there"—has to be wearing a badge of loyalty to the particular ideological regime that the person or the culture supports: in this case, the belief that certain evil individuals—rapists, child molesters, snuff movie makers, serial killers, psychopaths—are responsible for the horrors that take place daily in our society. The rest of the information—that crime is caused by social policy and institutional legislation, that snuff movies do not exist, that Charles Manson was never at Cielo Drive that night in 1969—is considered suspect, and therefore either deliberately censored or unconsciously ignored.

Low-probability events, especially those that inspire this kind of horror, often jolt us into a process of primitive thinking, and it is a fundamental tenet of primitive thinking that rare individuals like Charles Manson are capable of wielding catastrophically evil powers. Anthropologists such as Mary Douglas (1992) have remarked that these powers—sometimes known as *fetish powers*—may either be purchased, or gifted by a relative or ally, or else—as in Manson's case—constituted by a charisma innate in the person's own self, supporting the successful leader in his symbolic regime (60–61).

As Manson was always searching for new recruits, almost anyone could join his side and win the protection of his fetish power. If the charismatic individual does not immediately deliver his promises, his supporters can wait until some new event can be made a crusading point for their leader's fetish power. From an outside perspective, the person who controls the most fetish power, when brought to the attention of the general public, becomes the greatest source of danger on the horizon.

Like Satán in *Snuff*, Manson's charismatic leadership, in contrast to the routinized procedure of Western society, impelled a reversion to ancient thought processes both in his followers and in those terrified by stories told about them. The charismatic fetish power of leaders like Manson has much affinity with that of traditional ancestor cults and their suppression of disorder anxiety through factional solidarity and the reinforcement of opposition. Within the cult itself, the fetish power of the leader is generally used to encourage collectivity and suppress factional fighting, but to those outside the cult, the fetish power is quite clearly the mark of a traitor, allied to alien conspirators, plotting evil against good citizens. Those outside the cult apportion blame for all misfortune on the cosmic plot of the fetish-holding leader and attribute bloodshed and disaster to his magic powers. In order to explain why a group of young, clean-cut, middle-class American girls turned to carnage and slaughter, instead of looking within itself, America looked to Manson—now a byword for black magic, hostile powers, and evil plots. In the Manson case, and in the snuff movie chaos of the mid-1970s, the culture in crisis cast from itself those elements which it was unable to control peacefully, then blamed those outcast elements for a catastrophic inner disorder of its own.

VI

The pattern that is beginning to emerge here discloses an interesting parallel between the ways in which "Manson" became synonymous with the chaos within American culture—particularly American youth culture—in 1969, and, partly by way of a response to this chaos, the ways in which the film *Snuff* became a totemic index for the snuff-movie crisis of the mid-1970s (itself initiated, ironically, by the rumors surrounding the Manson case). In other words, the Manson case provoked a crisis in meaning, which, in the years between 1969 and 1975, reshaped itself into a quest for the mythical "snuff movie," which itself found an appropriate outlet for blame in Shackleton's recut version of *Snuff*, a fictionalized version of the Manson case. This displacement of blame served a dual function.

Not only did it fit in neatly with Shackleton's outrageous publicity campaign, but it also refocused and redirected the guilt of an audience by implicating them in the taboo act of "killing the actress" (symbolically reenacting the murder of Sharon Tate), when—as the film reel appears to run out and the disembodied voice of the director asks the cameraman, "Did you get it all?"—they share complicity in the apparent production behind the "interior" film.

But to set up *Snuff* as a cultural scapegoat for the moral chaos of 1969 carries in its wake a major set of difficulties, not least of which is that it assumes an audience is easily convinced by a clumsily manufactured film with a tacked-on ending without any rationale or redemptive last-minute attempt at self-rescue by the female victim. It assumes an audience accepts without question the unmotivated illogicality of the two "temporal structures" that compete in *Snuff:* the ill-made reconstruction of the Manson saga laid side-by-side with a behind-the-scenes, hand-held-camera reconstruction of an apocalyptic episode in filmmaking. It also assumes a certain amount of sadism on the part of the film's audience, and it assumes an audience prefers a film appealing to the lower parts of the body, rather than the mind. And perhaps most significantly of all, by emphasizing the film's misogyny, it ignores the fact that virtually all the violence in *Snuff* is perpetrated by women on men or on other women. Any thoughtful spectator of *Snuff* will certainly recognize it as a badly made, low-budget B movie with a sensationally gruesome tacked-on ending—not the cinematic apocalypse of the 1960s.

But, of course, this is assuming all kinds of connections between *Snuff* the movie and "snuff" the rumor-panic that the movie quickly came to stand for. In fact, however, Shackleton's *Snuff* was, like the group of feminist activists standing in a circle outside the Rialto Theater on Broadway, a reaction to the snuff-movie rumor-panic. As it turned out, both Shackleton and the feminist campaigners picketing the theater needed *Snuff* to exist—or, at least, needed people to believe in the idea of *Snuff*—albeit for very different reasons and to support quite different agendas. Like the story of Manson, the story of *Snuff* is about the process of blame allocation and the many different social and moral functions that this ancient process serves.

To understand this procedure is to understand a great deal about the control of knowledge, the emergence of consensus, and the development of expectations. Both narratives involve a crisis in meaning, which is then displaced and redefined to protect the public good. The incidence of blame is a by-product of arrangements for persuading fellow members of the culture to contribute to it. In both cases, the process of blame allocation serves a moral function: The blame is expiatory. These kinds of purification rituals are necessary in order for the rest of culture to be exhorted all the more strongly to obey its own laws and to refrain from breaking its taboos. The fact is, however, that blame and taboo are two sides of the same coin—a coin that buys off moral and ethical pollution and social or religious defilement. What happened between 1969 and 1975 was simply that a new pair of magic words was introduced into the cultural vocabulary of blame: "Manson" and "snuff." Both words conjure up demons of legendary dimensions that possess all kinds of unholy powers: the power to corrupt innocent youth, the power to instigate bloodshed and butchery, the power to make myths and rumors come true. Once these demons had been released, their intimations of forthcoming apocalypse rendered utterly insignificant the facts—now so functionless and incidental that they have almost disappeared from view—that Charles Manson is technically innocent of the Tate-LaBianca murders and that no one at all was killed in the making of *Snuff*.

5 Once Upon a Time in Texas

> *The Texas Chainsaw Massacre* is a vile little piece of sick crap.... It is a film with literally nothing to recommend it: nothing but a hysterically paced, slapdash, imbecile concoction of cannibalism, voodoo, astrology, sundry hippy-esque cults, and unrelenting sadistic violence as extreme and hideous as a complete lack of imagination can make it.
>
> Stephen Koch, *Harper's,* November 1977

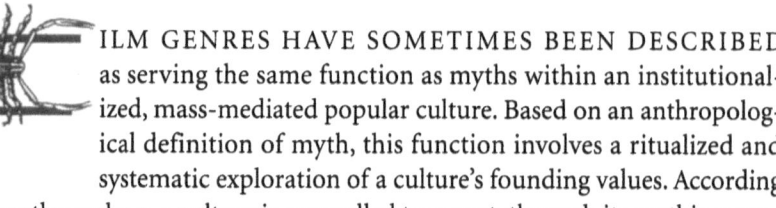

FILM GENRES HAVE SOMETIMES BEEN DESCRIBED as serving the same function as myths within an institutionalized, mass-mediated popular culture. Based on an anthropological definition of myth, this function involves a ritualized and systematic exploration of a culture's founding values. According to anthropology, a culture is compelled to repeat, through its mythic narratives, the symbolic tale of its origins. These stories generally deal with the particular series of semiotic and iconographic elements that represent a culture's value systems, rituals, ethical conflicts, and moral inconsistencies. Within this narrative framework, different film genres can be said to provide a number of variations on the classical structure of myth. The western, for example, has much in common with the epic; the horror film in particular relies for its innate symbolic resonance on the structure of the fairy tale.

The many functions of the fairy tale within modern society have been explored in depth by such scholars as Bruno Bettelheim (1976), Carl Jung (1936), Jack Zipes (1955), Marie Tatar (1992), Marina Warner (1996), and others. It is generally agreed that fairy tales have much to teach their readers about the condition of human consciousness, about the inner problems of human beings, and about the solutions to their predicaments. More specifically, according to Bettelheim (1976), the fairy tale helps its young reader to master the psychological problems of growing up—problems, as Bettelheim explains, that involve "overcoming narcissistic disappointments, Oedipal dilemmas, sibling rivalries; becoming able to relinquish childhood dependencies; gaining a feeling of self-worth, and a sense of moral obligation" (6). Through its ambivalent plot and archetypal polarization of human characteristics, the fairy tale entertains the child, enlightens the child about himself or herself, and fosters his or her personality in development. In its narrative and allegorical capacities, the fairy tale, it has been claimed, enriches the child's existence in a multitude of diverse ways.

In Freudian terms, the importance of the fairy tale relates to the fact that such stories unfold within an animistic universe, governed by the belief that spirits, good or bad, inhabit all things and that thoughts and wishes are all-powerful over physical reality. Animism is the force that forges the mind of the child and also the mind of the neurotic, and it represents the primitive incarnations of all cultures. Freud (1919) argues that none of us has passed through this animistic phase of development without unconsciously retaining certain residues of it that are still capable of manifesting themselves in those feelings of fear and terror that he refers to as versions of the *uncanny*: "Everything that now strikes us as *uncanny* fulfills the condition of touching those residues of animistic mental activity within us and bringing them to expression" (40–41). This is the symbolic structure linking the fairy tale with the horror film. The fairy tale takes place in a primitive, animistic universe ruled by spirits and magic; the horror film also gives us glimpses of this animistic state of mind, but in a repressed, unconscious form and thereby only recognizable as terrifying, bewildering, and often malevolent.

Most traditional horror films share the functions of the fairy tale in that they serve to teach their (mainly adolescent) audience of the dangerous consequences of inappropriate sexual (and other) behavior, thereby working as a ritual process of acculturation for the modern adolescent, just as the fairy tale helps the child come to terms with many of the psychological problems of growing up. Most horror films, by affording their audiences uncanny glimpses of the fairy tale's animistic universe, lead them through the dangers of the adolescent sexual predicament, reinforcing the culture's taboos in a ritual display of rule-breaking galvanized by the instinctive libidinal stamina of the death-wish.

II

Occasionally, and often accidentally, certain films are made that transgress the structures and traditions of a genre, sometimes with notorious consequences. Such a film is Tobe Hooper's *The Texas Chainsaw Massacre* (1974), in which a sustained inversion of the symbolic rituals and motifs of the fairy tale creates an apocalyptic narrative of negativity and destruction, wholly unredeemed by any single element of plot, mood, or characterization. Through its systematic inversion of the fairy-tale structure, *The Texas Chainsaw Massacre* functions not, as do most horror films, to acculturate its adolescent audience into the difficulties of adulthood and the inconsistencies of human consciousness; rather, it serves to mislead, misdirect, and confuse its audience in a bewildering nightmare of violence and bloodshed.

The film begins with a fairy-tale warning:

The film which you are about to see is an account of the tragedy which befell a group of five youths, in particular Sally Hardesty and her invalid brother Franklin. It is all the more tragic in that they were young. But had they lived very, very long lives, they could not have expected, nor would they have wished to see as much of the mad and macabre as they were to see that day. For them, an idyllic summer afternoon drive became a nightmare. The events of that day were to lead to the discovery of one of the most bizarre crimes in the annals of American history. *The Texas Chainsaw Massacre.*

A group of teenage friends are enjoying a day out in their camper van: Sally Hardesty; her wheelchair-bound brother, Franklin; her boyfriend, Jerry; and their friends, Kirk and Pam. During the trip, the radio reports a series of bizarre grave robbings in local cemeteries. The friends, worried about the grave of Sally and Franklin's grandfather, stop at one of the cemeteries, but Sally is unable to locate his grave. Moving on, the friends pick up a "weird-looking" hitchhiker with a huge birthmark and twisted face, who proceeds to disgust them with tales of the local slaughterhouse (where Sally and Franklin's uncle also works). The hitchhiker then takes Franklin's penknife, slits open the palm of his hand, and then turns the knife on Franklin. Thrown out into the road, he smears the van with blood, laughing and cursing.

Pulling into an isolated garage, Kirk discovers that they are short on fuel and that there will be no gas delivery until the following morning. The friends drive a short distance to a run-down house by a creek, once owned by Sally and Franklin's grandfather. Sally and Jerry explore the old house, leaving Franklin downstairs, while Pam and Kirk set off for a swim. Discovering that the creek has dried up, however, they decide instead to investigate a neighboring house that they believe may have a gas pump. Pam remains in the garden while Kirk goes inside. Here, he is attacked and killed with a meat cleaver wielded by a huge masked figure in a leather apron. Pam, looking in the house for Kirk, discovers a room full of bizarre artifacts and human remains. She, too, is attacked by the masked man, dragged into a back room, and impaled on a meat hook. Pam is followed by Jerry, who, exploring the house, discovers Pam's dead body in a meat freezer, then is killed himself by an ax blow to the head.

Meanwhile, back at the van, the sun has set, and Sally and Franklin decide to go together in search of the others. Sally pushes Franklin up the hill in his wheelchair, but on the way the pair is attacked by the masked man—Leatherface—wielding a buzzing chainsaw, and Franklin is killed. Sally, chased into the house, runs into the attic, where she discovers what appear to be the decomposing bodies of two people and a dog. She escapes by hurling herself through the window and runs to the garage for help. Here, however, instead of helping her, the garage owner attacks her with a broomstick,

Sally (Marilyn Burns) escapes through the forest, *The Texas Chainsaw Massacre*. © 1974 Charles Grigson. All Rights Reserved. Courtesy of BFI stills, posters & designs

puts her in a sack, and drives her back to the house, where she is tied to a chair at the dinner table and tortured and tormented by a whole family of slaughterers, including the hitchhiker, until she once again manages to escape through the window. In the light of dawn, she limps, blood-splattered, to the highway, pursued by Leatherface with his buzzing chainsaw. She then flags down a truck, which runs over the hitchhiker on the way. The driver, in a vain attempt to rescue her, is killed by Leatherface, but not before a brief fight during which Leatherface is injured by his own chainsaw. Moments later, Sally flags down a second truck and manages to climb in the back, leaving Leatherface swinging his chainsaw through the air with rage and frustration.

III

As with many horror films, the basic narrative structure of *The Texas Chainsaw Massacre* has elements in common with a number of popular fairy tales. It is not difficult to spot structural parallels with Jack and the Beanstalk (the ascent into a secret world, ruled by an ogre; the descent back into the "real" world at daybreak, given chase by the ax-wielding giant); Goldilocks and the Three Bears (the golden-haired girl encountering a bestial family sitting around their table at dinner[1]); Beauty and the Beast (the beautiful daughter "stolen" by the ugly beast and dragged off into his own world); Bluebeard (the "dreadful room" with its terrible secret); Little Red Riding Hood (the girl lured into the house by a monster in disguise); and, perhaps most of all, Hansel and Gretel (children lost in the woods, stumbling upon an attractive house owned by a cannibalistic brute, who kidnaps them and attempts to use them for food).

Other elements of the film's structure incorporate a number of random fairy-tale symbols and motifs: the forest, the broomstick, the woodcutter's ax, lost children, the child in a sack, the bucket, the dinner table, the farm (and its cows, chickens, and pigs), the giant, grandparents, the disguise, the "escape" back into the "real" world at sunrise. And just as the lost children comprise one family group—two young couples and a brother and sister—the fairy-tale family is paralleled by the wizened and macabre family of men: Grandpa (virtually a corpse), their dog (mummified), Father (the garage owner), Leatherface (the eldest son), and Hitchhiker (the younger son). The clan construction of the chainsaw family reminds us, as Christopher Sharrett (1984) points out, that the story takes place in Texas, "a state brimming with folklore and key signifiers of frontier experience: the Alamo, Davy Crockett, cattle drives, frontier justice, Indian wars" (270). But, due to the pathological inversions of this perverse folktale, Leatherface's mask is made not out of buckskin, but human flesh.

From the very opening of the film, there are intimations of anarchy and disorder. Sally tries to restore a sense of stability, but she cannot even locate her grandfather's grave. By the time of her capture, the narrative has descended into a dark carnival of chaos and hysteria. Order and control have been abandoned; the potential violence of the dinner party recurrently lapses into absurdity as Grandpa, too weak to grasp the hammer, is unable to deliver his famous killing blow. All dialogue is drowned out by Sally's uncontrolled screaming, which does not abate as the film ends but transforms itself into hysterical laughter. Narrative stability evaporates right from the film's outset, when the radio report about grave robbing diverts Sally and her friends from whatever trip they were planning to take on that "idyllic summer afternoon" and leads them instead into the *other* film: the unconscious of the traditional fairy-tale narrative.

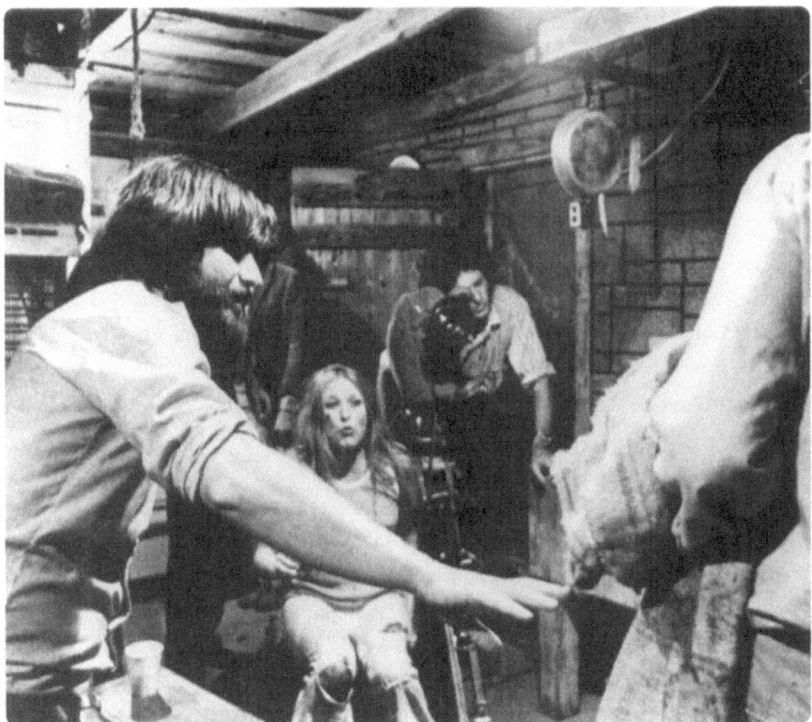

Director Tobe Hooper on set, *The Texas Chainsaw Massacre*. © 1974 Charles Grigson. All Rights Reserved. Courtesy of BFI stills, posters & designs.

The fairy tale is controlled by a mythic order and a ritual narrative script. The story of Hansel and Gretel, for instance, embodies the child's anxieties about abandonment, separation anxiety, being deserted or devoured, suffering from starvation, or being punished for greediness. But the children are victorious in the end, when Gretel achieves freedom and independence for both, and the witch is utterly defeated. By embodying the child's anxieties, fairy tales help him or her to understand and overcome these difficulties, as well as to come to terms with Oedpial tendencies within the family by separating and projecting various aspects of the child's own personality and those of, for example, his or her parents into different characters in the story. Because fairy tales begin from an animistic standpoint, they lack the aspect of involuntary repetition characteristic of adult manifestations of the animistic—in the uncanny images of the horror movie, for example. Most horror films share the positive, pragmatic functions of the fairy tale in that—when they *do* allow unconscious material to come to awareness and work itself through in our imaginations—its potential for causing harm is greatly reduced. The traditional horror film—as Bettelheim (1976) explains of the fairy tale—generally works to serve positive acculturating purposes (7).

Tobe Hooper's classic piece of horror inverts this mythic order and upsets the ritual narrative script—and on a cosmic level. The inverted fairy-tale narrative is not simply a tale of personal tragedy; rather, like all fairy tales, it works to universal dimensions. This apocalyptic sentiment is suggested first by the film's "documentary" aspect. On one level at least, the film is meant to be approached as a "true story" and has many of the stylistic aspects of the documentary, such as the opening "explanation" and the specification of an exact date printed on the screen (August 18, 1973). In fact, the story is based very loosely on the bloodthirsty exploits of Ed Gein, a mild-mannered and retiring grave robber from Plainfield, Wisconsin, who also provided some of the inspiration for the character of Norman Bates in Robert Bloch's original story for Hitchcock's *Psycho* (1960). *The Texas Chainsaw Massacre* is compelled to repeat a fixation on a nonregenerative apocalypse, an end to history, a cosmic destruction ultimately denied by the film's ending. Sally's escape, however, is not a forestalling of the apocalypse but simply a postponement of the end of ritual violence. Her escape signifies a return to the cycle of horror, never to be redeemed by any sense of an ending. As Christopher Sharrett (1984) points out:

> The denial of causality and emphasis on ritual structures suggest an atmosphere that is both primitive and modernist in spirit. The "primi-

tive" aspect refers to the ritual atmosphere surrounding the film's horrors and the way characters interact in a situation of chaos; the "modernist" aspect denies the primitive belief in a cyclical view of history and asserts instead an absolute dead end without possibility of renewal or even resolution. (262)

The mythic dimensions of Hooper's film are constituted by four separate groups of images: Firstly, elemental images of solar fire during the opening credits are counterbalanced by visions of a huge moon, then again, at dawn, by images of a gigantic, blazing sun. These images are compounded by the lunar-style symbol smeared in blood on the side of the van by Hitchhiker, a symbol that starts to make Franklin nervous. Secondly, the use of totemism brings a cosmic element to the narrative in the opening shots of exhumed corpses propped into bizarre tableaux. Leatherface's mask of human skin and the recurrence of bones, teeth, skulls, and other human offal provide symbolic resonance. Thirdly, a prescient chorus to the drama appears in the form of an old laughing drunk in the cemetery. "Things happen hereabouts," he tells the teenagers. "I see things. You think it's just an old man talking. Them that laughs at an old man knows better." This choric warning is echoed by a macabre series of images—a dead armadillo lies on its back in the road; a huge hornet's nest has been built in the corner of the room in the old house where Sally used to stay before her grandmother died. An apocalyptic series of disasters is reported on the radio news, which includes, apart from exhumations and grave robbery, references to an "eighteen-month-old daughter kept chained up in the attic." Finally, Pam spends the journey reading horoscopes aloud from an astrological magazine, and the forecast, as she warns her friends, is far from auspicious. Saturn is in retrograde, its powers of malignancy increased. Franklin's horoscope forecasts "a disturbing and unpredictable day." Sally's is even worse: "There are moments when you can't believe what's happening to you is really true. Pinch yourself, and you might find out that it is."

IV

The traditional fairy tale is based on a narrative structure composed of symbolic and iconographic elements that are, according to Carl Jung (1936) in *Archetypes and the Collective Unconscious*, fundamentally universal, as the basic elements of human consciousness are held in common by all humankind. Every child is born of a mother, has to grow up, attain independence, and win a mate; and yet details of such a progress will vary from culture to culture. In a similar way, variations will be found in the manifestation of acrchetypal elements within each culture and even within each genre—elements that *The Texas Chainsaw Massacre* ritually inverts, one by one. Perhaps the best-known and most important fairy-tale archetype is that of the Wise Old Man, the benevolent Father in "Hansel and Gretel" and in "Beauty and the Beast," who in other fairy tales takes the form of the good Grandfather, the Wizard, or the Wise King, giver of judgment and knowledge, sharer of wisdom. According to Jung, the Wise Old Man represents the factor of intelligence and knowledge or superior insight.

The counterpart to this pillar of wisdom in *The Texas Chainsaw Massacre* is the mute, ax-wielding Leatherface, the Wise Old Man's devilish shadow. With a huge, bloated body, his tangled, curly hair, his leather apron,

The Chainsaw Family, *The Texas Chainsaw Massacre*. © 1974 Charles Grigson. All Rights Reserved. Courtesy of BFI stills, posters & designs.

and his mask made from pieces of human skin, Leatherface communicates through a series of grunts. After the murder of Jerry, he runs off swinging his meat cleaver and squealing like a pig.

In many ways, Leatherface bears a number of similarities to a set of abject Hindu ascetics known as the Aghori. Polluted and contaminating Wise Old Men, the Aghori are filthy mystics who dress sometimes in the skins of beasts and sometimes in human flesh; many of them are simply insane, in the medical sense. The Aghori perform austerities at, and live in, the cremation ground or cemetery, sometimes in a mud shack, into the walls of which are set human skulls. They may go naked or clothe themselves in shrouds or skin taken from a corpse; they wear necklaces of bones around their necks, and their hair falls in matted locks. Their eyes are conventionally described as "burning red," and, as with Leatherface, their demeanor is awesome. Another "inverse" Wise Old Man, the true Aghori is entirely indifferent to what he consumes; he drinks not only liquor but urine, and eats not only meat but excrement, vomit, and—also like Leatherface—the putrid flesh of corpses. According to anthropologist George William Briggs (1938), the Aghori "roams about in dreadful cemeteries, attended by hosts of goblins and spirits, like a mad man, naked, with disheveled hair, laughing, weeping, bathed in ashes of funeral piles, wearing a garland of skulls and ornaments of human bones, insane, beloved of the insane, the lord of beings whose nature is essentially darkness" (153).

V

A second recurrent archetypal element of the fairy tale is the house, the rooms inside the house, and their internal decorations. Houses—either the family house or an isolated house discovered in the middle of a forest—play a significant part in many of the best-known fairy tales, including Little Red Riding Hood, Jack and the Beanstalk, Beauty and the Beast, Goldilocks, Bluebeard, The Three Little Pigs, and Hansel and Gretel, where the house is made of gingerbread. Rooms within the house figure prominently in Little Red Riding Hood, Goldilocks, Beauty and the Beast, Hansel and Gretel, and Bluebeard, where the virgin entrusts the girl with the keys to thirteen rooms, twelve of which she may open, but not the thirteenth. The internal decoration of rooms plays a significant part in Hansel and Gretel, Goldilocks, and—again—Beauty and the Beast, where inanimate objects, including items of furniture, have human properties and comfort Beauty in her loneliness.

Two houses are featured in *The Texas Chainsaw Massacre*: the dilapidated cottage owned by Sally and Franklin's grandparents, and the house of horrors inhabited by the family of slaughterers. The latter, like most fairy-tale houses, is attractive and welcoming from the outside, with a brightly lit porch, a swing, and the possibility of a gas supply. Inside, however, things are different. The house is almost totally in shadow. Downstairs, it has been divided into two sections: a thick steel door separates the front room and hallway from the slaughterhouse at the back. The front room is decorated with a gruesome selection of human offal; the floor is scattered with bones; skulls and more bones hang suspended from the ceiling; feathers and human teeth lie on the floor; bizarre sculptures made from skulls and jawbones are mounted at the windows; the corners of the room are covered in cobwebs; and, hanging from the middle of the ceiling, a huge chicken is stuffed into a tiny cage. Outside in the yard, tin cans, cups, and pieces of metal are strung from the bushes and trees. Elsewhere, a pig squeals faintly.

Upstairs in the attic (which is also used as the dining room), the main decoration consists of the mummified corpses of Grandma and Grandpa (who revives upon tasting fresh blood sucked from Sally's slit finger in a grotesque parody of Hitchhiker's gleeful self-mutilation in the van) and the stuffed corpse of their dog. This is the room in which the armchairs, quite literally, have human arms. During the dinner party sequence, the dinner table is festooned with bones, skulls, scalps, and other graveyard detritus, around which buzz a number of thick black flies. During this parody of the fairy-tale feast—the film's most protracted and frightening sequence—the food about to be consumed is Sally herself. Leatherface, smartened up for the occasion in evening dress and black tie, keeps leaning over to peer at Sally through his mask. The rest of the family all sit round in their allotted, neatly laid places, and whoop, cry, and gibber in a bizarre parody of Sally's terrified screams. Eventually, Grandpa, "the best" killer, is brought out to deal the blow: Sally is undone from her chair and led to kneel at his feet with her head over a bucket.

According to Jung in *The Archetypes and the Collective Unconscious* (1936), the motif of the house in fairy tales stands for the unavoidable entrapment of our minds in archetypal relationships and modes of thought. Sometimes the house is replaced by the symbol of the maze hiding its secret—the minotaur, symbol of man's duality and mortality, the half-man, half-beast to whom young people are sacrificed.[2] As Bettelheim (1976) notes in *The Uses of Enchantment,* the house is the central image of the "residues and traces" of a previous animistic worldview, with the motif of the forbidden room connoting sexual knowledge. The mysterious house in *The Texas Chainsaw Massacre* is not a house of life and knowledge but a house of death, whose counterpart may be found—again—in anthropological sources. Its division into living space and slaughterhouse recalls the Tikopian house in Polynesia, one half of which is not actually used as living space because, as Andrew Stathern (1982) explains, the former occupants of the house are buried underneath the mats that cover the floor (117).

Human remains are also frequently used decoratively within such cultures, but generally with some regenerative symbolic significance. Among the Melpa of the West New Guinea Highlands, for example, the jawbones of pigs are hung up on fences in commemoration of sacrifice, and, as anthropologists Maurice Bloch and Jonathan Parry (1982) explain, at death—prior to the influence of Christian missions—the skull of an important man and some of his limb bones might also be taken as relics and established in a *peng manga* ("head house") (28). And for the Doubains of Melanesia, all creation is the metamorphosis of one thing into another. Yams, for example, are transformed people, and they retain many of their human characteristics. They have ears and hear, are susceptible to magic charms, walk about at night, and give birth to children. In such societies, as in the fairy tale, human relics are associated with the regenerative properties of the corpse, and other inanimate objects are given life by spirits and magic, as is usual in the animate universe. Bettelheim (1976) points out that the fairy-tale hero proceeds for a time in isolation, just as the child often feels isolated. He is helped by being in touch with primitive things—a tree, an animal, nature—as the child feels more in touch with these things than do most adults, as Bettelheim explains (11). In "Beauty and the Beast," the human element attributed to inanimate objects allows Beauty to befriend them, and they comfort her while she is away from her sisters and her father.

This symbolic process is again inverted in *The Texas Chainsaw Massacre*. Here, rather than inanimate objects having special, magical powers of life, even living things are reduced to mere objects, as in the armchair made out of human arms and the table ornaments composed of human remains. Instead of imagining a world animated by spiritual magic as in childhood and primitive cultures, *The Texas Chainsaw Massacre* presents a world not only antipathetic to "normality," but forged out of an aversion, finally, to life itself, showing existence drained of all value: an ultimate, apocalyptic threat to the vital principle.

VI

Most fairy tales deal in one way or another with family relationships and the transition of power and authority through generations. For example, many center around a family in which one of the parents is an "evil" substitute or else is missing completely (as in "Snow White," "Hansel and Gretel," and "Jack and the Beanstalk"). Others, such as "Beauty and the Beast," begin with the death of a mother or father, which creates a number of ongoing problems, just as it does in real life. Yet other fairy stories, as Bettelheim (1976) notes, tell of an aging parent who decides that the time has come to let the new generation take over. But before this can happen, the successor has to prove him or herself capable and worthy (8). Fairy tales that deal with orphaned children or animals (such as "The Ugly Duckling") represent, according to Freud, a displacement of the child's fantasy in which both his parents are replaced by others of better birth. Freud claims that this exaltation of the parents is a reminder of the time when the child believed his or her parents to be supreme, noble, and strong (1923, 3).

The Texas Chainsaw Massacre presents us with two separate families: the "good" family of children and their evil counterparts. The children are closely interlinked: Kirk and Pam are a couple, Sally and Jerry are a couple, and Franklin is Sally's brother. There are also references to Sally and Franklin's father, their grandfather—the former owner of the old house by the creek—and their uncle. It is not quite clear to what extent the family of slaughterers are related to one another, as there are no female members of the family (with the exception of Grandma, now a corpse). Basically, the males of the family are all retired—but still practicing—slaughterhouse workers, made redundant by the mechanization of the local slaughterhouse, who have decided to use their skills on human prey ("A whole family of Draculas!" exclaims Franklin in the van). Hitchhiker, the youth of the family, seems to be the grave robber, responsible for the macabre series of exhumations reported on the local radio. Leatherface, his older brother, follows in the steps of his grandfather as the family butcher of carcasses, and Father, the garage owner, is "nothing but the cook," who sells human barbecue at his roadside store. "I can't get no pleasure in killing," he complains to Hitchhiker during the dinner party. "It's just something you gotta do. Don't mean you gotta like it."

Anthropologists have drawn attention to some of the ways in which those who bear the responsibility of disposing of corpses serve an important and practical function as cultural scapegoats. Lowest in the hierarchy of the Cantonese society, for example, are those menial laborers employed to handle the corpse and dispose of clothing, bedding, and other materials most directly associated with death. The corpse-handlers, according to James Watson (1982), are considered "so contaminated by their work that villagers will not even speak to them; their very glance is thought to bring misfortune" (157). The same pragmatic scapegoating is seen in the Hindu attitude toward the Aghori, whose fascination with decomposition, according to anthropologist Johan Huizinga (1955), is sometimes regarded as a spasmodic reaction against the excessive sensuality of their culture, particularly in its younger

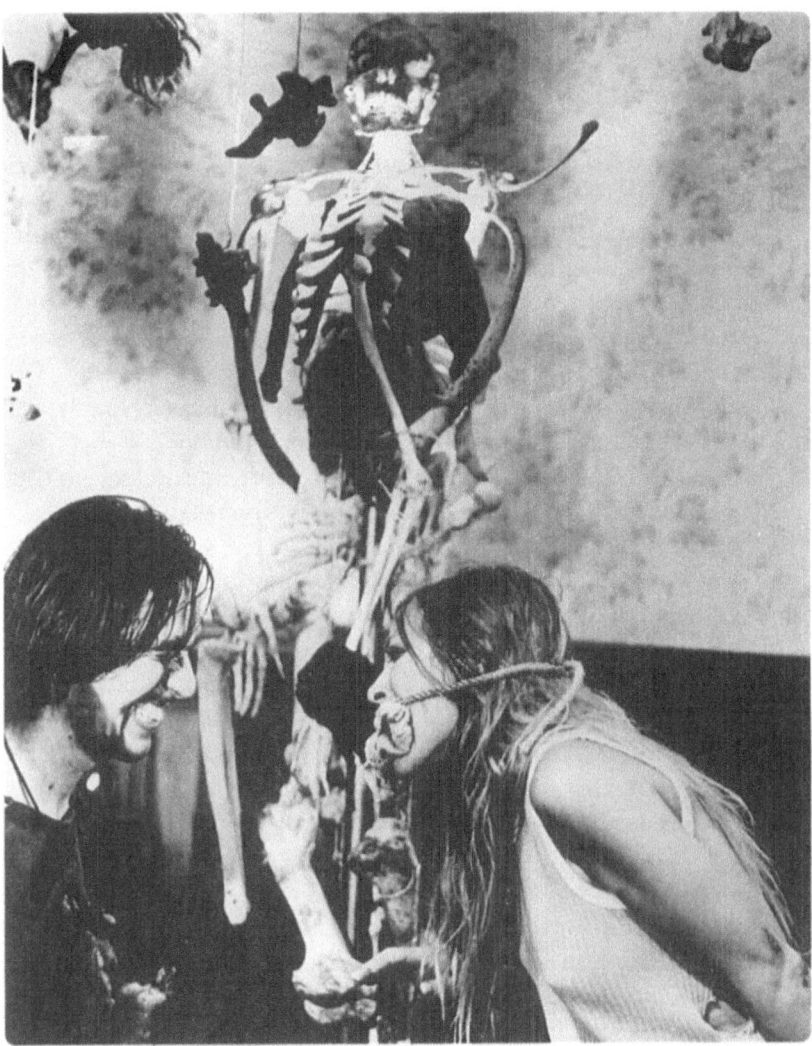

Hitchhiker (Edwin Neal) and Sally (Marilyn Burns), *The Texas Chainsaw Massacre.* © 1974 Charles Grigson. All Rights Reserved. Courtesy of BFI stills, posters & designs.

generation (65). By systematically embracing death and pollution in life, the Aghori aim to suspend time, to enter what George William Briggs (1938) explains is known as *samadhi*, an eternal state in which death has no menace.

Similarly, the death of the parent or the displacement of parental power in the fairy tale not only helps the child come to terms with death, especially the anticipated future death of the parent, but also dramatizes the natural transition of power and authority from generation to generation, thereby exploring the eventual takeover of the new age. In *The Texas Chainsaw Massacre*, this transition is blocked and inverted: Traditional values are refuted and negated by monstrous parent figures who destroy children. Robin Wood (1979) has noted how the "terrible house" of the chainsaw family signifies "the dead weight of the past crushing the light of the younger generation" (188), an obliteration that has no redeeming or regenerative qualities whatsoever. According to anthropologist Jonathan Parry (1982), there is a Hindu expression *alp mrityu* (meaning "death in life") that is used as a synonym of an "untimely death," such a death being always *ipso facto* degenerative, in any narrative or culture (83).

While, on the one hand, the monstrousness of the chainsaw family suggests a parallel with the stultifying bonds and tensions of the "normal" family that most of the film's adolescent viewers are currently dealing with, on the other hand, critics have drawn attention to the alienation and breakdown within the Hardesty family itself. There are two scenes of crisis: the first when Franklin, unable to climb the stairs to join the others in his father's old house, is left outside spitting, crying, and imitating his sister's laughter; the second when Sally's frustration with Franklin leads to a violent argument and scuffle over the possession of the flashlight. Critic David N. Rodowick (1984) argues that, in scenes such as these, the bourgeois family "manifests a degree of violence which equals or exceeds that of its 'monstrous' aggressors, effectively implicating the family in the monstrosity it is trying to combat" (322).

VII

The final fairy-tale motif mocked and inverted by *The Texas Chainsaw Massacre*'s apocalyptic economy is that of cannibalism. In fairy tales like "Little Red Riding Hood" and "Goldilocks and the Three Bears," the threat of cannibalism is modified into a threat of being devoured by human creatures in animal form. In stories like "Jack and the Beanstalk" and "Hansel and Gretel," cannibalism is threatened directly, though the threat is never carried out—at least never upon the tale's protagonists. Like many forms of death and violence in the fairy tale, cannibalism seems to be generally associated with regenerative functions. In this form, the threat of cannibalism helps the child to come to terms with his fears of punishment for oral greediness and—correspondingly—his own fear of being devoured or "swallowed up" by the parent. The same is true of cannibalism in its anthropological manifestations. On a symbolic level at least, the consumption of sacred flesh during the Eucharist involves, as Christopher Sharrett (1984) explains, "replenishing the spiritual aspect of a culture and reminding society of its sense of communion" (265). This regenerative notion is also the basis for scalping and tribal head-hunting, where the killer takes the substance of his enemies in order to recharge his or her own strength and power, or, as anthropologist Martin Horner (1962) explains, where the very act of killing gives the killer the power of his or her victim.

In *The Texas Chainsaw Massacre*, however, the cannibalism is gratuitous and purposeless. Hitchhiker's graphic description in the teenagers' van of the making of head cheese (boiling the cows' heads, scraping out their flesh, muscles, eyes, ligaments, and so on) leads to an act of self-mutilation that parodies this family's means of sustaining and nourishing itself by slaughtering people and robbing graves, then either consuming the bodies themselves, or, as Robin Wood (1979) points out, selling them off as barbecue (152). Pam's body is strung up on a meat hook, then transferred to the deep freeze. Jerry and Kirk are both killed with a meat cleaver. The sacrifice of these children inverts the regenerative ritual of cannibalism: It is empty of any kind of cultural or pragmatic signification in the sense usually associated with collective violence and other acts of ritual aggression, as Christopher Sharrett describes (1984, 266).

VIII

In fairy tales, this kind of terrible punishment is not so much a deterrent to crime as a means of persuading the child that crime does not pay. Morality is promoted not through the fact that virtue always wins out at the end of the story, but because the bad person always loses, and, as Bettelheim (1976) has noted, because the hero is most attractive to the child, who identifies with him in all his struggles (26). In *The Texas Chainsaw Massacre*, however, humanity is completely powerless, and the annihilation is complete. There are no heroes or heroines, only victims and villains. Sally Hardesty *would* be a heroine if there were anything rational or calculated she could do to escape her situation, but there is nothing, and, when she does escape, is it purely by accident. In this fairy tale there are no clues, no magic passwords, no treasures to rescue or battles to fight, because this is not a narrative governed by any kind of logical order. Neither victims nor slaughterers have any kind of control over themselves or each other, and this lack of control is cosmic and universal. Malevolent predictions come true. Not one of the young victims has any control over his or her destiny, suggesting that our defense against horror is finally subject to the forces of an arbitrary fate. Robin Wood (1979) has described *The Texas Chainsaw Massacre* as a "collective nightmare," which "brings to focus a spirit of negativity, an undifferentiated lust for destruction that seems to lie not far below the surface of modern collective consciousness" (191). Christopher Sharrett (1984) agrees:

> The idea of "redemption" that occidental man has assigned to the spirit of art, underlined by the "great works" continuing the concepts of sacrifice and the revivification of society, is parodied here, even if the parodic process is itself unconscious. Tobe Hooper's film is one of the cinema's strongest statements of the general paucity of myth and communal belief in the contemporary world. (272–73)

The Texas Chainsaw Massacre is perhaps one of the only stories of true horror that our culture has produced. The film's narrative disorder, illogical sequences of action, and apocalyptic sense of destruction are ritualistic, but without the regenerative or collective functions generally associated with ritualized violence. In the fairy tale, virtue is as omnipresent as evil; good and evil are both given body in the form of some figure and their actions. But in this fairy tale there is only evil: The good that exists is defeated, annihilated, or driven away. The morality of the fairy tale is inherent in its potential for assurance of success. Most fairy tales teach us about the possibility of mastering life's difficulties. A fairy tale that misleads, bewilders, confuses, and ultimately delivers the expectation of defeat is a dangerous story indeed.

6 Cannibal Holocaust: The Last Road to Hell

IN 1979 A FILM WAS RELEASED THAT SOLIDIFIED the merging and fusion of two fascinating cult cycles in the history of offensive films. Ruggero Deodato's *Cannibal Holocaust* was the first "cannibal mondo" film, standing at the crossroads of the cannibal cycle of the late 1970s and early 1980s and that other celebrated Italian cinematic tradition, the mondo movie. The cannibal cycle was initiated by Deodato's own *Cannibal* (1976) and followed by Umberto Lenzi's *Eaten Alive* (1977), Sergio Martino's *Prisoner of the Cannibal God* (1978), and Lenzi's *Deep River Savages* (1981). Distinctive features of this end-of-the-decade European excursion into anthropophagy include footage set on location in a generic "South America," some aggressive misogyny, and—most of all—a high proportion of stomach-turning sequences, with (genuine) animal mutilation and (faked) human disembowelment providing a large part of the revulsion quota. These sagas of exotic adventures abroad all bear in their wake a cortege of summary clichés shared—at least in part—by Deodato's scandalous cannibal epic: the humanitarian professor, the cynical guide, the cruel and primitive savages.

The second current in Italian shock-cinema flowing through *Cannibal Holocaust* was explosively sparked off in 1962 by Gualtiero Jacopetti and Franco Prosperi's infamous *Mondo Cane* and followed up by a number of bizarre and exploitative imitators. Alternating between pseudodocumentary and episodes of debased fiction, the mondo films of the 1960s won themselves a scandalous reputation for cinematic realism by focusing on semiauthentic, semifabricated clips of footage that claimed to lift the veil on the hidden turpitudes of our pathetic world. Critics of *Cannibal Holocaust* were not slow to pick up on the way Deodato appropriated the Italian mondo tradition and, while pretending to denounce it, made a film that was, in its way, even more gruesome, exploitative, and scandalous.

Others complained about the film's structural incoherencies, its naïveté of mise-en-scène, improbable scenarios, audacious schema of identification, and factual complacencies. *Variety* ("Cannibal Holocaust" 1985) condemned the "patently phony tale of cannibalism and the white man's mistreatment of native tribes." F. Gere in *Cahiers du Cinéma* bemoaned the "abysmal construction" of a film "that allows its director to simulate moral condemnation of the footage he has created expressly for our entertainment and credulity, making daring implications (though never fully affirming them) of the 'authenticity' of certain sequences."[1] Only a few of the film's reviewers were able to acknowledge (and, even then, only very fleetingly) the violent, excessive, fascinating intelligence behind a film that progressively but deliberately breaks down the boundaries between spectator and camera, between spectacle and violence, between shock and freedom, thereby questioning the nature of cinema, of voyeurism, and of the rights of the filmmaker to fictionalize reality and to realize fiction. As reviewer Jean-Louis Cros (1981) put it, "The title alone is enough to stop one in one's tracks."

II

Four young television reporters have disappeared during the filming of a documentary about a stretch of South American jungle known as the "Green Inferno," which is peopled by primitive cannibals. The television team—Alan Yates; his girlfriend, Faye Daniels; Jack Anders; and Mark Tomazzo—are well known for their grim, shocking, and realistic documentaries. Two months later, a search party sponsored jointly by New York University and the "Pan American Broadcasting Corporation" is sent out to find them. The search party is led by the somewhat implausible Professor Harold Monroe (played by porno veteran R. Bolla, aka Salvatore Basile), "NYU's noted anthropologist" and specialist on primitive cultures. Accompanied by a native guide and a man named Chako (Ricardo Fuentes), a mercenary of ambiguous nationality, Monroe sets out for the Green Inferno to experience a series of jungle adventures, including a close escape from a jaguar attack, the witnessing of a savage rape, and the discovery of the partially decomposed body of Fillippe, the documentary team's guide. Finally, Monroe and his colleagues make tentative contact with the Tree People, or the "Yanomomo,"[2] the tribe that has killed the documentary team. As proof of this, they find the bodies themselves, propped into a fetishistic tableau of decomposing corpses crawling with worms, huge spiders, and swollen beetles. Miraculously, however, their boxes of film are still intact, and it is these that Monroe and his team bring back with them to New York.

The television executives at Pan American want to begin screening the initial part of this "lost footage" right away, but Monroe insists on first revealing a little more about the ethics of Yates and his crew. Through brief interviews with family members and clips from previous documentaries, we learn that Yates is a highly unethical egotist, who, in the past, paid African troops to stage executions for his camera. We learn that on the African trip he killed tribesmen and staged massacres for his documentary team and was apparently unstoppable in his quest for the violent and excessive scoop. Knowing something of these illicit methods, the television executives then sit down to analyze the subsequent jungle expedition footage scheduled to be broadcast the following Wednesday night on BDC-TV as "The Green Inferno."

From this point, the filmmakers—Alan Yates (Robert Kerman), Faye Daniels (Francesca Cilardi), Jack Anders (Perry Perkamen), and Mark Tomazzo (Luca Giorgio Barbareschi)—are the real focus of *Cannibal Holocaust*, as we are shown the newly discovered footage, shaky, scratched, and unfocused though it is. This documentary, which takes up the second half of the film, is a cinematic coup. We first see footage of the four colleagues fooling around at their camp in a clip that establishes not only the amateur character of an expedition involving no special equipment in a terribly inhospitable environment, but also—and more subtly—that the team is using a pair of separate, handheld cameras. Developed and projected, film from these cameras has captured the horrible truth: that Yates and his team did not hesitate to manipulate the scenes of violence and cruelty they filmed, thereby becoming victims of their own egotistical drive for exploitative sensation.

The camera crew spends six days walking through the jungle in search of the Tree People. Their guide, Fillippe, catches a huge turtle, which he and Jack skin and mutilate with a pocket knife while Faye vomits over a tree stump. When Fillippe is bitten on his toe by a poisonous snake, the team has no hesitation about hacking off his entire leg on-camera, then burying his fatally mutilated body in the leaves. Eventually, the rest of the team comes across a single member of the Yanomomo tribe, whom Yates shoots in the leg so he can lead them slowly to the rest of his people. Arriving at the village, Yates tortures and shoots a wild pig, then rounds up the Yanomomo into grass huts and torches the whole place. Other atrocities witnessed are the forced aborting of a human fetus and the clubbing to death of its mother, the abandonment of tribal elders on the verge of death, the rape of a Yanomomo virgin by Mark, Jack, and Alan, and the later discovery of the same woman impaled to death on a stake, which enters through her vagina and emerges through her mouth. In the battle that finally ensues, Jack is captured, castrated, and tortured by the Yanomomo before being eaten alive. A similar fate awaits Mark and Faye, while Alan Yates, professional to the end, continues filming until his own head is bashed in.

Back in the BDC-TV studios, the producers decide that the material must be destroyed, and Professor Monroe, wandering out into the New York streets, wonders to himself just who the *real* cannibals are. One final coda: The end credit suggests that the television station's projectionist illegally

Alan Yates (Gabriel Yorke) in the "green inferno," *Cannibal Holocaust*. © F.D. Cinematografica. All Rights Reserved. Courtesy of Cult Epics.

smuggled out the footage we have just been shown after Professor Monroe had ordered it to be destroyed—and for this, the projectionist was allegedly fined the sum of $10,000.

The controversy surrounding the release of Deodato's film centered, perhaps predictably, around its use of "authentic" footage, most notably in the killing and mutilation of animals—with all its associated implications of a vicious and abhorrent attitude toward living human beings and the possibility that some of the on-camera "atrocities" are in fact, as the filmmakers claim, "authentic." These intimations are enhanced by the poor quality of the film-within-a-film: shaky handheld camera work, numbers flashing up on the screen, flickering lights, and the constant physical and verbal references to the camera by the documentary team. And, as Kerekes and Slater (1996) point out, "it doesn't seem to matter that a wavering tree branch or the ever-reliable pop, start, or film hiccup should occur always at the most technologically advantageous moment—that is, when Faye's head is about to be lifted from her shoulders or Jack is about to have his chest split asunder by the savages" (70).

The *coup de grace*—in many countries, at least—was provided by a series of scandals associated with the film's distribution. Firstly, a French magazine, *Photo*, published an article entitled "Grand Guignol Cannibale," suggesting that *Cannibal Holocaust* was, in fact, a "genuine" snuff movie, in which men were *really* dismembered, beheaded, castrated, and *mangiati vivi*. In Italy on February 8, 1980, four weeks after it opened, *Cannibal Holocaust* was confiscated and declared obscene by the High Court. It was later banned outright under an old law forbidding the torture of animals, although Deodato fought the decision, and in 1983 the film was released back into Italian cinemas in its entirety. In Britain, however, the film was banned under the so-called "Video Nasties" Act, and a copy of *Cannibal Holocaust* confiscated in Birmingham in April 1993 prompted predictable outcries about "snuff movies" (see Kerekes and Slater 1996, 69). As a result of these calumnies, *Cannibal Holocaust* was a huge *success de scandale* in Italy and elsewhere in Europe. And in Japan, at least according to the film's director, *Cannibal Holocaust* is second only to *E.T.* as the most successful production of all time.

III

Deodato's film, then, consists of two separate narratives: the story of Yates and his team disappearing in the jungle, and the story of Monroe and his team on their quest to discover the lost film footage. The protagonists of these two narratives are set in opposition to one another. Yates represents the worst extremes of mercenary capitalism—a man who, in the quest for monetary rewards, has no hesitation about involving himself in the most ignoble excesses, including the torture and mutilation of his fellow human beings. Monroe, on the other hand, stands for decency and humanitarianism—his brave genius represents the values of an idealized American democracy. Yates's story is one of chaos, anarchy, violence, and the apocalyptic collapse of moral boundaries; Monroe's is one of wary restoration and resolution. The structural system that both these narratives deal with is one as old as cannibalism itself, as old as mankind: the system of give and take. What the "lost footage" documents is the collapse of the exchange system, that most basic and primitive ritual of civilization. Monroe's narrative then begins, albeit tentatively, to restructure these social codes by warily initiating a very simple but fundamental structure of exchange. In other words, *Cannibal Holocaust* presents us with two short narratives: the "improper" film (which, to confuse matters somewhat, comes second chronologically) —a story of taking and taking back—and the "proper" film—a restorative narrative of give and take.

IV

The film footage taken by Yates and his crew, given the title "The Green Inferno" by BDC-TV, is a terrible warning of what happens when the most primitive structures of human civilization collapse. It is a tale of flesh debts, cannibal vendettas, morally unsanctioned gifts, collapsed boundaries, and the violation of all rites of exchange.

Appropriately enough, from what we can gather about the documentary crew, they are all the products of failed parenting or broken homes. Alan Yates, as we know, is an unscrupulous double-dealer, capable of staging massacres and executions for the camera, obsessive in his quest for the ultimate scoop. From brief clips of the team clowning around theatrically, we learn that he has persistently refused to marry his long-term girlfriend, Faye; a crew member who dropped out of the documentary team at the last moment describes Alan as "pushing his people to the limits, demanding everything, including *blood*. . . . God have mercy on his soul, he was one ruthless son of a bitch." Faye's sister, a nun, informs us that not only was Faye adopted as a child but she changed her name from the one her adoptive parents had given her. Jack's abandoned hippie wife, living on welfare with her fatherless child, is interested only in asking her interviewer whether "you guys think I could get any bread out of this?" Finally, Mark's father, Mr.

Tomazzo, a hardened and cynical blue-collar worker, reveals simply that he has disowned his son long ago ("My son was no good... that son of a bitch, my son is dead.") These brief interview clips are enough to establish what we have already surmised: that Yates and his team represent the most decadent extreme of the Age of Aquarius. Adrift from their homes and families and without any moral ties to speak of, they are united only in their obsessive quest for the scoop—and the financial rewards it might bring them.

In the same way, we learn that this is a group of people who have no respect for public and private boundaries, nor for the dignity of the individual human body. Their expedition knows no notion of privacy, and there is no personal act that does not find its way into the film. We first see Faye emerging nude from a shower, filmed by Mark, while Jack wrestles with her, steals her panties, and throws them across the room ("A crew of clowns—they had a great sense of the theatrical," comments Monroe in the BDC-TV viewing room. "Like I said, they were real professionals.") Later, when the gruesome mutilation of the turtle prompts Faye to seek a private corner in which to vomit, the camera follows her, filming the act with relish. She is even filmed defecating in the forest, something she accepts with equanimity ("I had to wait in line, with the rest of the animals," she laughs). Later, Alan is filmed urinating and Mark shaving. When his massacre of the Yanomomo has excited Yates erotically, he is filmed pulling off Faye's jeans and making love to her violently—a precedent for the later gang-rape of a young Yanomomo girl, a "little monkey," who is raped by Jack, Mark, and Alan, each taking a turn to hold the camera.

And then, of course, there are the private moments of bodily death, made public by the ever-present camera. When Fillippe is bitten by a snake, Alan gleefully films the fatal mutilation of his leg and the cauterization of the bloody stump. Other private acts made gruesomely public include the induced abortion and execution of a native woman; the Yanomomo girl's impalement on a stake; the death, castration, and mutilation of Jack; and the decapitations of Faye and Mark; finally Alan, achieving the ultimate scoop, manages to catch his own death on-camera. Historians and anthropologists have often pointed out that this collapse of public and private boundaries, allowing the public to impinge on the private and vice versa, is one of the hallmarks of a decadent civilization.

Another characteristic of the team's degeneracy is its unflinching indulgence in animal mutilation—the chief reason for the banning of *Cannibal Holocaust* in Britain. Snakes, spiders, and small birds are killed as a matter of routine, but the turtle mutilation is another matter. Still alive as Fillippe dismembers it and prizes the shell off its back, its feet continue to flap and twitch, and its head, lying some distance away, continues to gasp and croak.[3] Later, on arriving at the Yanomomo village, Alan kicks a wild piglet around to make it squeal helplessly before shooting it in the side.

Thus, we are introduced to the documentary crew—a team which has set about shooting this footage for reasons no more altruistic than the desire to win awards ("Keep rolling—we're gonna get an Oscar for this!")—and all the financial benefits that such success can bring ("This's gonna make us rich and famous!" yells Alan. "This's gonna make us lots of money!"). For Yates and his team, crossing the border between Brazil and Peru seems to represent the breakdown of those moral boundaries that protect human dignity, self-respect, and privacy: The Green Inferno is a zone of transgression and taboo. Here, even the primitive human ritual of give and take is reduced to a cruel farce. Yates and his team all take from the jungle—carving up the turtle, shooting the pig, pinning rare butterflies to a board—but have nothing to give in return. They take the service of Fillippe, their loyal guide, and repay him with a cruel and violent death. They take a monkey from the trees, kill it, and throw its head into the jungle. When a brave Yanomomo tries to take the head for food, they pepper him with bullets, forcing him to move slowly enough for them to follow him to his native village. Taking burning brands to the villagers' huts, they herd up the natives like cattle and burn down their homes. They take film footage of a private ceremony of execution, take the virginity of the Yanomomo girl in a particularly brutal gang-rape, then take more footage of her bizarre ritual impalement.

Purely for the sake of the microphones, Alan comments hypocritically on the grotesque tableau before him ("It's unbelievable, it's horrible, I can't understand the reason for such cruelty. . . . It must have something to do with some bizarre sexual rite, or with the profound respect these primitives have for virginity.") Finally, of course, the Yanomomo wreak their fatal and legitimate revenge on their persecutors by taking part in the ancient and symbolic practice of cannibalism, thereby taking their enemies' lives.

As anthropology has often testified, there is nothing bizarre, taboo, or forbidden about cannibalism—particularly exophagy (the eating of members of a foreign or enemy tribe)[4]—so long as it takes place for a morally sanctioned reason. These are many in number. Early humans, for example, indulged in exophagy as a preferred form of protein consumption, eating human marrow and brains without much more compunction than they ate deer, otter, or wild sheep. According to anthropologist Reay Tannahil (1975),

CANNIBAL HOLOCAUST: THE LAST ROAD TO HELL

hunters in some parts of the world were even accustomed, after killing their human prey, to eat its most perishable parts raw (the heart, liver, brains, the fat behind the eyeballs) before they got down to the task of carving up the carcass into pieces that could be easily transported (7). However, according to Tannahil, when humans learned to cultivate the soil, settled down, and became farmers or pastoral nomads, the need for supplementary food began to diminish; and, as law and religion developed and became institutionalized, there gradually grew up a climate of opinion that was opposed to the casual eating of human flesh (29).

A second morally sanctioned reason for cannibalism is extreme necessity and sheer hunger. Cannibalism was known to occur out of desperation among the inmates of German concentration camps during World War II. In Belsen, according to historian Raul Hilberg (1961), a former British internee engaged in clearing away dead bodies gave evidence that "as many as one in ten had a piece cut from the thigh or other part of the body.... On my very next visit to the mortuary I actually saw a prisoner whip out a knife,

Professor Harold Monroe (Robert Kerman) and a TV company executive, *Cannibal Holocaust*. *Cannibal Holocaust*. © 1980 F.D. Cinematografica. All Rights Reserved. Courtesy of Cult Epics.

cut a portion out of the leg of a dead body and put it quickly into his mouth" (175). The best known of all such cases is probably the Andes plane crash of 1972, replayed in the 1993 movie *Alive!*, when sixteen injured young Uruguayans survived seventy days in the bitter heights of the Andes by eating the flesh of companions who had been killed in the crash and a subsequent avalanche.[5]

Thirdly, ritualistic cannibalism can be morally sanctioned for a number of magico-religious reasons: to facilitate conception, for example, or to absorb the virtues of others. Cannibalism for the symbolic purposes of absorbing the strength of others has been reported among the Aborigines of Australia, the Maoris of New Zealand, the Hurons and Iroquois of North America, the Ashanti of Africa, and the Usochi of the Balkans (Tannahil 1975, 24). Austalian Aborigines, for example, indulged in cannibalism for a great number of symbolic reasons. It was a sacrificial ritual, good magic, a symbol of revenge, a sign of respect for the dead; it gave strength and courage, and some tribes are said to have believed that it facilitated conception, as the life of the dead man passed into the woman's body from which it was born again. The Tibetans were said to practice only symbolic endophagy: When a tribesman's father was about to die, all the relatives met together to feast on the dead body. Such ideas as these, combined with a belief that the soul possessed a life-essence as transferable as blood, also help to illuminate both the practice of headhunting and the cult of skulls (see Roheim 1925, 391).

What happens in *Cannibal Holocaust*, however, is something rather different. The Yanomomo's mutilation, decapitation, and consumption of the four reporters takes place for reasons neither of protein lack, nor as the result of extreme necessity, nor for morally sanctioned magico-religious reasons. Cannibalism itself is neither necessarily violent, nor fearsome, nor taboo, but what happens in Deodato's film is a different kind of cannibalism altogether: the extreme and terrifying reaction of a society whose moral boundaries have been forced to collapse, whose foundations have been forcibly shaken, and whose basic system of exchange has been exploited and abused. This is the kind of cannibalism whose morally unsanctioned nature would have led it to be seen in the same category as witchcraft, as the exhumation of decaying flesh to eat from graveyards, or—later—as psychosis. This is the repayment of flesh debts, transmuted into a violent quest for total vengeance, an ultimate demonstration of hatred or scorn. This kind of psychosis—resulting from the collapse of social and moral boundaries—is far from unknown. Ojibwa Indians, for example, suffer from a bizarre mental disorder technically known as the *wiitiko* psychosis—also known as *witigo* or *wendigo*—an acute anxiety state marked first by melancholy, then by a distaste for ordinary food, and finally by an obsessive desire for human flesh that ends in homicidal cannibalism (see Parker 1960). The cannibalism of the Yanomomo in *Cannibal Holocaust* functions as payback homicide intended to shame and insult the anarchic foreigners. It is cannibalism that takes place as a hysterical reaction to moral and social collapse. Reduced to a grossly psychotic level, the Yanomomo begin to act out primal myths on these foreign bodies.[6]

Cannibal Holocaust is an "improper" film because it is a film of chaos and warning. It warns of the consequences of social breakdown, of moral collapse, and of the failure of the system of exchange, demonstrating what happens when the system of give and take is replaced by a selfish and aggressive ritual of taking and taking back. The system of exchange has become a system of vendetta, of morally sanctioned thefts, of the payment and repayment of flesh debts. In an ironic twist, the BDC-TV projectionist, joining in the chaos, steals the footage and smuggles it out of the projection booth instead of destroying it, as Monroe tells him to, thereby preserving this moral tale of near-apocalypse for our gleeful entertainment and horror. It is not surprising, then, that the film ends with Monroe gazing around the streets of New York City, wondering just "who the *real* cannibals are."

V

In the first section of *Cannibal Holocaust*—the narrative of Monroe's search party—we are told that the apocalyptic transgression of Yates and his team has cast an "evil spell" over the Green Inferno. Upon capturing a Yanomomo warrior, whom Chako recognizes from his symbolic body markings to be "the son of a shaman who has been consecrated to the spirit of a jaguar," we are informed that "the Yanomomo are not really cannibals, and their assault on Yates and his team was, in fact, part of 'a religious ceremony to chase the spirits of white men out of the jungle'"—a ceremony that, apparently, is still in process. It is the task of Monroe and his search party to disperse this evil spell by enacting a narrative of propriety and ordered exchange, thereby reestablishing the solid boundaries between public and private, the "proper" system of give and take, which Yates and his team did so much to destroy.

Firstly, unlike the crack team of scoop-hunters, Monroe is—however implausibly—carefully characterized as an "official," and his search party is formed with altruism rather than exploitation as its motivating force. The trip is sponsored jointly by New York University and the Pan American Broadcasting Corporation. Monroe is described as "NYU's noted anthropologist, specialist on primitive cultures," and is first seen walking across the lawns of an appropriately collegiate-looking institution. His status as the brave and humanitarian representative of an idealized American democracy is ratified by the mercenary Chako, who comments, on first being introduced to Monroe, that "you anthropologists and missionaries are made of special stuff.... I would give anything to be somewhere else."

Secondly, Monroe's narrative begins tentatively to reestablish the "civilized" social boundaries between public and private worlds. Although the camera lingers in voyeuristic close-up over Chako picking fat slugs off Fillippe's corpse and Monroe vomiting at the sight, the Yanomomo's private ceremonies are never interfered with. When the search party encounters a Yanomomo warrior enacting "a ritualistic punishment for adultery"—the rape and murder of a native woman with a nail-encrusted gourd—Monroe tries to intervene but Chako holds him back, reminding him that this kind of punishment is considered a divine commandment, and "if he had not killed her, the tribe would have killed him." At the Tree People's village, Monroe and his team observe the rites of the warriors from an unobtrusive hiding place at an appropriate distance, never intervening, anxious that the Yanomomo still behave toward them "with a mixture of fear and distrust." "We were permitted to observe the execution of one of their warriors—death by mutilation," whispers Monroe into his tape recorder. "From the way the criminal was destroyed, he must have done something horrible to incur the wrath of his own people. It's not clear if this was just to pay a debt of honor to us, or only to demonstrate how they dispense justice." Monroe, Chako, and their guide, Miguel, mix with the Tree People only at certain times, when invited to join in particular ceremonies. Otherwise, they keep to their own tent. But perhaps the most solid indication that Monroe's narrative is one of social order and the reestablishment of boundaries is his attitude toward the developed rolls of film. The executives at BDC-TV attempt to persuade Monroe, as an "eyewitness," to host the screening of "The Green Inferno," to "let the public know the truth" and "let the public judge." But Monroe, knowing this to be a voyeuristic invasion of what is essentially a private apocalypse, orders the material to be destroyed.

Thirdly, everything that is taken from the jungle or its inhabitants is shared, restored, or replaced with gifts of equal value. This civilized process of give and take is established right from the outset by a series of communal exchanges between Chako and Monroe. At the camp, when Monroe asks

Chako to switch off his tinny radio, he does so without question, offering to share his beer supply with the professor, which Monroe politely declines (and not without reason: "A skunk must have pissed in it," gags Chako, spitting the beer out into the jungle). This symbolic exchange is later repeated at their encampment in the Yanomomo village, when Chako offers to roll Monroe a cigarette but the professor, again amicably, declines.

These private rituals of exchange are symbolically acted out on a public level between Monroe's team and the Yanomomo. In this part of the narrative, the system of exchange takes place in the context of public drama—with nothing secret about it—and is directly associated with public esteem, the distribution of honor, the sanctions of religion, and respect for the dignity of the human body. When Miguel catches a muskrat with his bare hands, although he slits its throat with almost as much relish as Fillippe skins the turtle, he shares the pickings equitably, tossing the muskrat stomach to their Yanomomo guide, which the guide scoffs raw, sniggering to himself in glee. His dessert is a line of white powder—presumably cocaine —shared with him by Chako, albeit with the intention of stopping him from escaping that night, as they are by now very close to the Yanomomo encampment and their guide can "already smell his own." The next day the search

VHS cover for U.K.release of *Cannibal Holocaust* by Cult Epics. © 1980 F.D. Cinematografica. All Rights Reserved. Courtesy of Cult Epics.

party arrives at the village, in range of the tribal drums. So as not to alarm the Indians, Chako and Miguel conceal themselves behind a log, sending Miguel (who takes off his trousers and remains naked) and the Yanomomo guide as their welcome party. The villagers then shoot a series of arrows at Miguel's feet—a symbolic gesture that is, according to Chako, supposed to "demonstrate their good intentions."

Monroe, however, remains dubious ("I don't know about this," he remarks anxiously. "I think they want us for dinner tonight.") His concern is not groundless. Although Miguel and the guide are welcomed into the village with a chattering celebration, as soon as the Indians catch sight of the white men, chaos ensues. The natives begin screaming and wailing, tearing at the ground, gesticulating wildly toward a pile of skulls and the muddied corpses of two native women—their lives taken from them by Yates and the anarchic path of destruction he brought in his wake. Fortunately, Miguel, familiar with the laws of the jungle, relieves the tense situation by simulating a series of magical gestures with his flick-knife, which he finally gives to the Yanomomo chief as a token of friendship and goodwill: a gift. "It's alright now, professor," says Chako to Monroe, and he is correct. That evening the search party is welcomed with a ritualized meal in which a cauldron containing a thick, pasty, white liquid is passed around from the villagers to their guests. The next day the liaison is reinforced when Monroe, "naked and unfettered," decides to join a group of young native women chasing and frolicking in the river.

Upon discovering the existence of the cans of film footage, however, Monroe is faced with an enormous problem. To the Yanomomo, Yates's film cans are a totemic fetish commemorating the tribal massacre, and they are not willing to give them up although "they hadn't an inkling of what was really in those cans," as Monroe explains later to a BDC-TV executive. "They just knew that they were a threat. The Yanomomo understood how important these film cans were to Alan Yates and his crew.... They thought this silver box contained their power—a power which, I must say again, caused much damage and violence." Knowing how valuable the silver cans are to the Yanomomo, Chako is ready to give up and return to the border, but Monroe can't bring himself to turn back empty-handed. First, he tries offering firearms in exchange, but the Indians are unimpressed. Finally, he decides to try an experiment, playing a tape recording he made the night before of the Yanomomo chief's magic wailing, backed by the beat of tribal drums.

Slowly but gradually, the natives begin to emerge from their treetop hideaway, grunting and chanting excitedly. A dead body is lowered from the treetop, covered in blood: the evening menu. "You did it, godammit," cries Chako. "They just invited us for dinner!" The exchange has been accepted: film cans for tape recorder. The deal is ratified that evening when Chako and Monroe, to the accompaniment of the tape-recorded wailing, are invited to participate in a cannibal feast—this time a celebration, a ceremony of chanting and dancing, of jubilant mutilation where the Yanomomo pluck handfuls of raw, dripping, entrails from the fresh corpse and hand them to the pale dinner guests to bite into. Monroe—like Yates, professional till the end—manages to join in the spirit and partakes, with Chako, of the magic feast. The curse is lifted. "They thought that since I was capable of capturing the human voice I was also capable of capturing their spirits," he explains later, in the television studio. "This convinced them that I was the only one capable of breaking the evil spell that had been cast over the tribe by the murder of the whites."

VI

As *Cannibal Holocaust* is so clearly conservative in its narrative impact, so obviously the depiction of structural systems collapsed and restored, so straightforwardly an illustration of the morally sanctioned gift cycle upholding the social cycle, it is difficult to understand why reviewers considered it to be such a destructive and disturbing film. Clearly, this is a movie with much to be desired in terms of formal qualities, acting talent, narrative plausibility, character development, and so on; but to condemn *Cannibal Holocaust* for its moral and ethical implications seems to be somehow beside the point.

A major objection of the film's critics seemed to be its scenes of explicit violence and cruelty. Richarde Lelande (1981), in *Image et Son*, declared himself shocked by a film in which humans are "rounded up, . . . mutilated, decapitated, flayed, degraded" (39–40). J. Zimmer (1981) also in *Image et Son*, describes the film as beating all the records of ignominy: "rapes, feasts of raw flesh, gross shots of decomposing corpses, interminable flayings and diverse mutilations are depicted with a great luxuriance in sordid details to culminate in an apotheosis of voyeurism in which the team cameraman films the atrocious agonies of his companions" (49–50). *Variety* condemned "Deodato's inclusion of much extraneous gore effects and nudity, as well as the genre's usual (and disgusting) killing of animals on camera" ("Cannibal Holocaust" 1985, 74). Alain Garsault (1981) in *Positif* commented that Yates and his team "appear well-placed amidst the source of horror, which is so atrocious to the sensibilities of the television executives that one of them orders it to be burnt—after we have seen it, of course" (65). F. Gere (1981) in *Cahiers du Cinèma* claimed that "the sole but not negligible effort of the spectator consists partly in overcoming his repulsion at this defiling of phobic objects and traumatizing scenes, partly not in abandoning himself to the only desire that this film excites: the desire for censorship" (32–36).

Other critics had more of a problem with the film's ethics, particularly its alleged racism. Jean Roy in *Cinéma 81* described *Cannibal Holocaust* as "a racist and fascist film which was made in this way to shock us by the inclusion of everything we find degrading," and he had just one question to ask: "How much did they pay the unfortunate Indians to make us believe that they are nothing but vulgar beasts?" (125–26). Garsault in *Positif* (1981) mentioned the film's "aggressive misogyny and ... old racist cliches" (35). Richard Lelande (1981) ridiculed the "generic guise" of the "wild Yanomomos" (39)[7], and F. Gere in *Cahiers du Cinèma* was primarily offended by "an explicit racism which, I must say, I haven't seen the like of for some time" (63).

Above all, however, the film's critics were united in outright disgust at what they considered to be studied hypocrisy in the way the film purports to condemn that which it takes a voyeuristic delight in displaying. "The anthropologist declares that it would be odious to show such films to the public," comments Roy in *Cinèma 81*, "[but] what do you think the spectator is shown for the next hour and a half? The famous ignominious footage, with occasional breaks to tell us how disgusting it all is. And yes, it certainly is" (125). *Variety* ridiculed the film's "liberal" message about civilized man's cruelty to primitive peoples as "ludicrous" and "old hat" (72), a criticism with which Garsault agreed in *Positif* (1981):

> A product of overkill in the domain of horror, *Cannibal Holocaust* would merit no more than an accusing silence, were it not for the enormous hypocrisy of its director, Ruggero Deodato, and producer, Gianfranco Clerici.... The last phrase of the dialogue—"I wonder who the *real* cannibals are"—carries with it an assertion that is not only clichéd, but has rarely been employed with such total and evident bad faith. The discredit it places on these filmmakers is worse even than that inspired by the lengths they have gone to find out how they can excite the most repulsion in the contemporary spectator. (35)

And F. Gere (1981), who begins his review by suggesting that—were it not for the accompaniment of so much hypocrisy—one might be able to find something likable and amusing in "this mixture of formal carelessness and intellectual naivété," becomes more and more scathing and critical in his vitriolic indignation at the film. He concludes with the most vicious attack of all: "Of Ruggero Deodato one can only say, as the English said of Mussolini in 1940, 'if you see this man, cross the street'" (63).

VII

To respect and obey social rules, we need to understand why those rules are in place. To understand why those rules are in place, we need to see what happens when they are broken. Therefore, we break the rules in fantasy: in narratives, which are acceptable and sometimes cathartic versions of broken rules. We keep to the rules because we have seen what will happen if we don't.

Cannibal Holocaust presents us with a pair of obviously fictionalized, obviously simplistic morality tales: stories that tell us the wrong way and the right way to behave oneself in society. When simple rules are broken, the horror and disgust experienced by those observing the consequences reinforce those basic rules. Of course, this horror and disgust is sometimes lascivious and voyeuristic: The whole point of a rule is that it is a sanction against *human desire*—against what we, as human beings, want and need, sometimes consciously, sometimes unconsciously. Lasciviousness and voyeurism are fundamental characteristics of the "unfettered" human being.

Cannibal Holocaust is not about racism, nor the mutilation of animals, nor exploitative cruelty, nor explicit voyeurism. This is a film about dissolving redundant relations, about libel and blood libel, about shame, blame, courtesy, conduct, public and private rituals, behavior and respect, about the most simple and basic law of human civilization: the law of give and take. The "improper" narrative—Yates's expedition—is not only a narrative but a libel, in the original sense of the term: a libel not just against foreigners, but against humankind in general. The regular strategy of rejection, according to anthropology, starts with the libel—whether this be the simple food libel (the libeled group eat disgusting foods), the sex libel (the demeaned category is promiscuous, effeminate, or incestuous), libel involving violence or perversion, escalating, if the determination to exclude is fixed, to the blood libel (the demeaned category is murderous and even cannibalistic—see Douglas 1992, 86). The "proper" film, however, is a narrative of resolution and restoration, reassuring us that humankind is not, in fact, "other" by nature—not barbaric, murderous, enslaved to desire, sensual, or ineducable; but amicable, restrained, equitable, generous, and humane. If part of the "improper" film involves explicit and voyeuristic pleasure in cruelty and barbarism, it is only in order for the "proper" film more fully to clear the rubble in preparation for new social relations to be restored. The "proper" film illustrates that the best way of maintaining the social structure is by allowing the periodic redistribution of structural forces.

VIII

Contemporary critics and reviewers of the film did not seem to realize that Deodato's cannibal saga is, in fact, a film of restoration and redistribution rather than a film of chaos and destruction. Deodato's gleeful voyeurism seems to have distracted most from attending to the film's restorative implications, preferring instead to condemn it as a tale of racist hypocrisy. Or perhaps the film's narrative structure detracts from its restorative impact. In other words, the reversed chronological order—showing Monroe's "proper" narrative before Yates's "improper" film—perhaps leaves the spectators with a final taste of chaos and destruction, rather than order and repair. Or perhaps there is a third reason.

In fact, *Cannibal Holocaust* consists not of two films, but of three. At BDC-TV in New York City, Monroe studies one of Yates's earlier documentaries, "The Last Road to Hell," to get a little more background information about the team of ill-fated filmmakers. "The Last Road to Hell," it is claimed, was made by Yates and his team a year and a half earlier, in Africa. This flickering black-and-white footage, with a haunting and romantic soundtrack, consists of images of blacks being slaughtered at the hands of a Third World dictatorship. A firing squad cuts down a line of men; piles of corpses lie abandoned in the road; men and women are tied to posts and executed; trussed-up cadavers are tossed casually into the back of a truck; the mutilated and the dead are laid out in a public square. For this section of the film, Deodato utilizes actual news footage; according to Kerekes and Slater (1996), "the atrocities meted out in this archive material are undoubtedly real" (68).

"Pretty powerful stuff, huh?" asks the BDC-TV executive. "Well, just to give you an idea how Alan and the others worked, everything you just saw was put on.... That was no enemy army approaching. Alan paid those soldiers to do a bit of 'acting' for him," implying, of course, that the entire massacre and series of executions was "set up" and paid for by the filmmakers. In the fiction of *Cannibal Holocaust*, "The Last Road to Hell" is intended to be a "genuine" snuff movie. In fact, it is a series of news-footage outtakes of "real live" deaths.

"The Last Road to Hell" serves a number of significant narrative functions. Principally, through its irrefutable realism, the sheer numbers of bodies mown down, the understated tone, and the unsensational, undramatic depiction of fast, simple executions, this footage throws into perspective the only too patent phoniness of what Richard Lelande (1981) referred to as "*l'enfer vert Deodato-Amazonien*" (39), with its flickering, scratched, elaborately unfocused, dramatically "amateurish" cinematic style. In other words, "The Last Road to Hell" is a testament to the *actual* transgression of all those rules that "The Green Inferno" merely *pretends* to break, particularly those of voyeurism and the public appropriation of what is essentially a private moment—the moment of death. The *real* genuine footage slips by quickly, briefly, undramatically, and with little attention drawn to it; the *fake* "genuine" footage, on the other hand, is announced elaborately, exotically, melodramatically. In return, it attracted elaborate, exotic indignation from the film's critics. The *staged* voyeurism of "The Green Inferno" plays at breaking the rules of cinematic intrusion, which "The Last Road to Hell" breaks for real, explaining to us why this pseudovoyeurism is necessary. "The Last Road to Hell" is the secret token hidden inside *Cannibal Holocaust*, which categorically endorses, consolidates, and sanctions the film's narrative consequence. "The Last Road to Hell" is a fleeting and crucial glimpse of the unimaginable reality that *Cannibal Holocaust* (falsely) disguises itself as. When the very rules we unconsciously desire to break are actually broken without our knowledge, it slips by unnoticed but leaves a highly unpleasant taste in the mouth: a taste we then indignantly attribute—and quite wrongly—to the central narrative of *Cannibal Holocaust*. No wonder so many critics made such a meal of it.

IX

Deodato is the unfortunate inheritor of a long tradition—that of attributing to any individual the establishment considers dangerous the most unattractive characteristics that could be imagined. In Deodato's case, these are voyeurism and exploitation; earlier individuals were (and still are) almost automatically accused of cannibalism. It is very easy for people to regress to these kinds of primal modes of magical and mythical thinking, including the perception of archetypal images or biblical injunctions. Sometimes these modes of thinking are used as techniques of rejection, as well as ways of dealing with marginal categories, such as primitive peoples or those who tell frightening stories about them.

In trying to account for the large numbers of uninfected skeletons discovered in the leper graveyards of Western Christendom and the Latin Kingdom of Jerusalem in the East, cultural anthropologist Mary Douglas (1992) maintains that people of the period may have been trying to cure a real social blight by isolating an imaginary disease (19). Others, such as anthropologist Bryan Turner (1984), argue that more likely they were confusing a real disease with imaginary sins. It is highly possible that a similar process is in place with regard to *Cannibal Holocaust*. Indignantly condemned for hypocrisy and voyeurism, Deodato has committed none but imaginary sins. In fact, by telling a story about a collapsed system of exchange, of public and private boundaries falling in on one another, about theft, blame, and libel, *Cannibal Holocaust* causes its audience to reconsider the significance of moral and social forces. Through this reconsideration, it maintains the strength and vitality of our shared process of social exchange: the simple system of give and take.

7 Mondo Movies: Recarnivalizing the Taboo

THE MONDO FILM FIRST BECAME POPULAR IN THE 1960s, when films like *Mondo Balordo* (1964), *Mondo Bizarro* (1966), *Mondo Freudo* (1966) and *Taboos of the World* (1963) tried to capitalize on the huge success of the seminal mondo film, *Mondo Cane*, released in 1962. The mondo films of the 1960s featured (often faked) catalogs of bizarre practices from around the globe, such as dog-eating in the Philippines, tribal fertility rituals, and the activities of South American cargo cults. The mondo movies of the last three decades, however, are far more vivid and explicit than the films comprising the original bandwagon of the 1960s. The new films consist of compiled camera footage of murders, suicides, assassinations, and other real-life disasters. The mondo films of the last three decades, such as *True Gore* (1987), *The Shocks* (1988), *Video Violence* (1986–1987) and *Savage Zone* (1985), are composed of unedited police and news camera footage too graphic to be shown on television, including shootings, stakeouts, air crashes, and vehicle wrecks. Other mondo compilation films, such as *The End* (1972), the *Faces of Death* series (1978, 1981, 1985, 1990, 1995, 1996), and *The Killing of America* (1981), rely heavily on amateur or police camera work, Vietnam war footage, stills of murder and suicide victims, mortuary scenes, and close-ups of dead bodies. The footage is occasionally held together by a loose documentary-style commentary, but often it is left to speak for itself or is backed up by an appropriate (or sometimes rather inappropriate) musical soundtrack.

Originating in the United States, these new mondo movies have a massive cult following, and such films are also produced in Europe, China, Japan, and elsewhere. Certain "classic" popular clips or sequences of footage, such as those of the Kennedy assassination and the Hillsborough Stadium disaster (when overcrowding led to the deaths of more than one hundred soccer fans), show up again and again, from film to film. Some films in particular are highly sought after but rather difficult to obtain. In addition to people interested in "true crime," their audiences tend to comprise the same thrill-seeking adolescent males that flock to see most other forms of offensive films.

II

One of the more fascinating examples of mondo films is Sheldon Renan's *The Killing of America* (1981), produced by Mataichiro Yamamoto and Leonard Schrader (brother of the screenwriter, Paul Schrader). Unlike many other mondo films, *The Killing of America* includes a documentary-style script that attempts to provide some kind of commentary on the presented footage, rather than simply linking shots according to circumstances of death (assassination, murder, suicide) or connecting unrelated footage through a suitable sound track. If *The Killing of America* is somewhat more intelligent and self-conscious than the average example of such films, it is representative of the genre in its obsession with open-wound sequences, its use of slow-motion repeats, and its unflinching presentation of graphically disintegrating human bodies.

The Killing of America opens with a grim promise, with the words printed on the screen as they are spoken, as though for extra emphasis: "All of the film you are about to see is real. Nothing has been staged." The documentary-style voice-over then goes on to relate a series of crime statistics: that America has twenty-seven thousand murders a year, that it is the only country to have a higher murder rate than countries at civil war (such as Cambodia and Nicaragua), that it produces a murder victim every twenty minutes, and so forth. The voice-over backs up footage of police shootings, scenes of bodies on slabs in a mortuary, and incidents of extreme violence at race riots. The following section incorporates footage of the attempted assassination of President Reagan, during which a secret serviceman is lifted off his feet by a bullet to the stomach—this is shown several times, and in slow motion—followed by slow-motion footage of the Kennedy assassination. The shooting of Lee Harvey Oswald is also shown in slow motion, as

MONDO MOVIES: RECARNIVALIZING THE TABOO

are race riots following the assassination of Martin Luther King Jr., police street shootings, and the killings at Kent State University in Ohio, where the army opened fire on students protesting against the Vietnam War.

This section also includes footage of U.S. soldiers shooting Vietnamese civilians—in particular, a close-up shooting in the head and a close-up of the dead body—as well as George Wallace (Nixon's electoral rival) being shot in the back of the head (in slow motion), the assassination of Robert Kennedy, and a (brief) contemporary interview with his assassin, Islamic fundamentalist Sirhan Sirhan. We are also shown security camera shots of a supermarket holdup and shooting in slow motion and close-up, stills of murder victims, footage of a large hotel fire, and footage of on-camera suicides, with people throwing themselves from buildings, hanging themselves, and shooting themselves in the head, followed by close-up stills of the dead bodies.

The next section of the film moves on to chart the rise of the serial killer, with the documentary voice-over condemning the lenience of prison sentences, the madness of the urban streets, and the frightening yearly crime statistics. Film in this section includes footage of an urban sniper, photos of his dead body, and photos of the bodies of his victims. It also includes footage of "Son of Sam" serial killer David Berkowitz in police custody, and the Jonestown massacre, a mass cult suicide in Guyana (with authentic soundtrack). This is followed by film of a terrorist taking over a television station and taking the newscaster hostage, serial killer Ted Bundy in court, an interview with Ed Kemper, "the Co-Ed Killer," on death row describing his killings, the exhumation of the bodies of murder victims, more police shootings in slow motion, open-wound sequences, and close-ups of dead bodies. The film ends with the words: "While you watched this movie, five more of us were murdered. One was the random killing of a stranger."

The Killing of America is an arresting film. Even though these "live" deaths are generally much less vivid and drawn-out than the graphic fictional instances of on-screen death, what shocks in the mondo film is a combination of the sheer numbers of killings witnessed, along with the frisson of shock in the realization that what is being shown, however unsteady the camera work and picture quality, is really happening "in the flesh." What is especially absorbing about this film is the strongly reactionary and moralistic tone of its documentary voice (criticizing the unlimited availability of weapons, sympathizing with police problems, and so forth), coupled uneasily with a compulsion to repeat particularly disturbing images again and again, in slow motion and from a variety of different angles. The typical mondo movie—like the films of the *Death Scenes* series, for example—comes to terms with its presentation of gratuitous violence in a generally unproblematic way, through the use of an explanatory, deadpan voice-over (or, as often, blankly descriptive subtitles). This uncomfortable juxtaposition of a paternalistic, moralizing voice-over with a voyeuristic relish in the more brutal scenes of bodily fragmentation gives the final impression of a film not really at ease with itself, its direction, or its intent.

III

A movie far more successful in coming to terms with its own purpose and design is the blistering *Death Scenes,* produced by Nick Bougas, written by Nick Bougas and F. B. Vincenzo, and released by Wavelength Productions, a Californian corporation, in 1989. *Death Scenes* is introduced and narrated by the famous occultist and former leader of the Church of Satan, Dr. Anton Szandor LaVey, who describes the film in his wandering introduction as "a road map featuring the many avenues by which we encounter death . . . a brutally graphic collection of crime scene photographs . . . a tattered collection of horrid indiscretions, a true necronomicon." "What mysterious force draws us to such a dark, challenging subject?" inquires LaVey in his sardonic monotone. "That is a question that you the viewer must ask yourself, for you have chosen to join me in this unnatural participatory ritual, this tour of relentless human folly."

The film is basically a catalog of grisly police stills of death scenes in 1930s and 1940s Los Angeles, arranged according to manner of death. LaVey, a spectacularly deadpan narrator, explains the circumstances of the death presented in each picture, all the time backed up by psychotic calliope music. The first section of *Death Scenes*—suicides—includes still photographs of bodies killed by shotgun blasts, dynamite, self-immolation, carbon monoxide poisoning, hanging, hara kiri, the slashing of veins, and starvation. The second section—murder-suicides—includes photographs of death by evisceration, bludgeoning, torture, drowning, stabbing, and decapitation. The film's chief segment presents graphic photographs of murder scenes, including bodies found in trunks; bodies with their throats slashed; bodies that have been burned, beaten, and battered to death; mafia shotgun murders; more decapitations; child murders; the victims of sex crimes; policemen killed in action; and a selection of discarded and mutilated torsos. The penultimate series—accidents—includes the bodies of a dentist and his patient killed by the inhalation of nitrous oxide, bodies killed in fires, and a catalog of auto wrecks. The film concludes with footage of war scenes, military executions, and scenes from prisoner-of-war camps. *Death Scenes* runs for roughly eighty minutes, includes over eight hundred photographs, and was popular enough to lead to a successful sequel.

What makes *Death Scenes* a more unified and integral film than *The Killing of America* is its unflinching attitude toward the violent deaths of the exhibited cadavers. Instead of the didactic and condemnatory voice-over so at odds with *The Killing of America*'s perverse repetition of footage, *Death Scenes* includes a soundtrack and direction that are clearly at ease with the film's chief purpose: to shock and thrill the voyeur. The careful montage of photographs ensures that the viewer does not become overwhelmed; instead, the narrative pitch is allowed to build in intensity, reserving the most harrowing images until the end of each sequence and leaving the viewer with a morbid anticipation of what will be next. The background circus organ music, rather than detracting from this intensity, serves to enhance the film's mood of uncanny abandon. Much of this is due to the words and narrative delivery of LaVey, whose wry summary of each death scene is laconic without becoming droll. He concludes his dark narrative with a brief rhetorical coda:

> Ladies and gentlemen, what, if anything, is to be gained by reviewing this grim series of images? Do we find further proof that crime does not pay, or a greater realization? Only through the bold confrontation with man and his mortality can we fully comprehend the importance of living life to its fullest, to pursue in true fashion the admirable goal of life with honor, death with dignity.

IV

An execution by firing squad is followed by screams, the sound of police sirens, and radio static. Various shouts and cries of horror are followed by color stills of bodies mangled by car accidents and video footage of bodies leaping from a burning building as alarm bells ring and ambulance lights flash. A brief glimpse of news outtakes from the Hillsborough Stadium disaster and a clip of Vic Morrow's death on the set of John Landis's section of the movie *The Twilight Zone* (1976) give way to Marilyn Monroe pouting and blowing kisses at the camera, juxtaposed with a still of her bloated dead body lying on a slab at the morgue. Over the image of a skull are superimposed the words of the film's title: *Death Scenes 2*.

Produced by the same team responsible for the original *Death Scenes*, *Death Scenes 2*, in both black-and-white and color, was released by Wavelength Video in 1992. Sharing—in certain places—the same psychotic calliope soundtrack music of its predecessor, the second *Death Scenes* has little else in common with its source and suffers from the absence of its cynically morbid impresario, Anton LaVey. The sequel begins with a thinly disguised advertisement for its predecessor relayed over some alluring footage from the original movie:

> In our previous presentation, noted author and former crime scene photographer Anton LaVey provided a thoroughly fascinating tour of a massive personal scrapbook compiled long ago, by a Los Angeles homicide detective, that chronicled a seemingly endless array of startling photographs, and offered a rare and insightful view of big city crime. There was even a side-trip down the bloody back streets of glamorous Hollywood, where stardom, and even mere dreams of stardom, came at quite a price. Also examined were the trigger-happy bootleggers, who made the twenties roar, as well as infamous depression-era bank-robbers, whose bullet-ridden corpses were routinely displayed like trophies to the eager press. But what of the restless decades that followed? The countless haunting images from both the television and video age in this production are intended to further examine the compelling elements of cruel fate, and malicious mayhem, and, in the process, perhaps gain a new understanding of the often bloody events which have shaped our world over the last half-century.

We have been warned. The main difference between *Death Scenes* and *Death Scenes 2* is that the sequel utilizes far fewer stills and more action footage, on both film and videotape, with an appropriately dour voice-over credited to one Harold Wells. The effect of using videotaped color footage mixed with black-and-white stills is to make the film appear rather more voyeuristic than its predecessor, more gratuitously violent and explicit, and less of a studied essay on the inevitability of death. But this is not to say that it is any less of a fierce and powerful film.

The sequel proper opens with stock sequences of graphic images from World War II. Clips of U.S. troops proudly setting off to war are juxtaposed with pictures of charred corpses on the battlefield and stills taken from Ernst Friedrich's antiwar museum's gallery of grotesque images of war casualties and amputees. Standard war footage is intercut with shots of fields strewn with bodies, the remains of prisoners in concentration camps, and weeping women cradling the bodies of dead children. Further bodies are piled into a mass grave buzzing with flies, stacks of mutilated cadavers are tossed into death pits, and airplanes crash burning to the ground, all to the accompaniment of appropriately heavy organ chords in a minor key ("additional music" is attributed to George Montalba). An inter-title reads "Three cheers for war—noble and beautiful above all!" Mussolini addresses crowds of followers, then is pictured strung up on piano wire in execution. Goebbels speaks to all Germany, then is shown as a corpse. The dead body of Hitler is pictured in the bunker. The next section then returns to the United States and shows footage of mobsters and mafia killings after the prohibition era, the executions of rival gang lords, the smuggling and selling of illegal narcotics, and the deaths of various syndicate leaders. The film then cuts to moving footage and mortuary stills of recent drug-related homicides and gangland killings in the United States, as well as in the underdeveloped supply countries.

The next section of the film is set in the 1950s. Footage of suburban teenagers dancing to rock and roll is intercut with further footage of race riots and violence and some of the "unforgettable atrocities" perpetrated by and upon the U.S. troops in Korea. Korean soldiers are beaten to death with clubs, shot, burned to death, or executed by firing squad, then piled into huge mass graves. Terrorists and radicals abroad are faced with public execution. The film then moves on to show edited highlights from a series of driver's education films made in 1955 and shown in U.S. high schools in an attempt to stop speeding from being considered glamorous. This series of films, with titles like "Signal 30" and "Red Pavement," catalog the grisly aftermath of actual car crashes, including trains that have crashed into cars at railway crossings and the victims of reckless driving and speeding, with the original grimly uncompromising voice-over doing the honors: "We are cold, cruel and harsh, you say. You shouldn't be allowed to see and hear this. But how else could we give a better lesson on care? See for yourself how sordid and sickening impending death can be, and see for yourself the weapon in this case—the steering column."

The 1960s brings us a whole series of assassination footage, including the deaths of John F. Kennedy, Lee Harvey Oswald, Robert Kennedy, the Dominican dictator Rafael Trujillo, Malcolm X, Ché Guevara, and Martin Luther King Jr. Footage of race riots and the Kent State University killings leads to a series of stills from Vietnam followed by black-and-white film footage: Vietnamese are massacred, drowned, or otherwise executed. A helicopter carries a huge net full of corpses. "Yesterday they were living, breathing bodies," the voice-over reminds us. "Today they are just a sanitation problem." But "even the parade of ghastly images from the battlefields of Vietnam would not brace Americans for the deadly and ever-growing phenomenon in their midst," the somber commentator remarks. "Some of the nation's most grisly and senseless incidents of mass murder would occur during the 1960s." Court footage of the "Boston Strangler" Albert De Salvo and mass murderer Richard Speck follows, accompanied by stills of their victims. This section also includes the much-trumpeted footage of the Manson murders, which involves police videotape of both the Tate and the LaBianca crime scenes, close-ups of each victim's death certificate, and stills of their bodies at the crime scene and in the morgue, all to the accompaniment of loud, dramatic piano chords and a jittery violin.

The section that then follows deals with the deaths of the "Hollywood greats," using stills from life shown next to stills from corpses at the morgue or—occasionally—at the scene of death. Included in this sequence are shots of Rudolph Valentino, Elvis Presley, Marilyn Monroe, Jayne Mansfield, Ernie Kovacs, Lenny Bruce, Sal Mineo, Bela Lugosi, Tyrone Power, Grace Kelly, and Natalie Wood. This is followed by lengthy footage of the death of stunt man Vic Morrow and two extras on the set of John Landis's section of the movie version of *The Twilight Zone* (1976). Morrow, the voice-over reminds us, was "killed in a freak accident—one that was captured by a host of horrified cameramen." The rather undramatic footage of the accident is then shown at least six times in succession, from a variety of different angles, in slow motion, and even in a frame-by-frame sequence, accompanied by a series of melancholy piano chords and a horror film–style drumbeat. This section is rounded off with a city coroner's photograph of bodies at the scenes of their death and in the morgue, including some of the victims of serial killer Jeffrey Dahmer.

A brief excursion into the world of Mexican crime magazines follows. "In Mexico," we are told, "at any corner newsstand, one can find an array of colorful crime journals, which feature graphic and uncensored photos"—many of which we are then shown, in the form of color stills—"depicting every imaginable form of mayhem." These stills are set to the repetitive organ music (Saint-Säens's "Danse Macabre") from *Death Scenes*, intercut with bizarre headlines such as "Macabro!" This section then cuts to recognizably contemporary scenes of soccer violence at the Heysel Stadium in Belgium and fatal scenes of overcrowding from Hillsborough. "In the past several decades," we are reminded:

MONDO MOVIES: RECARNIVALIZING THE TABOO

advances in video technology have revolutionized the coverage of world events. The placing of live mobile cameras in the most troubled and remote corners of the globe has brought a new sense of immediacy to the reporting of breaking news. Modern-day disasters, war atrocities, and other tragic events are often broadcast as they happen, giving viewers a privileged glimpse of history in the making. We now end our chronicle with a random sampling of this era's most compelling and unforgettable images—an everlasting testament to the eternal power of fate and the continuing folly of man.

These "compelling and unforgettable images" include a rodeo rider being dragged around the ring, then crushed to death under the hooves of his horse; a racing car crashing and the burning body being tossed on to the track; lynchings, hangings, clubbings, and executions in South Africa; and—to the accompaniment of slow and heavy organ chords—more bodies leaping to their deaths from a burning building; a CCTV recording of a mugging and murder in a store; and, finally, the live, on-camera suicide of disgraced Pennsylvania state treasurer R. Budd Dwyer, who was facing an indictment on charges of corruption. Dwyer stands as though to give a speech, removes a small pistol from an envelope, shoots himself neatly through the mouth, and slumps to the ground, blood streaming from his nose, as his colleague tries to calm the frenzied press reporters and cameramen ("All right, settle down, don't panic, please, don't panic, someone call an ambulance and a doctor and the police ... don't panic please, dear god in heaven.") The film concludes with shots of bodies being piled into an anonymous mass grave, intercut with the birth of a stillborn child's decapitated head and the morbid button logo—in red letters—"We Shall Overkill."

Where *Death Scenes*, with its relentless parade of black-and-white stills, gives the impression of a thoughtful meditation on the unquestionable potency of death, *Death Scenes 2*, with its mixture of still and moving footage, appears far more graphic, more detailed, more contemporary, and—in certain places at least—more shocking. In sequences of film or video footage, the awkwardly shaky handheld camera, uneven soundtrack, and often vague picture quality all serve to increase (rather than detract from) the impact of the scenes. Whereas *Death Scenes* catalogs the physical collapse of the human body in death, its sequel proclaims the indignity of the death process, with its unholy cortege of bodies falling, staggering, keeling over, struggling to escape. This is death as it happens, death in your face, as bodies twist and turn, crack and bleed, bend and fall. Almost as shocking and riveting as the deaths themselves are the observers' reactions to them, from the valiant rescue attempts at the Hillsborough stadium, to the chaos and abandon accompanying Dwyer's on-screen suicide and the defeated gesture of a member of a crowd that has gathered to watch bodies hurling themselves from a burning building like so many rag dolls—he simply turns away, hiding his head in his arms in a gesture of utter dismay.

While lacking deliberate artistic consciousness in the arrangement and composition of its garish tableaux, *Death Scenes 2* contains some contemplative and often ironic collations of images and frames. Publicity shots of laughing, pouting film stars are intercut with shots of those same faces, pale and swollen, so bloated as to be almost unrecognizable, lying on slabs in the morgue. Underworld victims of gangland killings of the 1940s and 1950s are unexpectedly connected to their contemporary equivalents: striking color shots of street murders, drug-related homicides, and desperate narcotic deals gone violently awry. In the case of the Tate-LaBianca killings, the prosaic one-dimensionality of the victims' death certificates stands in stark, pale contrast to the bodies themselves, hideously bloodied and littered with countless stab wounds, especially the heavily pregnant Sharon Tate, whose swollen and discolored torso is grotesquely bedecked with a thick hangman's noose. In another tableau, Leno and Rosemary LaBianca lie unclothed and undignified on their bedroom floor, a knife and fork sticking out of LaBianca's chest and undecipherable words carved into his torso with the thin blade of a kitchen knife.

The soundtrack and voice-over are significantly less successful in *Death Scenes 2* than in its original. The rattling calliope playing "Danse Macabre" in the background of *Death Scenes,* though initially inappropriate—Kerekes and Slater (1993) describe it as "kitschy . . . often more suited to a fairground carnival than a catalog of death" (207)—in fact works to a deliberately unsettling counterpoint with the images as they unfold, transforming the film's litany of corpses into a ghastly circus parade. Montalba's "additional music" to *Death Scenes 2* creates a far more mundane effect, although the sober piano and nervous violin are perhaps more appropriate to its dual sequences of black-and-white stills juxtaposed with fast-moving video footage. In addition, LaVey's baroque narrative monologs, spelling out in austere and somber tones the method and manner of death in each case, are quite unmatched by Wells's voice-over to *Death Scenes 2,* wherein attempts to imitate LaVey's forbidding tone and fustian recital simply don't add up. Wells claims that the sequel's archive materials will usher the "brave and curious" into "a spellbinding trip through the reality that is our world today." Spellbinding it may be, but, whereas the sepia-tinted black-and-white stills of the original are distanced enough from the present day to inspire an almost sublime feeling of fascination and awe, the "on-screen" crimes and atrocities of *Death Scenes 2* place this film squarely in the realm of morbid gore.

V

Directed by Conan Le Cilaire in 1978, *Faces of Death* launched a series of sequels, including *Faces of Death 2* in 1981 and *Faces of Death 3* in 1985, both of which are interesting only for their inclusion of fabricated, pseudo-"authentic" footage alongside shots of cadavers piled in the morgue, animal mutilation, auto wrecks, train crashes, and so on. Presented by bogus pathologist "Dr. Francis B. Gröss" (played by Michael Carr), this "documentary" purports to be an investigative journey around the world to seek out new perspectives on the "various faces of death" collected by the pathologist over the last twenty years.

The original *Faces of Death* consists of two distinct types of footage: "genuine" outtakes from news reports, other mondo films, nature documentaries, sports coverage, and war scenes, alongside faked, pseudo-"authentic" footage purported to be taken by local news stations, close-circuit television networks, and amateur camcorder enthusiasts. This kind of patented footage is also used in most of the sequels to *Faces of Death* and in other imitations, such as *Savage Zone* (1985), whose images consist mainly of unconvincing and unremarkable sequences of fabricated "incidents."

What is especially fascinating about *Faces of Death* is the way in which the genuine and "hoax" sequences play off one another to negotiate their own "authenticity." Genuine footage is usually undramatic, unsensational, and diverse in nature. The film begins, for example, with segments of still footage from the catacombs of Guanajuato in Mexico, where "the dead were mummified due to the rich minerals in the earth." Off-key piano chords can be heard and neon *son et lumière* illuminates the twisted, preserved cadavers of men, women, and children—"their faces frozen with a final vision." Staying in Mexico, we are next shown footage of "the most brutal sport of all," in which two pit bull terriers tear one another to death to the accompaniment of inappropriate piano music. From Mexico, we are taken to the Amazon jungle, where "death becomes a mandate of survival," and "there is no shelter for the weak." Dull nature documentary footage of spiders and insects is followed by an undramatic piranha attack on a swimming snake, set to Mexican dance music, where the snake skeleton left floating on the water belies Gröss's remark that "death occurs in a matter of seconds, and nothing is wasted." Elsewhere in the Amazon, "Jivaro savages" deep within the river basin use a blowpipe to kill a monkey and roast it over a fire before dancing around the head of an enemy warrior. From Africa, stock footage includes shots of Masai warriors killing a cow, drinking its blood, then chewing on the raw bones.

Further authentic footage comes from the slaughterhouse, where a chicken is decapitated with an ax (to the tune of "Old Macdonald had a Farm") and sheep and cow carcasses are bled to death, carved up, and skinned to inappropriately light-hearted music ("As consumers, we're spared the process, and only deal with the finished product," remarks Gröss, cynically). Later scenes of intensive seal-culling focus on the skinned, bleating pups, while Gröss describes how "the island is transformed into a battleground of naked carcasses" (and vows "never to wear the skin of an animal" on his back ever again). We are next taken to a chief coroner's office and introduced to bodies piled up on carts in the hallway, faces split open and skinned, brains removed and weighed, corpses embalmed with injections of preservative fluid and lying in piles in the refrigeration room (and all this

VHS cover for U.S. Release of *Faces of Death* by International Trading. © 1978 F.O.D. Productions. Courtesy International Trading.

MONDO MOVIES: RECARNIVALIZING THE TABOO

cut with syrupy classical music and Gröss's ruminations on the possibility of his own violent death). Further on in the film, we are taken to a cryonics clinic to witness bodies being frozen in capsules filled with liquid nitrogen.

A meeting of the "Children of God" gives us footage of cultists bouncing, shaking, nodding, speaking in tongues, and snake handling. A suicide, "Mary Alice Brighton," leaps to her death from a building to the accompaniment of an insensitive musical introduction ("a-one, a-two, a-one two three four.") Drowned, bloated bodies are pulled up on to a beach to lively dance music ("I find this kind of death particularly tragic," remarks our host, "that caused by sheer stupidity.") Volcanoes erupt, earthquakes split the land, a flood hits Pennsylvania, and a tornado strikes Mississippi, all to the accompaniment of jaunty tunes. People drop thirty-five stories to their death from a burning building, trash piles up on the beach, and animals lie squashed by the roadside. Stock World War II footage follows—of missiles exploding, Hitler rallying his troops, and the mushroom cloud over Hiroshima. "I personally don't know if this situation could repeat itself," ruminates the meditative Dr. Gröss, "but if it does, we all deserve a life in hell."

The section on disease brings us nature documentary-style footage of rats and vampire bats, followed by news footage of people dying from a cholera epidemic in India, and famine and malnutrition in Biafra, followed by an operation on a cancerous dog. Finally, the accidents section, including the most graphic sequences of authentic footage, begins with footage of a skydiver whose parachute fails to open and who crashes to death at eighty miles an hour. The camera lingers over the debris of a train derailment, closing in through the twisted metal in its quest for pieces of mangled bodies. A woman cyclist is crushed under a truck, and after her body has been removed, bloody detritus is scraped off the road and scooped into a plastic bag. A small plane crashes when its amateur pilot attempts a few stunts: "Arms and legs are strewn throughout the wreckage," and the bodies are lifted from the cockpit straight into a hearse. Finally, we are shown what happened when a commercial 747 collided with a light plane over a residential section of San Diego. As the camera seeks out the remains of bodies "mutilated beyond recognition"—feet, hands, amputated limbs, and decapitated heads strewn in every imaginable area throughout the neighborhood—Gröss describes how "the stench of death" has led the place to become "a virtual morgue." At last, Gröss enthuses, he has stumbled across "the most gruesome face of death."

Significantly, these diverse illustrations of "death... in all its faces" are liberally juxtaposed with sections of fabricated, pseudo-"genuine" sequences, which draw for their impact on their "appropriation" of the accidents of fate, witness response, amateur camera work, and jumpy soundtrack well known to any audience accustomed to watching news outtakes, "reality" programming, lurid "case studies," and ratings-winning, on-air ambulance-chasers, all a staple of contemporary *tabloid vérité*. Some of these sequences are just clumsily played out, such as the "restaurant scene" in which an implausible group of tourists tuck greedily into the brains of a "live" monkey, brought squealing to the table in a special trap. Others, such as the embarrassingly ludicrous "true life" footage of an "alligator attack," use standard amateur techniques to validate the sequence with the official stamp of "authenticity"—namely, various panicking "patrol officials," shouting crowds, children's faces being turned away from the scene, a blanket being thrown roughly over the "body," a shaky handheld camera (bearing the designation "New's Watch"), and the final, familiar hand-over-the-lens routine leading to an abrupt blackout (a technique utilized to far greater effect in the final sequence of the Findlay/Shackleton *Snuff*—see chapter 4).

More professional "amateur" sequences are quite clearly based on well-known pieces of film footage. The "assassination" of a heavily bearded "Islamic fanatic" is a fictionalized composite of two real-life sequences. It contains resonances of R. Budd Dwyer's infamous on-camera suicide featured in *Death Scenes 2*. In this case, a speaker almost identical to Dwyer, speaking in French, introduces the "fanatic." This introduction is mixed with the Robert Kennedy assassination footage (a staple of the mondo genre). Generally, this footage is followed up with clips from an interview with Sirhan Sirhan, as in *The Killing of America*. In this case, however, the "assassination" is followed up by an interview with assassin "François Jourdan," wearing a balaclava helmet and displaying his personal assortment of handguns, his voice "disguised" through sound distortion. This is followed by fabricated footage of "Mike Lawrence," a "serial killer run amok," clearly based on the shootout between Charles Whitman and the Texas police force featured in *The Killing of America*. This, too, has all the hallmarks of spurious "authenticity": women's screams, police sirens in the background, the sound of random shots being fired, breaking glass, passing traffic, police radio static tuning in and out, shaky handheld camera footage, the final shootout, and the bloodied bodies of Lawrence's "family" strewn around the kitchen floor, followed once again by the now-familiar hand-over-the-lens shock *vérité* finale.

Two later sequences seem to be based on the self-immolation of Quang

Duc protesting the pro-Catholic Saigon government's unjust treatment of Buddhists, which is featured spectacularly midway through Jacopetti and Prosperi's *Mondo Cane 2*. The first is footage supposedly "shot by a Canadian tourist in the Middle East" of an execution by scimitar, in which the trunk of the "victim," separated from his head, fails even to bleed; the second is a man allegedly setting himself alight in protest against the construction of a nuclear energy plant. Ironically, as Kerekes and Slater (1993) have discovered (168–70), the immolation of Quang Duc in *Mondo Cane 2* is *itself* an elaborate reconstruction of an actual event, so what *Faces of Death* presents us with is, in fact, the paradoxical phenomenon of professional footage passing itself off as amateur by imitating other professional footage that passes itself off as amateur—as though the *pseudo-vérité* had become a genre in itself, with its own particular aesthetic codes and conventions. *Faces of Death* also contains a pseudo "stunt car accident" based on any number of real stunt tragedies accidentally caught on camera; but this particular example stands as ironic harbinger. In this case, the crashing car, panicking film crew, and "death on impact" bear an uncanny resemblance to the on-camera death of Vic Morrow on the set of *The Twilight Zone* ten years later, replayed at such length in *Death Scenes 2*.

In order to allow humankind to "stop and question the whole meaning of justice," Gröss generously decides to let us witness the "genuine" execution of the theatrically nervous "Larry Da Silva"—named, presumably, in the hope that the sound might revive some half-forgotten memory of the name of the Boston Strangler, Albert De Salvo. The soundtrack becomes indecorously buoyant and light-hearted, as two men in black come to fetch "Da Silva" from his cell and walk him down the hall toward the electric chair. His eyes are taped shut, a helmet is fastened on his head, and his body is strapped into the electric chair in anticipation of the charges that will jolt theatrically through his drooling body. A doctor enters the cell with a stethoscope and shakes his head in an exaggerated way, leading to further electric jolts until streams of fake blood pour from the victim's eyes and down his face. "A strange smell, like almond blossoms, permeated the witness room," claims Gröss, gleefully.

A similar sequence, exploring "the world of cults," seems to base its "credibility" on the fact that the "cult leader" bears a notable similarity to Charles Manson. "As he explained his beliefs and methods," claims Gröss, "I realized I was dealing with a maniac." The cult, supposedly from San Francisco, apparently believes that "the power to everlasting life is held in the internal organs of the dead"—a pretext for all kinds of "cultic activities" to be enacted on a "dead body," which is carved open with a knife, the internal organs removed, and eaten raw. "The ritual ceremony culminated in an orgy," adds Gröss lasciviously, but we can only assume that he made his excuses and left, as—predictably—the by-now familiar hand-over-the-lens routine prevents any further filming of the imminent Satanic debacle.

Another fabricated sequence, toward the end of the film, is based rather closely on the accidentally captured authentic footage of a tourist in a national park being eaten alive by a feeding lioness, which is featured in a number of mondo movies, including Antonio Climati and Mario Morrà's *Savage Man . . . Savage Beast* (1975). Kerekes and Slater (1993) describe the original sequence in its entirety:

> The event is recorded on Super-8 by other tourists filming from adjacent vehicles. Dernitsch leaves the car from where his wife and children observe. He approaches the solitary lioness unaware of the proximity of a second animal. The shots volley between scenes of Dernitsch struggling and bloody beneath the animals, and the reactions of his family in their car. The most troubling shot is that of the lions tearing at unrecognizable pink meat, while above their bobbing heads protrudes Dernitsch's leg; trousers and socks still in place but minus his shoe. When the park ranger arrives all that remains of the unfortunate sightseer is placed in a plastic bag. His camera is retrieved and the few seconds of unimpressive footage that cost him his life are shown (180–81).

The sequence in *Faces of Death* based on the Dernitsch footage is set amid generic mountain scenery. The footage was allegedly recorded—exactly like the Dernitsch footage—by two separate sets of tourists with Super-8 cameras filming from adjacent vehicles: The tourist, "Bob," creeps up on a large grizzly bear, which takes very little time to turn, attack, and eat him alive. As in the Dernitsch footage, we are shown the reaction of his family in his car, interchanged with shots of the grizzly. The final shot of the Dernitsch footage shows a lioness with the dead man's camera in its mouth; in the *Faces of Death* sequence, the bear is seen ambling away into the woods with a rubbery-looking "severed limb" hanging from its jaws. Incidentally, the conspicuously fabricated "alligator attack" in an earlier sequence of *Faces of Death* appropriates a similar image of a transitional object: It concludes with a shot of the game warden's battered hat lying on the bank of the river.

"It's violent . . . but only as death is finally violent," boasts the original publicity slogan for *Faces of Death*. Actually, there is no violent death recorded in *Faces of Death*—no *authentic* violent death, at any rate, apart from that of animals. Nonetheless, what is interesting about this film—something that recurs in each of its sequels and in all mondo films of this style—is the way in which it appropriates the images, soundtrack, and mise-en-scène of existing "live" death footage, even down to the most trivial "authenticating" detail, and sets them up as "classics" of accidentally captured amateur or home video footage. Certain tropes, images, and incidental details have henceforth come to represent semiotic designations of "authenticity" in all subsequently prefabricated "live" footage, from the initially out-of-focus visuals and shaky handheld camera to the predictable and final hand-placed-over-the-lens and the well-rehearsed mantra of all self-respecting professional "amateur" video footage, "Get that goddamn camera out of here!"

VI

Users and critics of pornography have amply testified how the simulated erotica of soft-core porn is commonly more effective, more arousing, and certainly more cinematically visual than hard core's representation of "real" human bodies engaged in "actual" sexual intercourse. If Jean Baudrillard (1983) is right that the boundaries between the "real" and the simulacrum have become so blurred that the simulacrum has, in many cases, taken the place of the "real"—at least in memory—then it is beside the point to try to distinguish between them. If the represented is often so much more powerful than the "real," then why is it that this particular area of "reality cinema" —the footage of "real," on-screen death—should somehow retain its power to shock in an arena so full of graphic and challenging competitors? After all, mondo accrues at least some part of its power via truth claims.

The answer is twofold. Firstly, as André Bazin has argued (1967), the unique power of the photographic image lies in its ability to present the actual object itself, freed from the conditions of space and time that govern it. Linda Williams (1989) has pointed out that this is the essence of hard-core pornography: the decontextualization and deracination of the moment of orgasm, a moment temporarily echoing the safety and security of the womb in its—albeit transitory—lack of subjectivity. Perhaps it is this same drive toward the unity of oblivion that fuels the momentum of the mondo movie. If, as Georges Bataille argued in 1927, life signifies discontinuity and separateness and death signifies continuity and nondifferentiation, then the desire for and attraction of death suggests also a desire to return to the state of original oneness with the mother. The annihilation of the "other" in mondo movies signifies a kind of fleeting fulfillment: a return to the self as a coherent and unitary entity, always imagined, but impossible to achieve. Mondo is dedicated to capturing the visual evidence of the mechanical truth of bodily disintegration caught in involuntary spasm, the ultimate and uncontrollable confession of bodily collapse at the moment of death: a possibility already imagined by André Bazin in his essay "The Ontology of the Photographic Image" in the collection *What Is Cinema?* (1967). Because desire cannot exist without lack, the only possible end of desire would ultimately be the annihilation of the "other": that is, the graphic portrayal of on-screen death. In this sense, mondo gives rise to both a yearning for and a terror of self-disintegration, signifying the obliteration of the self of the protagonist in the film, as well as that of the observing spectator, a fact that has important consequences for the positioning of the audience.

Secondly, mondo is more conspicuously shocking than other forms of offensive films because—while maintaining many of the qualities of mainstream body-horror, also obsessed with bodily openings (but not "real" ones)—it either allows fictive storyline to merge with "truth" or else it ignores cohesion of film footage completely, thereby dissolving genre barriers altogether. Mondo has virtually no similarities with film narratives involving the construction of characters and plots with recognizable psychological, social, and political environments, as is typical of the slasher movie, for example. As in the Grand Guignol of late nineteenth-century French street theater, subtlety, psychology, character, sustained narrative, and so on are all sacrificed to the shock effect and the prevailing images of bodily disintegration. On the other hand, neither is mondo similar to any other kind of documentary or even experimental film. Its repetitious parade of clips of unknown people facing bodily violence in incomprehensible contexts does share a few of the characteristics of some other nonfiction cinema mythology, however, including films from the library of Nazi propaganda, such as *The Eternal Jew* (1933).

Like the fragmented bodies it depicts, in fact, mondo is itself—to use Julia Kristeva's (1982) term—"abject," a casualty of the norms of ontological propriety: decategorized, falling loosely somewhere between the genres of slasher and documentary, between entertainment and edification, between moralizing diatribe and testament of sexual perversion. At odds in the cultural scheme of things, mondo is so much more disturbing than traditional kinds of offensive films because it is itself discreditable and contradictory, refusing to fit into any existing cultural category.

VII

There are, of course, a number of moral issues at stake here. Its voyeuristic carnivalization of violent and tragic deaths has caused the mondo film to be anathematized by popular and "high" film critics alike. The exhibition of violent death for public diversion is nothing new, as any glance at the history of popular entertainment will reveal—from Roman games and "satyr plays" to crucifixion, torture, and public execution. However, recent developments in the visual media, by allowing us a permanent public testament to all kinds of private tragedies, have placed this issue in an entirely different arena. The ubiquity of home VCR and DVD players, as well as the Internet, means that the spectator can now witness death in private, again and again, at different speeds, and from a variety of angles, exactly as it happened "in the flesh." Mondo is generally considered to be the most offensive kind of film because, essentially, it makes the violent death of the human body into a private leisure pursuit. To consider the mondo film in terms of Bakhtinian carnivalesque is not to gloss over these, or any other, moral issues. Indeed, the core of the Bakhtinian method is the impossibility of separating the aesthetic from the moral and political, which is evident in Bakhtin's own controversial refusal to ignore moral and ideological components.

Films like *Death Scenes* and *Faces of Death* are quite clearly not made for public cinema release, but for viewing in the privacy of one's own home. Like many other leisure-time activities, home video can be conceived as a carnivalized site, in that engagement in the activity demands a special, "sacred" time in the flow of secular ("working") time and a temporary suspension in the flow of secular time. The television screen itself is also a kind of sacred space within secular space, and, besides, like so many other forms of leisure-time activity, home video is regulated festivity. There is something quite ironic about the fact that the Bakhtinian carnivalesque involves rigid regularities, discrete groups, graduated hierarchies, and so on, which brings up the question of just how carnivalesque this kind of structured, rigorous, hierarchical festivity really is. It could be argued that the mondo film, in particular, is really only a parodic catharsis, which links up with the idea of carnival as a kind of safety valve, with an essentially conservative social function. It would be unwise to forget that the potential of carnival for radical rebellion is, in the end, politically limited, as it is, after all, *licensed* misrule—a contained and officially sanctioned rebellion—after which everybody goes straight back to work.

Where mondo goes beyond the potential of other kinds of offensive films is in its unique, all-encompassing, non-narrative presentation of a carnivalesque procession of bodily deformities and perversions. In the liminal period of carnival, participants are allowed to display all those things—such as the insides of the human body—that can destroy society and that all the rest of the time must be kept under control if society is to continue unaffected. All the rules that usually govern social life are suspended. Taboos can be broken without serious long-range sanctions, as long as they are broken within the carefully defined limits of the carnival.

In his study of Rabelais, Bakhtin (1968) argues that the crux of the carnival is its attitude toward the human body and the life of the body. In Rabelaisian carnival, the anatomical structure of the human body is revealed in action—and becomes a character in its own right. "But it is not the individual body, trapped in an irreversible sequence, that becomes a character," notes Bakhtin; "rather it is the impersonal body, the human race as a whole, being born, living, dying the most varied deaths" (173). The odd-looking carnival body is a body in the act of becoming, which is never finished or completed but continually breaking, building, and changing. Carnival ignores the impenetrable surface that closes the limits of the body as a separate and completed phenomenon, displaying "not only the outward but also the inner features of the body: blood, bowels, heart, and other organs" (173).

Medieval carnival habitually featured lengthy catalogs of bodily parts and pieces, extensive anatomizations of the different layers and levels of bodily life. Bakhtin draws our attention to an episode in Rabelais in which human bodies are transformed into "minced meat," containing a long and detailed anatomic list of wounded members and organs, broken bones and joints: the very image of a "bodily harvest" (208). Indeed, the theme of the original *carnem levare* was the theme of the feast, involving images of the slaughter of cattle and the disemboweling, dismemberment, and devouring of the shattered body—images that are later transferred to the anatomic description of the generating womb. These carnival images would have been far less striking than their equivalent modern representations in the mondo movie, however, because the eyes and imagination of medieval people were more accustomed to the grotesque body.

At other times, carnival displays a number of typically incongruous forms of exaggerated bodily parts that completely hide the normal members of the body, thereby providing visions of either dismemberment or bodies distorted and enlarged to gigantic dimensions (see chapter 1). Carnival, like Mardi Gras, presents us with images of characters with monstrous bellies, humps, huge noses, abnormally long legs, or massive ears. In a similar way, the mondo movie catalogs bodies that are swollen and distorted by death, with bloated features, discolored skin, and disembodied limbs. *Death Scenes* and *Faces of Death* each include a series of images of drowned bodies dragged from the water, and *Death Scenes* includes images of bodies enlarged and swollen by carbon monoxide poisoning, and scarred and inflamed by knife and gunshot wounds. In such carnivalesque scenarios, the human cadaver is wrenched and distorted into an outrageous travesty of its noncarnival shape.

VIII

The aim of carnivalesque discourse, according to Bakhtin in *Problems of Dostoyevsky's Poetics* (1984), is to bring the world closer in order for us to examine it more fearlessly: "to feed on dense experience: to be with the smell of real human bodies" (47). Medieval carnival was the drama of bodily life: birth, growth, copulation, eating, drinking, defecation. During the carnival, death is put in its "own place" in the world and thereby established as an unavoidable aspect of life itself. This is exactly the case in mondo. In its temporary flaunting of taboos, the mondo movie can demonstrate the biological inevitability of death in fantastic anatomical detail, in all its clarity and precision, as part of an impersonal understanding of the living and struggling human body. In Rabelaisian carnival, "death does not interfere with life; rather, it appears as merely one aspect of this life, and is made out of the same stuff of life itself" (195). The carnival's obsession with death is possibly related to widespread folkloric assumptions concerning the regenerative power of the fresh corpse and the idea of healing the death of one by the death of another. Death in folklore and oral literature has always been related to the birth of new life, fertility, and growth.

Other thinkers, such as Freud (1919) and Otto Rank (1952), have charted the connections between the fear associated with thoughts of death and the terror of birth. Rank suggests that the shape of the coffin, the rituals connected with burial, and so on all reveal an unconscious conception of death as a return to the mother's womb, as—according to Rank—the final spasms of death exactly repeat the first spasms of the organism in the act of being born. Carnival draws our attention to death as a moment that is entirely drawn into the cycle of life. During the medieval carnival, according to Bakhtin (1968), "death and death-throes, labor and childbirth are intimately interwoven" (151), and, thereby, the deeply ambivalent nature of the death-wish is exposed.

Anton LaVey claims, in his self-penned soundtrack to *Death Scenes*, that our fascination with such vivid and graphic images of violent bodily collapse lies in our unconscious understanding of how such representations can remind us of the universal inevitability of death and thereby invite us to live our lives more fully, to confront "life with honor, death with dignity." This is either simplifying the case or overstating it, but there is a case to be made that the frisson of horror evoked by a road accident or a local murder is a sensation that is, essentially, both existential and life-affirming. The popularity of films like *Faces of Death*—like the renown of the Roman games and public executions—must lie, at least to some extent, in the archetypal folkloric connections between violent death and bodily regeneration.

IX

Films like *Death Scenes* and *Faces of Death* may perhaps be most clearly understood as a site of Bakhtinian carnival in their appropriation and use of a series of inversions. According to Bakhtin (1968), carnival is a time of ritual reversal, an institutionalized time of upheaval when the world is turned upside down, ordinary people become horrifying monsters or animals, and the dead are resurrected. The element of relativity and *becoming* is emphasized, in opposition to the immovable and extratemporal stability of the medieval hierarchy. A principal function of medieval carnival is the emphasis on the importance of inside out and upside down in the acts and movements of the body. Bakhtin refers to carnival as a parody of truth in a world that is "turned inside out" (95); he describes the representations of these inversions, in typically evocative locutions, as images of "tripe life" and "tripe death," in which portrayals of death, birth, food, and excrement "are all drawn together and tied in one grotesque knot; this is the center of bodily topography in which the upper and lower stratum penetrate each other" (163). In a comparable way, carnival curses depict a body that is turned inside out, causing the anus to protrude: "Curses always indicate a downward motion, directed to the ground, the legs, the buttocks" (166). Carnival curses and oaths are typically based on grotesque images of the human body anatomized and dismembered. In representations of "tripe life" and "tripe death," notes Bakhtin, "the limits between animal flesh and the consuming human flesh are dimmed, very nearly erased" (221). "We always find [in medieval comic images] the defeat of fear presented in a droll and monstrous form, the symbols of power and violence turn inside out, the comic images of death and bodies gaily rent asunder. All that was terrifying becomes grotesque" (91).

In the carnival of offensive films, mondo movies depict upheaval and reversal not only in their inversion of the traditional realist film narrative, but in the way their entire structure is based on a series of anatomical inversions that carnivalize the site of the body. The impetus of mondo is sustained by a compulsion to exhibit the inverted body, the body reversed, opened up, upside down, inside out. This series of anatomical images is essentially an obsessive reiteration of the human body *out of control* and thereby—as in comedy—made ridiculous.

Yet the images of medieval carnival need to be considered within their own somewhat broader context of presentation, where mock death and disfigurement—the horrors of the body—are staged with real actors and other representational artists to a broad audience with widely shared beliefs about their meaning. As a seasonal affair associated with Lent, medieval carnival recited the degradations of the body precisely to contrast its functions with higher spiritual and human social consciousness and longing. As Bakhtin points out, the carnival audience of an established caste system clearly understood this context. In marked contrast, the audience for the mondo film—apparently desperate for some facsimile of macho proving ground—is small and subcultural. And yet Bakhtin was also clear that the liminal state of carnival could function psychologically, as a state of mind or psychic moment of transgression and transcendence. This "carnival consciousness," then, can be inspired by all kinds of dispensable and forbidden cultural forms, however remote from the medieval source of the inceptive carnival moment.

X

Bakhtin points out that one of the most expressive features of the carnival is the way in which, at carnival time, death becomes comic, as in the Rabelaisian mocking of death. Rabelaisian carnival presents a number of examples of the absurd or *clownish* portrayal of death, and the image of death itself takes on humorous aspects: "Death is inseparable from laughter" (1981, 196) and so we arrive at the representation of "*cheerful deaths*" (196). Films like *Death Scenes* and *Faces of Death* help us to understand how certain essential aspects of the world are accessible only to the reflex of laughter. Folkloric laughter liberates the consciousness from the confines of its own discourse and, hence, creates freedom. "Seriousness burdens us with hopeless situations, but laughter lifts us above them and liberates us from them. Laughter does not encumber man, it liberates him" (144).

Much of Anton LaVey's voice-over in *Death Scenes*, for example, takes on a wryly playful vein. Without ever being openly vulgar or distasteful, his gently ironic account of each corpse's decease succeeds in cynically mocking the dignity of the human body and all the taboos and rituals with which we surround its collapse and demise. LaVey remarks on the "inventive approaches" of "overambitious" suicides, for whom "commonplace firearms did not suffice"; points out "a sterling example of matricide," "a remarkably brutal bludgeoning"; he notes how one woman's head has been "cleaved neatly in two." He describes the suicide of a legal client who killed his incompetent attorney as "moving for a dismissal of his own design." "Objection sustained," he comments on a similar scenario, "as yet another disgruntled client vents his wrath on two attorneys whom he felt mishandled his defense." The assailant who murdered a Japanese man for thirty cents and his wristwatch is described by LaVey as currently "serving time" in San Quentin. A woman is bludgeoned and dumped outside a laundry by her lover because "she declared their romance was all washed up," and the bloody tableau of a man murdered by the owner of a corner food stand over payment of a ten-cent hot dog is referred to by LaVey as "a sight few would relish."

Clearly, *Death Scenes* involves a deliberate and parodic kind of bad taste that helps the audience deal with the horrors of death, possibly relating to fantasies of immortality. Bakhtin emphasizes the *libidinal* nature of laughter and its associations with tension, with bad taste, and with the mocking of death. During the carnival, there is a close and intrinsic connection between ritualistic violations, ritualistic laughter, ritualistic parody and clownishness. Comedy, tied to the gross realities of life, takes its place in permanent conjunction with death. For example, Bakhtin draws our attention to the comic presentation at the carnival of mimicked death throes: "hanging tongue, expressionless, popping eyes, suffocation, death rattle ... spasms, tensions, sweat, convulsions of arms and legs" (1968, 353–54). The abjection attached to similar representations of the "opened body" and the absence of bodily order in the mondo movie signals the many connections between the horrific and the comic in the way that both manifest the return of the repressed in the guise of bodily miscontrol. Bakhtin is one of the few philosophers to draw explicit attention to the interrelated nature of horror and laughter.

XI

The main function of laughter during the carnival seems to be to *uncrown* or *contemporize*. Films like *Death Scenes* and *Faces of Death*, in their deliberate mocking of the human body and its undignified collapse, involve what Bakhtin would describe as a "necessary" uncrowning, a removal of the venerated object (the dead body) from a distanced plane and an assault on, or destruction of, the distanced plane in general. This uncrowning is essentially allied to blows and abuses that are universal and never assume the character of merely personal invective. By allowing death to seem ridiculous and therefore less "venerated," the mondo movie can access the very nature of what it means to be human. Offensive films are a kind of carnivalesque theater for the cultural expression of violence and misrule, which serves the purpose of symbolic as well as performative disorder. This disorder seems to be instinctual in nature, containing a level of aggression and violence that seems to bespeak the libidinal associations between the horrific and the farcical, between laughter and bloodshed.

The king of uncrowning and disorder is the secret carnival devil, or the Lord of Misrule, whose function, according to Bakhtin, is to stand as an ambivalent image, like the fool and the clown, representing the destroying and renewing force of the lower bodily stratum. Like Anton LaVey of the Church of Satan, the mystery devil is an ex-official figure whose ambivalence and whose material bodily form make us clearly understand his transformation into a popular mischievous trickster who ties together both horror and laughter. The psychotic carnival music backing LaVey's narration in *Death Scenes* is an index of his status as a folk devil, abusing and taunting the dead. At other times in the same film, the role of the Lord of Misrule is played by the dead bodies themselves, which, in the gross physical transformation of bodily death, come to resemble the carnival clown or the harlequin, who "sweats and gapes.... His face is swollen, his eyes pop.... The gaping mouth, the protruding eyes, sweat, trembling, suffocation, the swollen face—all these are typical symptoms of the grotesque life of the body" (1968, 304, 308).

It is significant that the part of the body that is represented most vividly in *Death Scenes*, as in the *Faces of Death* series, is the face and head. Mondo is replete with images of faces torn open; heads blown up; mouths, ears, and noses draining blood. One image in *Death Scenes* shows us a man who has shot himself in the head with a revolver and whose separated brain has left his body and sits on the floor, right at the forefront of the picture. "Curiously," remarks LaVey, "the brain which had made the frantic decision to kill only a few moments before now lies peacefully on the planks of an old wooden porch." Another image, of a car accident victim, presents us with a truncated torso whose decapitated head lies some yards away, face upward, in the middle of the road. "Of all the car crashes on view in our source," comments LaVey, "this one is undoubtedly the most novel. This decapitated head landed neatly in the center of the road with a serene facial expression which totally belies the obvious fury of the crash." Other tableaux present monstrous visions of facial collapse like so many broken masks. These are highly carnivalesque representations. In the carnival body, there is no opaque surface, only cavities and heights. According to Bakhtin (1968):

> Of all the features of the human face, the nose and mouth play the most important part in the grotesque image of the body: the head, ears and nose also acquire a grotesque character when they adopt the animal form or that of inanimate objects. . . . But the most important of all human features for the grotesque is the mouth. It dominates all else. The grotesque face is actually reduced to the gaping mouth; the other features are only a frame encasing this wide-open bodily abyss (316–17).

The fundamental disrespect for death that is peculiar to all these images of the contemporizing and uncrowning of the human cadaver derives from the carnivalesque mocking of relics, which was comic in medieval literature—especially Protestant satire—where the dismembered bodies of saints became an occasion for grotesque images and enumerations of various parts of the bodies (350). In the carnival of offensive films, the role of the holy relic is played by the dignified living human body, which is aped and travestied by an obsessive litany of bodily collapse.

XII

Many of the critics writing on the traditional horror movie—including Clover (1987), Dika (1990), Krasniewicz (1992), and Prince (1988)—believe they have stumbled upon a critically neglected yet essentially radical genre, whose dismissal as "inconsequential" or "lacking in value" allows it to exert a considerably progressive influence in such areas as schemata of identification, gender representation, and the mechanisms of subjectivity. No longer, however, is the horror movie a critically despised genre: Recent years have seen an enormous number of articles and critical studies on all kinds of horror movies, both mainstream and (at one time at least) obscure. This recent interest in the "repressed" and "taboo" slasher movie is, however, simply a scapegoat for film scholars and cultural theorists to avoid dealing with *genuinely* taboo movies. Fascination with the horror movie conveniently diverts interest from the kind of cinema nobody wants to talk about: the "other" film, the repressed of the traditional horror movie—the mondo film.

When considering the subliminal associations between film and dream, it is important to remember that Freud came to dream interpretation out of concern with psychoanalytic needs and in the effort to utilize dreams as symptoms. If the mondo movie can be seen as the "other" of the mainstream horror film, then it can be concluded that the images presented in mondo are catalogs of nervous disorders and psychotic symptoms: the repressed complexes of traditional horror-film narrative. The final and most shocking of the mondo film's catalog of grotesque inversions is its inversion of the liminal and the subliminal by transferring elements of the unconscious into the filmic narrative. The mondo film is an externalized diagnosis of the many sicknesses successfully repressed by the traditional horror film. In its terrifying carnivalization of the site of the body, of the spasm of death, and of that moment in which horror merges with laughter, the mondo film—for those able to appreciate its progressive nature—fulfills all the functions of the horror-film narrative, but more explicitly, more offensively, and more defiantly.

8 An Experiment in Time: Gaspar Noé's *Irréversible*

> Watching the shied core
> Striking the basket, sliding across the floor
> Shows less and less of luck, and more and more
> Of failure spreading back up the arm
> Earlier and earlier, the unraised hand calm,
> The apple unbitten in the palm.
>
> Philip Larkin, "As Bad as a Mile."

EGINNING WITH A FAILED GESTURE—A MISSED attempt to land an apple core in a trash can—the poet realizes this was no unlucky shot. He traces his failure back from the gesture, back up the arm itself, earlier and earlier—to when? To the moment the thought was formulated, or earlier? To the moment of conception?

When do quirks of personality become ingrained? When do the choices we make betray a pattern?

When Gaspar Noé's film *Irréversible* was shown in competition at Cannes in May 2002, it apparently provoked fainting and a walkout by around 250 of the 2,400 audience members. According to press reports,[1] fire officers were called upon to give oxygen and other forms of medical attention to twenty people, most of them women, who were supposedly nauseated not only by the film's scenes of explicit violence but also by the frenzied, restless camera work in the opening moments. Audience members were also apparently upset by the film's frequent use of profanities directed at homosexuals and women, and a much-publicized seven-minute scene (often described as taking ten or twelve minutes—and, indeed, it seems that long) in which Italian actress Monica Belluci is anally raped. Fire Brigade spokesman Lieutenant Gerard Courtel commented that "in 25 years of my job I've never seen this at the Cannes festival. The scenes in this film are unbearable, even for us professionals."[2]

AN EXPERIMENT IN TIME: *IRRÉVERSIBLE*

Response to the film, as the director no doubt expected and desired, was extreme. Noé, an Argentinian-born resident of France, was flayed alive in the French media. When the film screened at one American festival, he was threatened with violence—an ironic response to a film about the catastrophic effects of aggression. A press release from the New Zealand Society for Community Standards, written by someone who had clearly not seen the film, described *Irréversible* as containing a "highly sexualized and graphic 10-minute long rape and sodomy scene," and added that "the script consists almost entirely of expletives directed against homosexuals and women."[3] And yet the film was passed uncut not only in the United States, but also in the more morally conservative climates of Australia and Britain.

Irréversible is meant to shock, and it does. Critics in general dismissed the film; many despised it. The prevailing attitude was summed up by Lisa Schwartzbaum in *Entertainment Weekly*, who described the film as a "vacantly outrageous orgy of graphic rape, revenge and gay-bashing." "I think people felt violated," said Patrick McGavin, film critic for the *Chicago Tribune*, after the film's press screening at Cannes. "It's ugly, and there's a lot in it that's gratuitous. It's profoundly unsettling. It goes too far."

While some might argue that not enough "profoundly unsettling" films get screened today, at Cannes or elsewhere, Noé's masterpiece got short shrift from critics too offended by the film to appreciate its complexity. For example, James Quandt (2002) in *Cinemascope* dismissed the film by claiming that its director is simply out to shock:

> Noé has only one trick in his bag—anti p.c. provocation—and when he attempts to portray "normality" . . . he suffers an utter failure of imagination, falling back on tired tropes of French cinema. . . . Noé stands bravely *seul contre tous*, especially against anyone who prizes ambiguity, complexity, and moral vision. . . . *Irréversible* leaves us with only one enigma: why it was made. (46–48)

II

The film consists of a dozen long, apparently unbroken shots, and it begins with a short prologue spoken by Phillipe Nahon, the violent and dissolute butcher who is the main character in Noé's two previous films, the forty-minute *Carne* and the feature-length *Seul Contre Tous*.[4] Naked, fat, and repugnant, the butcher is squatting on his bed with a companion when he hears police sirens outside the gay club (The Rectum) beneath his sordid Paris apartment and comments that the club's patrons are always killing one another. "Time destroys all things," he explains to his equally repugnant companion, as the camera constantly swirls and dives, providing us with only the most fleeting, temporary moments of clarity.

The film then moves to the interior of The Rectum. Marcus (Vincent Cassel) and Pierre (Albert Dupontel) are hunting down a male prostitute known as Le Tenia—The Tapeworm (Jo Prestia)—who has just raped and tortured Marcus's girlfriend, Alex (Monica Belluci). The furious Marcus violently barges into room after room, disrupting scenes of anonymous sex and beating the participants in a long display of unrelenting violence. When a person resembling Le Tenia is found (though he is actually the wrong man), he is beaten to death by Pierre, Alex's ex-boyfriend, who smashes up his face with a heavy fire extinguisher. Throughout this protracted sequence, the camera literally never stops shaking, moving from side to side, bobbing, weaving, moving in and out of focus, bouncing off walls, turning upside down, gliding through buildings, showing us nothing and showing us everything. Its movement seems to echo the chaos and violence of the situation and the characters' drugged, out-of-control state of mind. The sound of the attack is the stuff of nightmares.

Moving back in time, we see Marcus savagely beating up a Chinese taxi driver and a transvestite hooker while looking for The Rectum, while Pierre —a philosophy professor—pleads with him not to be so violent. Moving back in time again, we witness Alex walking into a dark underpass and getting brutally raped and beaten by Le Tenia. We then see the situation preceding the rape—a party, at which Marcus plays around with other girls, causing an irritated Alex to walk home on her own.

Gradually, the film explains the reasons and motivations for the scene in The Rectum, as the frenzied camera slowly begins to relax and allow us to make sense of the plot. Finally, a more natural, unobtrusive directorial style comes into play, and we see Marcus as a calm, pleasant young man. We witness Marcus, Pierre, and Alex joking around as they take the subway to the party, then we are shown a long romantic sequence in which Marcus and Alex lie around in bed together, indulging in love play and play fights, laughing and kissing. The film ends with a scene in which Alex, newly pregnant— though she has yet to learn the fact—lies happily reading in a park surrounded by picnicking families and playful children.

The second half of the film comes as something of a relief after all this violence, mainly because it gives us a chance to see the actors whole, alive, and unbloodied. Moreover, the fact that we know what's about to befall these people turns the story into a tragedy. Noé seems to be suggesting that they carry the seeds of their own undoing within them. Understanding the relationship between Alex and Marcus changes the way we regard Alex's rape and the murder in The Rectum; after we have been sickened by the depiction of revenge, we start to wish for it. Noé seems to be making a point here about the way we are manipulated by the chronological structure of narratives.

III

Those critics who so readily dismissed *Irréversible* as racist, vacant, and homophobic seem to believe that the film's scenes of violence and reverse chronology are simply tricks and gimmicks, rather than a fundamental part of its meaning. *Irréversible* is not, in fact, a story told backward, but a complex study of the nature of time. Its director is perhaps less interested in cause and effect than in the form of time itself, and this is part of what distinguishes *Irréversible* from many other "reverse chronology" narratives, the best-known of which may be Harold Pinter's *Betrayal* (1983) and Christopher Nolan's *Memento* (2001).

Critic Noah Cowan (2002) makes the case that the film challenges us to reconstitute a standard narrative by providing us with the missing piece. He argues that the film's reverse chronology prevents us from becoming emotionally invested in its attractive bourgeois couple by refusing to preface their "descent into hell" with all the foreshadowing that such narratives demand. He writes:

> By putting the lovey-dovey stuff at the end, Noé identifies it as the actual problem. This ridiculous, idealized notion of heterosexual reproduction is a form of narrative deceit, and should be considered the object of horror; they are perpetuating all the bourgeois myths of safety and protection that Noé hates so much through the privileged act of making babies. He completes his earlier joke: time *should* destroy this. (49–50)

Cowan's reading of the film suggests that it needs to be considered according to the chronology we see on screen and not, as most critics have judged it, as though it begins at the story's temporal beginning and ends at the story's temporal end. Cowan's reading suggests that, according to Noé, the violence and brutality of human beings creates the need to perpetuate the blind lie that is romantic love. This is an interesting position, but perhaps rather one-dimensional. *Irréversible* contains many signs and clues that suggest the film is rather too complex to be read as a mere nihilistic antiromance.

Part of the significance of the film's structure is, of course, bodily. We begin in the realm of the anal (The Rectum)—a dark, destructive, macho place—in search of Le Tenia (The Tapeworm). Alex is anally raped, and the sequence in the dark, rumbling passages of the subway also have an anal quality. As the film continues, we progress—as Freud might say—to a more mature realm, that of the vaginal. Alex and Marcus make love, and, when Alex tests herself with a home pregnancy kit, she learns she is expecting Marcus's child. The final sequence, an abstract montage of flashing lights and mesmeric colors, seems to counterbalance the chaos of the opening scene by taking us into the uterus itself, back to the moment of conception and even earlier.

IV

Especially significant in this context is the book Alex is reading in the final scene of the movie, when she lies by a sprinkler in a sunny park surrounded by children playing, one of them flying a red kite. The book is J. W. Dunne's 1927 treatise *An Experiment in Time*. In his review of the film in *Cinemascope*, James Quandt (2002) dismisses this important reference by suggesting that "the book is there to show our heroine is no bimbo, and to emphasize the non-linearity of the film's structure." He continues disdainfully: "Dunne's theories of time influenced Tolkien—appropriately a fave of adolescent males everywhere—and were derived from the flow and irrationality of dreams, and from Dunne's visions of disasters that eventually happened, which no doubt included *Irréversible*."[5]

In fact, however, Noé's inclusion of *An Experiment with Time* is not simply a glib allusion to "the non-linearity of the film's structure," but sheds a great deal of light on the movie's complex and intricate composition.

J. W. Dunne's *An Experiment with Time* was first published in 1927, though revised editions were published in 1930 and 1934. While Dunne was not a scientist, the book was initially well received among the scientific community and was also popular with the public. Dunne's theory is too complicated to discuss at length here, but it hinges on the notion that there are many "time states," two of which he refers to as "Time 1" and "Time 2." According to Dunne, Time 1 is the kind of time to which we are accustomed in our waking observation—that is, linear time, which moves steadily forward and involves states of the external world being experienced in succession. Time 2, however—which coexists with Time 1—is not linear but integrated in a kind of fourth dimension, where future, past, and present merge together. Dunne suggests that we experience most of our lives in Time 1—

linear time—but we can access Time 2 through our dreams, when our cognitive faculties cease to concentrate so intensely on the present moment.

In order to give a fuller picture of Time 2, Dunne cites from a work by C. H. Hinton, published in 1887, entitled *What is the Fourth Dimension?* In this work, the "fourth dimension" is described as "some stupendous whole, wherein all that *has ever come into being or will come co-exists*, which, passing slowly on, leaves in this flickering consciousness of ours, limited to a *narrow space* and a *single moment,* a tumultuous record of changes and vicissitudes that are but to us" (67). Dunne compares Time 2 to the "Everlasting Now" of Oriental philosophy. According to Dunne, our dreams, which always take place in Time 2, contain both precognitive and retrospective events that are confused and integrated, not necessarily distinguishable as one or the other. In Time 2, future, present, and past are experienced as superimposed rather than separate and linear, as they are in Time 1.

Dunne's theories are adapted from the known laws of physics, but his initial experiment was the result of a series of provoking dreams in which he experienced events that he subsequently reexperienced in waking life. In his preface to the reprinted edition of Dunne's book, philosopher Russell Targ explains how Dunne believed that "we live in an interconnected spider-web of space-time, in which the future [like the past] is an attractor pulling the present toward itself" (x). Thus, we often experience an effect before we understand its cause, just as we might come to a whirlpool in a river before coming to the boulder downstream that is causes it. Dunne believed that in dreams we often experience events before they occur—a phenomenon that Targ refers to as "retro-causality" (vii).

An Experiment with Time has been in and out of print sporadically since 1934, a fact which suggests Dunne's contributions to the metaphysics of space-time paradigms have now been dismissed by the scientific community. His work, like that of renegade philosopher Charles Fort, has been taken up not by the academy but by dilettantes and dabblers, kitchen mystics and bedroom metaphysicians. But even if mainstream science has rejected him as a crank, *An Experiment with Time* clearly had an impact on Gaspar Noé, since—in a way—*Irréversible* is an attempt to reproduce a similar experiment.

The structure of *Irréversible* consists of roughly eight separate segments, each lasting between five and twenty minutes. These segments are given in reverse order, but each individual segment runs forward, in linear time. In a recent interview with Matthew Hays in *Cinemascope* (2002), Noé commented, "You want to hypnotize with a movie. The hypnosis either takes you somewhere or it doesn't. You're in a trance or you're not.... If the hypnosis works well, the audience will get into your dream" (50).

States such as trances, dreams, and hypnosis are, according to Dunne, states in which we have access to Time 2, and yet our perceptive faculties endeavor to interpret the dream's "scenes" as a succession of three-dimensional views similar to those we experience in Time 1. Dunne believes that it is possible to separate the dreamer from the dream, in that what we *experience* as our dream (and recount upon waking) is, in fact, an attempt to make sense of Time 2 on the part of one whose perceptual faculties are accustomed to operating in Time 1. Dunne's account of the dreamer's experience closely resembles what the audience of *Irréversible* undergoes, as though, through his movie, Noé was attempting to recreate the chronological concatenation of Time 2 experienced from the perspective of Time 1:

> Nothing stays to be looked at. Everything is in a state of flux.... And, because of the continual breaking down of your attempts at maintaining a concentrated focus, the dream story develops in a series of disconnected scenes.... You are always trying to keep attention moving steadily in the direction to which you are accustomed in your waking observation... but attention relaxes, and, when you recontract it, you find, as often as not, that it is focused on the wrong place.... You start on a journey, and find yourself abruptly at the end. (104)

Certainly, the sense of time in *Irréversible* seems disjunctive, weird, and liminal; each segment seems full of impending catastrophe and transition. According to Dunne, dreams partake of both the past and the future, and thereby reveal that the future cannot be altered in any way by human action. Which brings us to the next question: To what extent, in Noé's vision, is the future irreversible?

V

The film's narrative seems characterized by a belief in inevitability and human helplessness in the face of a future that is as unchangeable as it is unavoidable, since—as Dunne suggests—it is already present. Certain signs and occurrences in the film's first, more violent scenes are later replayed in a romantic, affectionate context, suggesting some of the many complicated connections between what we call "romantic love" and the brutality of rape and murder. Le Tenia's brutal treatment of Alex, including the way he spits disgustedly into her face after raping her, is recalled by the friendly play-fighting between Marcus and Alex, during which Marcus spits into Alex's face as a joke. Their love play includes a mock version of anal sex, which cannot help but remind us of Alex's violent anal rape, and the banter that Marcus and Pierre engage in on the subway is all about Alex's capacity for orgasm, which again recalls her brutal rape. In Noé's vision, the play fighting and the real violence are no different from each other; both are continually present. Only human perception interprets one as distinct from the other. A sense of imminent catastrophe, as well as the unrecuperability of humanity, pervades all the "romantic" scenes involving Marcus, Alex, and Pierre. Consequently, the violence in the film sensitizes us in a profound way to what we are watching.

Irréversible is clearly influenced by J. W. Dunne's sense of the past and future as states that are constantly with us in the present, and to this extent the movie is inflected as much by fatalism as nihilism. Fatalism has been characterized by scholars Marilyn McCord Adams and Norman Kretzmann (1969) as "the view that whatever happens must happen of necessity and whatever does not happen of necessity does not happen at all. . . . It is generally taken to be an obvious consequence of fatalism that nothing a man does is ever really up to him. What he has done he had to do; and what he will do he must do" (3–4). Noé's characters are powerless to control any aspect of their future, all of them predestined from the outset to a fate from which they cannot escape—a fate which is irreversible.

Violent brutality and romantic affection are closely connected in *Irréversible*, but not in the sense that one causes or leads to the other. The connections simply exist: This hellish state is just the way things are. Humans, through their own efforts, cannot save themselves from their fate, which—in this case of Alex, Pierre, Marcus, Le Tenia, and a number of other characters, including Alex's unborn child—is destruction and disaster. Any attempt to save oneself from this disaster is rejected as futile, and yet people like Alex and Marcus continue to delude themselves into thinking that the future is in their hands.

VI

According to scholar Daniel Wojcik (1997), fatalism, nihilism, and powerlessness are the trinity of secular apocalyptic thought (201). In fact, the content, structure, and cause-effect relationships that characterize *Irréversible* closely resemble those of the traditional apocalyptic narrative, in which perceived threats, social turmoil, and anomalous occurrences are interpreted as signs that foretell of imminent worldly destruction. The effects of Noé's apocalypse may be limited to a small handful of characters, but its implications are inescapable. The social and cultural rituals human beings have developed to perpetuate the concept of "civilization" are meaningless acts of denial and repression. In crisis and trauma, human brutality reigns supreme.

The literal meaning of apocalypse is "an unveiling," usually in the sense of an unveiling of a state of affairs that has been present all along. Often, in apocalyptic narratives, what is unveiled is the future, which turns out to have its roots in the present moment. As philosopher and theologian Martin Buber (1957) notes, in apocalyptic thought "everything is pre-determined, all human decisions are only sham struggles" (201). This is certainly true of *Irréversible*, which is apocalyptic not in the spiritual sense, but rather is inflected by a strong mood of secular eschatology, since it uses scenes of apocalyptic violence as metaphors for modern anxiety. In *Irréversible*, rituals and institutions like romantic love, marriage, the family, and friendship are revealed to be no more than vacant shams, and we are left with a resulting sense of anomie, disorientation, lawlessness, and impending chaos.

In this sense, the narrative of *Irréversible* can be regarded as metonymic of twentieth-century thought, which has been characterized by the breakdown of previous meaning systems and subsequent feelings of disillusionment, meaninglessness, anxiety, and apathy. Throughout the twentieth century, tragedies, disasters, and situations of great concern, uncertainty, and threat have motivated people to attribute causality to external factors, whether God's will, the devil, fate, the government, one's parents, or the configuration of the planets at birth. In *Irréversible*, however, Noé suggests that in the twenty-first century we can no longer attribute violence and disaster to any cause outside the brutal nature of humanity itself. In Gaspar Noé's apocalyptic scenario, worldly destruction is considered immanent in human nature rather than externally prescribed, fulfilled by the actions and character of human beings rather than determined by outside forces.

The branch of apocalyptic thought most clearly evoked by *Irréversible* is "unconditional apocalypticism." This is the belief that history is predetermined and unalterable (or, in Dunne's case, perpetually present); the world is irredeemable by human effort, and its cataclysmic destruction is regarded as inevitable. Some writers and scholars attribute the strand of unconditional apocalypticism in twentieth century thought to the development of nuclear warheads and the bombing of Hiroshima and Nagasaki. After the invention of the bomb there was a sense that humanity could not reverse its inevitable path to destruction and that scientists had created an uncontrollable weapon that would ultimately destroy the world. "The bomb," according to Alfred Kazin (1988), "gave the shape of life, inner and outer, an irreversible change; a sense of fatefulness would now lie on all things" (1).

What the bomb symbolized to earlier writers and scholars is represented in *Irréversible* by human nature. Noé's apocalyptic vision presents us with a hellish, drug-addicted, anarchic society cursed by violence, fear, paranoia, and a sense of fatalism that time can only make worse. The veil has been lifted, and what it reveals is death-in-life, and life-in-death.[6]

Afterword to the Second Edition

> Another waterproof sheet was spread over the table in the manner of a tablecloth, with the corners turned up over a sort of mound—a heap of rags, scorched and bloodstained, half-concealing what might have been as accumulation of raw material for a cannibal feast.
>
> Joseph Conrad, *The Secret Agent*, 1920.

WHEN THE HALF-WIT STEVIE TRIPS AND FALLS while carrying a bomb intended to blow up London's Greenwich Observatory in *The Secret Agent*, Conrad spares us nothing. Like Chief Inspector Heat who is assigned to the case, we are forced to confront the "shattering violence of destruction" that transforms Stevie into a "heap of mixed things, which seemed to have been collected in shambles and rag shops," "a heap of nameless fragments." "Look at that foot there," demands the constable who was given the task of shoveling up Stevie's remains. "I picked up the legs first, one after another. He was that scattered you didn't know where to begin." The news of the explosion reaches Stevie's sister when she overhears Chief Inspector Heat informing her husband that Stevie was "blown to small bits: limbs, gravel, clothing, bones, splinters—all mixed together . . . they had to fetch a shovel to gather him up with," a description that leads her to imagine vivid fantasies of "a rainlike fall of mangled limbs."

The Secret Agent was based partly on the case of Martial Bourdin, who attempted to blow up the Greenwich Observatory on February 15, 1894, and, in doing so, accidentally blew himself to bits. The case was reported in great detail in the following day's newspapers. Over a hundred years later, the bombing of the World Trade Center in New York—a far greater tragedy—resulted in the deaths of almost three thousand people, yet despite the thousands of witnesses and hours of footage, media renditions of the World

Trade Center bombing are much less detailed than Conrad's fictional account of the death of poor Stevie.

Nevertheless, any discussion of the events of September 11 on American television is still characterized by highly overcharged rhetoric, including the widespread use of the word "horror." Conrad's account of Stevie's death, however graphic and explicit it may be, is completely uncontroversial because it takes a literary, rather than a visual form. In Western culture, particularly in America, we've come to associate "the horrifying" with visually explicit (rather than literary or imaginative) representations of violence, usually violence done to the human body (dismemberment, evisceration, decapitation, and so on). For anything to be considered truly horrifying, it has to be seen—and, preferably, rendered as graphic and lifelike in detail as possible.

However, despite all the rhetoric, television coverage of the events of 9/11 brought us no visual images to endorse these recurrent assertions of "horror." We saw planes crashing into the World Trade Center, which was spectacular. We saw the towers collapse, which was incredible. We saw huge clouds of smoke and piles of rubble, buildings covered in dust and ashes, people running in alarm through the streets of lower Manhattan. Later, we saw sobbing widows grieving over their missing husbands; we saw firefighters and police officers mourning their valiant colleagues—but "horror"? If "horror" is defined as visual representations of violence done to the human body, most NC-17 rated films contain more "horror" than any station's broadcast of the events of 9/11. If the American television coverage of the events of September 11 had been an Arnold Schwarzenegger movie, people would be asking for their money back.

This, however, is quite typical of the media discourse surrounding "images of violence," which is always enormously overblown. Even otherwise intelligent commentators seem to accept without question generalities about apocalyptic Japanese anime, violent video games, bloody carnage on the Internet, a rising tide of terrifying images on the television news. For example, Richard Restak, author of the scarily titled *The New Brain: How the Modern Age is Rewiring Your Mind* (2003), claims that "constant exposure to visual depictions of suffering, conflict and violence creates dysfunctional circuits within areas of the brain that mediate emotion," leading to "various forms of post-traumatic stress disorder (PTSD), desensitization, feelings of unreality and detachment that cause one to respond to real tragedy as if it were a film, and various audience reactions ranging from phobias to emotional burnout" (10). Be that as it may, how many of us actually experience "constant exposure to visual depictions of suffering, conflict and violence"?

Even the most hardened, video-game obsessed teenagers need to eat, sleep, go to school, and interact with their friends and parents. As for the rest of us, we may occasionally see the aftermath of a bombing on the evening news, or view pictures of wounded civilians in the newspaper, or catch a horror movie now and then, but, in general, we lead rather ordinary lives of uneventful domestic routine.

II

The case has been made that the very act of photography is an act of aggression. According to Susan Sontag in her book *On Photography* (1977), there is an implicit violence in the idea of wrenching something from its original context. Jean Baudrillard in *Simulacra and Simulacrum* (1995) has claimed that every photographed object is merely the trace left behind by the disappearance of all the rest, an "almost perfect crime, an almost total resolution of the world, which merely leaves the illusion of a particular object shining forth, the image of which becomes an impenetrable enigma" (24). Critic Paul Virilio's recent discussions of multimedia imaging condemn its seemingly omnipresent gratuitous hyperviolence. In his most recent book *Art and Fear*, Virilio (2003) is especially critical of the "Sensation" exhibition at the Royal Academy of Arts in London in September to December 1997, which featured such explicit and disturbing artworks as Damien Hirst's bisected animals and putrefying cow's head, the Chapman brothers' grotesque sculptures, Marcus Harvey's cruel nudes, and Mat Collishaw's Bullet Hole—a huge close-up of a head wound mounted on fifteen light boxes. This exhibition, argued Virilio, typified a new kind of commercial "realism" nurtured on superficial advertising hype. Others, such as critic John Molyneux (1998), were impressed by the way in which the exhibition forced its viewers into a confrontation with flesh and death, making dead flesh into "an objective correlative for a range of different almost conflicting ideas and emotions" (5).

But is the act of photography really always an act of violence? In the discourse surrounding visual images—especially images of "real events"—I believe words like "horror" and "violence" tend to be used very loosely. To see a passenger plane crashing into a building may be horrific in its implications, but the image itself is not an especially graphic or violent one, at least not by today's cinematic standards.

This carelessness about the concept of "violence" is precisely why I have difficulty accepting the many the "scientific experiments" regularly conducted in the attempt to "prove" that prolonged exposure to gratuitous violence in the media can lead to hostile behavior (most recently, for example, see the work of Eric Uhlmann and Jane Swanson, published in 2004 in the *Journal of Adolescence*). Over forty years ago, Hans Eysenck (1964) began publishing his studies claiming that violent media images lead to an increase in violent and aggressive behavior in viewers. Although Eysenck was attentive to some aspects of the transmission of media images—for example, repetition and saturation—his main concern was with violence as media representation. Those who have followed up Eysenck's original research often have a conservative political or religious agenda; they usually report that participants in the study were shown "violent films," as though such phenomena needed no further explanation, without any attempt to explain why particular films were chosen or to give reasons for the choice of these particular forms and manifestations of fictionalized violence.

Significantly, some researchers say that digital images typically carry less information than celluloid images and that they operate purely at the level of communication. On what affective level can the digital then be said to operate? Do digital images carry less violence than media such as analog photography? To what extent can digitality be said to bypass representation but still register viscerally? These and other questions need to be answered before we can speculate about the effects of violent images on the Internet and in other digital forms. Moreover, as any fan of Court TV knows, case studies "proving" one argument can always be matched by similar experiments confirming the opposite; indeed, there are plenty of examples of experimental research showing that the viewing of violent films has a cleansing, cathartic effect on the viewer, just as users of pornography are often adamant about its salutary effects on their relationships with women.

Many of my students are intelligent fans of horror movies who tell me they are tired of films being blamed for propagating violence and crime when there is so much real violence in the world, much of it the direct, deliberate result of world governments and national leaders, and most of it ignored by the press. Many of them tell me they feel insulted by the notion that they need to be protected from "violence in the media," when nothing is being done to stem far worse horrors in real life, especially in the Third World, including famine, genocide, and torture.

The films I am championing in this study may be disturbing, but none could be said to be consistently violent in the way that, say, Mel Gibson's *The Passion of the Christ* (2004) is consistently violent. Admittedly, some of them contain particularly violent scenes, such as the Rectum scene in *Irréversible*, but even these are surprisingly limited in frequency, considering the overall content of the films discussed in this book. *The Texas Chainsaw Massacre*, for example, despite its dramatic title and reputation, contains hardly any actual violence—only a tiny proportion of the bloodshed of mainstream films like *Saving Private Ryan* (1998). Believe it or not, I find consistently violent Hollywood blockbusters difficult to sit through—not because their violence disturbs me, but because my attention often starts to wander. I find it hard to focus on drawn-out fight and chase sequences made senseless by stultifying noises and deadening special effects. This, of course, is merely the end result of Hollywood's capitalist system of moviemaking, which consistently deals up action films aimed at the multiplex-going fourteen-year-old boys who are the main demographic market of today's film producers.

Significantly, recent war movies, such as *We Were Soldiers* (2002), *Black Hawk Down* (2001), and *Saving Private Ryan*, use highly realistic violent effects, often during battle scenes, in an attempt to suggest that this is exactly how it "really happened" (instead of giving us a sense of historical context and military strategy). In other words, the verisimilitude is a way of dulling our critical faculties and exciting our senses so that we will neither question the "truth" of what is being shown, nor pause to consider the ideological agenda behind it.

III

In fact, the best place to find the "violent images" that so repel family-values campaigners is not at the multiplex at all, but on cable television. If you'd decided to change channels during the repetitively screened footage of the World Trade Center bombing on 9/11, for example, you would have had little trouble finding the kind of graphic footage of human death so conspicuously absent from coverage of the terrorist attacks on New York City. If you'd tuned into the Discovery Channel, you might have been able to catch an episode of *Pile-Up!* or *Runaway Trains*, cable television shows both devoted to footage of violent and often fatal accidents. Or, perhaps you might have preferred to watch an episode of *Trauma: Life in the ER*, the Learning Channel's longest-running series, a fly-on-the-wall hospital show that allows us to experience a night on the emergency ward, including close-up, open-wound sequences from the operating theater. It seems to be a requirement of the show that each episode involves at least one fatality. Other, similar shows on the Learning Channel include *High Speed Pursuit!*, *Paramedics*, and *Code Blue*.

If none of this grabbed you, you might have been able to catch *COPS* on Court TV, a program notorious for showcasing scenes of real-life violence filmed by cameramen who follow an inner-city police force on their nightly rounds. On the other hand, *When Good Pets Go Bad* on Fox is always handy for footage of lions mauling overambitious photographers in safari parks or of foolhardy matadors being torn apart by bulls.

To find the most extensive coverage of real-life violent fatalities, however, you would have needed to tune into one of the most popular channels on cable television, the History Channel. Specializing in footage of wars, military campaigns, assassinations, and the bombing of large cities, the History Channel offers a round-the-clock diet of shows like *Great Blunders of History*, *The Wrath of God*, *History's Crimes*, and *Caught on Film*. The latter series has been especially popular, featuring rare footage of historical disasters, from student films of the Kent State University shootings and unedited images of the Andria Doria shipwreck to footage of the Nazi concentration camps of World War II. In fact, Holocaust footage is shown on television so frequently that scenes of skeletal prisoners pushing wheelbarrows full of dead bodies are familiar to us all. It's generally accepted that the viewing of such footage is a vital part of understanding the terrible horrors of the concentration camps, even if, inevitably, such footage soon loses its original capacity to shock.

Ironically—given the amount of violence shown daily on the History Channel—media commentators regularly express fears about "evil individuals" who might exploit scenes of "real-life carnage" for the sick pleasure of those voyeurs who collect such underground footage or charge people to watch it on the Internet. There seems to be a widespread sense of anxiety about the fact that this repressed material will make its way to that frightening place known as "out there," presumably alongside footage of animal torture and prepubescent children involved in sexually explicit acts. This belief is itself supported by the assumption that it is the evil people "out there"—pedophiles, psychopaths, snuff moviemakers, suicide bombers, Islamic terrorists, and other assorted sickos—who are responsible for the horrors that occur on a daily basis in American society.

The otherworld of "out there" used to be located underground, as in "underground footage," but now can be accessed just as readily through cyberspace, where all kinds of distasteful things are alleged to go on. The Internet is becoming increasingly mythologized, leading to a new sense of domestic isolation that has been dramatically heightened by the 9/11 attacks on American soil. The original antihero of the Internet used to be the anonymous and unknowable hacker, but this evil individual has recently been usurped by the computer-savvy fiend who caters to the sick tastes of perverted voyeurs. In media discourse, such characters are usually conceptualized as lurking around on the Internet, which can in turn be accessed through the computer terminals in our own homes. The computer screen is therefore regarded as a kind of magic portal—the gate of hell—through which computer viruses can escape to invade your home, turning your husband into a porn fiend and your children into the potential victims of drooling pedophiles, maybe even pedophile priests.

"The social changes which have followed the Internet explosion," writes computer expert John Ives (1998), "themselves quite abrupt, have led to stories which suggest near-apocalyptic scenarios in which innocent users find themselves at the mercy of forces beyond their control" (4). Ives explains how people's fear of the Internet's power to disrupt community stability and organization is typified by anxieties about computer viruses that are capable of physically eating their way through the materials of your hard drive or making your computer screen literally explode. To many people, especially those who don't understand how their computers work, the Internet is an unrestricted, unpoliced otherworld, where perverts swap tips, teenagers make suicide pacts, pedophiles lurk in the guise of pen pals, and the censored footage of 9/11 plays over and over again in an endless, blood-drenched loop.

IV

As always, the truth is a lot less dramatic. Television cameramen at the scene of any large-scale disaster, accident, or violent act regularly capture plenty of graphic material on tape. If, on return to the station, it is determined that this footage is too explicit to be broadcast, "DO NOT AIR!" will be written on the side of the tape in big red letters. If any of the material is deemed usable, it will be edited out of the tape and spliced into the broadcast.

People who work at television stations sometimes become curious about these "DO NOT AIR!" tapes. These people usually have access to duplicating facilities and will sometimes make their own copies of these tapes to take home. Temps or interns may make copies as souvenirs of their job at the television station; photographers may make copies in case the tape is needed as legal evidence or in case the footage can be screened at some future date. Copies of these tapes may be kept in the television news archives and sometimes in private collections, especially if the events they document are of potential legal or historical significance. Occasionally, an individual with access to such footage will obtain copies for a producer, who will then put

AFTERWORD

together a compilation of murders, suicides, accidents, assassinations, and other real-life disasters to be offered for sale to the public.

Far from being "underground," however, these tapes can be bought or rented at virtually any main-street video outlet under titles like *Death Scenes* and *Faces of Death*, two of the films discussed in chapter 7. It seems inevitable that repressed material from 9/11 will appear as part of one of these low-budget "shockumentaries" long before it becomes acceptable viewing on network television. The fact that it remains repressed, in fact, virtually guarantees a market for such footage.

Some of these "shockumentaries" are produced in other countries, contrived to play on anti-American sentiments. Future films of this kind will clearly make much of the "uncensored" footage of 9/11, if indeed such footage exists. There have already been reports of such tapes being shown on video in the Middle East and China. Apparently, in the immediate aftermath of the attacks, workers at a Beijing television station worked round-the-clock to produce a documentary they called *Attack America* (2002), which splices scenes from Hollywood films with shots of the events of September 11. As rescue workers pick through the rubble of the twin towers, according to journalist Damien McElroy (2001), "the commentator proclaims that the city has reaped the consequence of decades of American bullying of weaker nations" (10).

In his late essay *The Question Concerning Technology*, Martin Heidegger (1977) writes that "the essence of technology is by no means anything technological" (14). What Heidegger suggests in this essay is that what we call "technology" is fundamentally no more than an extension of the relationship between human beings, and to think of it in any other way is to engender the kind of passivity and mystification that characterizes public anxieties about "underground" videos and, in particular, the Internet. It is certainly true that still photographs of accidents and disasters, mainly grabs from "DO NOT AIR!" tapes, can be viewed online. Again, however, there is nothing "secret" or "underground" about these sites, among them rotten.com, gruesome.com, scarystuff.com, and trauma.softcoma.com; most of them are even free to use. Some feature repressed material from 9/11, both still footage and video streams, mostly of people leaping to their deaths from the windows of the World Trade Center.

It is often reported that people from cultures unfamiliar with photography sometimes display a morbid fear of the camera, believing that to take somebody's photograph is a way of stealing their soul. This is seen as primitive fetishism, but what could be more fetishistic than our own culture's superstition about the photographic image? In Western culture, the photograph is surrounded by enormous structures of mystery, anxiety, and taboo; it is an ideological commonplace that video images have the power to harm, traumatize, and seduce, to overcome all ordinary rational logic and human reason. The media regularly convey moral tales about pornographic films turning home-loving husbands into sex-obsessed perverts, about video violence turning teenage schoolboys into gun-toting killers. Evangelists have claimed not only that certain horror films are works of the devil, but that evil resides in the actual celluloid of these movies. All over the United States, people are currently serving custodial sentences for possessing photographic images considered so shocking and disturbing that those who own them are considered dangerous criminals and cannot be allowed to go free.

V

Authentic counterculture is shunned because it offends, puzzles, shocks, alarms, or outrages. The kind of countercultural cinema that is interesting to me is "counter" not because it affords an alternative to traditional or popular cultural forms, but because it turns this kind of culture on its head, revealing its seamy undersides. The films analyzed in this book are all examples of genuine countercultural forms. Firstly, they are all full of a powerful sense of self-conscious irony, representing profanely productive and deathless creations infected with the spirit of process and inconclusiveness, breaking up the otherwise grim atmosphere of traditional, "official" cinema, culture, and society. Secondly, these films all contain a ludicrous kind of creativity and vitality far from fatalism and pessimism, and it is this basic consolidating force that gives them such power. Thirdly, offensive films are an immediate, dynamic form of cinema associated with the physical body and bodily life, affirming a lack of distance between the real and the textual. The core of the identity of most kinds of offensive films is the everyday and obvious nature of the physical, bodily world. Finally, these are all films that affirm the primal connections between culture, narrative, and the human body, between simplicity and timelessness, between that which is rejected and its challenge to institutionalized forms. They are films that affirm the way in which play, pantomime, and masquerade can destroy epic distance and free the individual conscience from canonical practices and traditions.

In *Notes from the Underground*, Dostoyevsky (1864) explains, through the mouth of his narrator, that genuine freedom and anarchy can be achieved only through a rejection of the doctrine that two plus two equals four. Only by refusing to believe in the human systems of proportion, precision, struc-

AFTERWORD

ture, science, mathematics, and ultimately the power of civilization itself, can man ever be free. Freedom, in other words, comes from "throwing stones at the Crystal Palace." The films analyzed in this book all represent large rocks hurled against the Crystal Palace of traditional narrative cinema and its proportionate forms. Offensive films are part of the cinema of excess and extremity.

Wherever there is neurosis and repression, there will be a counterforce. Wherever there is traditional narrative cinema, there will be its cinematic counterpart—cinema *in extremis*. "Official" cinema and its outlandish opposite are two sides of the same coin, with the king on the front and the joker on the back. Official cinema, as a force of syncretic pageantry, is the impetus fueling diverse variants and nuances of counter cinema, depending on the time, the place, the people, and the particular example of cinema involved. The abandon of exploitation film is the force that forges the sideshow of offensive films, with their cultic and transgressive acts, each of which is an individual symptom of the anxieties of that sanctioned masquerade known as cinema. In order to find an authentically creative countercultural force, we need to look not in the art gallery, museum, or experimental movie theater, but in the chamber of horrors, the hall of mirrors, the freak show, the shadowy funhouse: This is where transgression and transcendence lie. What is so valuable about these kinds of films is their unconscious awareness of the repressions of official cinema and the importance of chaos and crisis. What these films have to teach us about the condition of being human is both frightening and repellent. In these offensive films, human consciousness is reflected not in the grand mirror of literature, nor in the order of cultural monuments, but in the nervous twitches of the death-spasm and the waste products of the autopsy.

Filmography

Abbot and Costello Meet Frankenstein, dir: Charles Barton, 1948.
Alien, dir: Ridley Scott, U.S. 1979.
Aliens, dir: James Cameron, U.S. 1986.
Alien 3, dir: David Fincher, U.S. 1992.
Alien: Ressurection, dir: Jean-Pierre Jeunet, U.S. 1992
Alive! dir: Frank Marshall, U.S. 1993
Basket Case, dir: Frank Henenlotter, U.S. 1982
Basket Case 2, dir: Frank Henenlotter, U.S. 1990
Basket Case 3—The Progeny, dir: Frank Henenlotter, U.S. 1992
Bell, Bare and Beautiful, dir: David F. Friedman and Herschell Gordon Lewis, U.S. 1963.
Betrayal, dir: David Hugh Jones, U.K., 1983.
Black Hawk Down, dir: Ridley Scott, U.S. 2001.
The Blob, dir: Chuck Russell, U.S. 1998
Blood Diner, dir: Jackie Kong, U.S. 1987.
Blood Feast, dir: Herschel Gordon Lewis, U.S. 1963.
Cannibal, dir: Ruggero Deodato, Italy 1976.
Cannibal Girls, dir: Ivan Reitman, Canada, 1972.
Cannibal Holocaust, dir: Ruggero Deodato, Italy 1981.
Cannibal Man, dir: Eloy de la Iglesia, Spain 1972.
Charles Manson, Superstar! dir. Nicholas Shreck, U.S. 1989.
Charlie's Family, aka *The Manson Family,* dir. Jim Van Bebber, U.S. 2003.
The Chance of a Lifetime, dir: William Castle, U.S. 1942.
A Clockwork Orange, dir: Stanley Kubrick, U.K. 1971.
Color Me Blood Red, dir: Herschel Gordon Lewis, U.S. 1965.
Cult of the Damned, dir: Robert Thom, U.S. 1970.
Damaged Goods, dir: Alexander Butler, U.K. 1919.
Dawn of the Dead, dir: George A. Romero, U.S. 1978.
Day of the Dead, dir: George A. Romero, U.S. 1985.
Day of the Locust, dir: John Schlesinger, U.S. 1975.
Death Scenes, dir: Nick Bougas, U.S. 1989.
Death Scenes 2, prod. Nick Bougas, U.S. 1992.
Deep River Savages, dir: Umberto Lenzi, Italy 1981.
Deep Throat, dir: Gerard Damiano, U.S. 1972.
The Defilers, dir: David F. Friedman, U.S. 1963.

Der Todesking, dir: Jörg Buttgereit, Germany 1989.
Dracula, dir: Tod Browning, U.S. 1931.
Eaten Alive, dir: Umberto Lenzi, Italy 1977.
The End, dir: Pol Ferbus, U.S. 1972.
The Eternal Jew, dir: George Roland, Germany 1933.
The Exorcist, dir: William Friedkin, U.S. 1973.
Faces of Death, dir: Conan Le Cilaire, U.S. 1978.
Faces of Death 2, dir: John Alan Schwartz, U.S. 1981.
Faces of Death 3, dir: John Alan Schwartz with Susumu Saegusa, U.S. 1985.
Faces of Death 4, dir: Uwe Schier, U.S. 1990.
Faces of Death 5, dir: Uwe Schier, 1995.
Faces of Death 6, dir: Uwe Schier, 1996.
Frankenhooker, dir: Frank Henenlotter, U.S. 1990.
Frankenstein, dir: James Whale, U.S. 1931.
Freaks, dir: Tod Browning, U.S. 1932.
Freddy's Dead—The Final Nightmare, dir: Rachel Talalay, U.S. 1991.
Friday the 13th, dir: Sean S. Cunningham, U.S. 1980.
Friday the 13th Part 2, dir: Steve Miner, U.S. 1981.
Friday the 13th Part 3 in 3D, dir: Steve Miner, U.S. 1982.
Friday the 13th Part 4—The Final Chapter, dir: Joseph Zito, U.S. 1984.
Friday the 13th Part 5—A New Beginning, dir: Danny Steinmann, U.S. 1985.
Friday the 13th Part 6—Jason Lives, dir: Tom McLoughlin, U.S. 1986.
Friday the 13th Part 7—The New Blood, dir: John Carl Buechler, U.S. 1988.
Friday the 13th Part 8—Jason Takes Manhattan, dir: Rob Hedden, U.S. 1989.
Friday the 13th Part 9—Jason Goes to Hell aka *The Final Friday*, dir: Adam Marcus, U.S. 1993.
The Gore-Gore Girls, dir: Herschel Gordon Lewis, U.S. 1972.
Graveyard Shift, aka *Stephen King's Graveyard Shift*, dir: Ralph S. Singleton, U.S. 1990.
The Gruesome Twosome, dir: Herschel Gordon Lewis, U.S. 1967.
Halloween, dir: John Carpenter, U.S. 1978.
Halloween 2, dir: Rick Rosenthal, U.S. 1981.
Halloween 3—Season of the Witch, dir: Tommy Lee Wallace, U.S. 1983.
Halloween 4—The Return of Michael Myers, dir: Dwight Little, U.S. 1988.
Hell Night, dir: Tom de Simone, U.S. 1981.
Helter Skelter, dir: Tom Griles, U.S. 1976.
The Hills Have Eyes, dir: Wes Craven, U.S. 1977.
Homicidal, dir: William Castle, U.S. 1961.
The House on Haunted Hill, dir: William Castle, U.S. 1958.
I Demoni, dir: Jerry Jameson, Italy 1970.
I Saw What you Did, dir: William Castle, U.S. 1965.
I Spit on Your Grave, dir: Meir Zarchi, U.S. 1977.
Insatiable, dir: Godfrey Daniels, U.S. 1980.

FILMOGRAPHY

Irrvérsible, dir: Gaspar Noé, France 2002.
The Killing of America, dir: Sheldon Renan, U.S. 1981.
King Kong, dir: Merian C. Cooper and Ernest B. Schoedsack, U.S. 1933.
Laura, dir: Otto Preminger, 1944.
Leatherface—The Texas Chainsaw Massacre 3, dir: Jeff Burr, U.S. 1990.
Lorna, dir: Russ Meyer, U.S. 1965.
Love in the Commune, dir: Wade Williams, U.S. 1970.
Macabre, dir: William Castle, U.S. 1958.
Manson, aka *Manson and "Squeaky" Fromme,* dir: Robert Hendrickson and Lawrence Merrick, U.S. 1972.
Memento, dir: Christopher Nolan, U.S. 2001.
Mr. Sardonicus, dir: William Castle, U.S. 1961.
Mondo Balordo, dir: Roberto Bianchi Montero, Italy 1964.
Mondo Bizarro, aka *Bizarro,* dir: Manfred Durniok, U.S. 1966.
Mondo Cane, aka *A Dog's Life,* aka *Mondo Cane no. 1,* aka *Mondo Insanity,* dir: Gualitiero Jacopetti and Franco Prosperi, Italy 1962.
Mondo Freudo, aka *The World of Freud,* dir: R. L. Frost, U.S. 1966.
Motel Hell, dir: Kevin Connor, U.S. 1980.
Natural Born Killers, dir: Oliver Stone, U.S. 1994.
Night of the Living Dead, dir: George A. Romero, U.S. 1968.
Nightmare on Elm Street, dir: Wes Craven, U.S. 1984.
Nightmare on Elm Street 2—Freddy's Revenge, dir: Jack S. Holder, U.S. 1985.
Nightmare on Elm Street 3—Dream Warriors, dir: Chuck Russell, U.S. 1987.
Nightmare on Elm Street 4—The Dream Master, dir: Renny Harlin, U.S. 1988.
Nightmare on Elm Street 5—The Dream Child, dir: Stephen Hopkins, U.S. 1989.
The Other Side of Madness, dir: Wade Williams, U.S. 1970.
Parents, dir: Bob Balaban, U.S. 1988.
The Passion of the Christ, dir: Mel Gibson, U.S. 2004.
Pet Sematary, dir: Mary Lambert, U.S. 1989.
The Pit and the Pendulum, dir: Roger Corman, U.S. 1961.
Plan 9 From Outer Space, dir: Ed Wood, U.S. 1959
Prey, dir: Norman Warren, U.K. 1977.
Prisoner of the Cannibal God, dir: Sergio Martino, Italy 1978.
Psycho, dir: Alfred Hitchcock, U.S. 1960.
Rosemary's Baby, dir: Roman Polanski, U.S. 1968.
Satan's Sadists, dir: Al Adamson, U.S. 1970.
Savage Man . . . Savage Beast, aka *Savage Temptation,* aka *The Great Hunting,* dir: Antonio Climati and Mario Morra, Italy 1975.
Savage Zone, aka *Dimensione Violenza,* dir: Mario Morra, Italy 1985.
Saving Private Ryan, dir: Steven Spielberg. U.S. 1998.
The Scarlet Trail, dir: John S. Lawrence, U.S. 1918.
Scream, dir: Wes Craven, U.S. 1996.

Scream 2, dir: Wes Craven, U.S. 1997.
Scream 3, dir: Wes Craven, U.S. 2000.
Shivers, dir: David Cronenberg, Canada, 1975
Shampoo, dir: Hal Ashby, U.S. 1975.
Shocking Asia, aka *Asia Perversa*, dir: Emerson Fox, Germany 1974.
The Shocks, dir: Kentaro Uchida, Japan 1988.
The Silence of the Lambs, dir: Jonathan Demme, U.S. 1991.
Snuff, aka *Slaughter*, aka *The Slaughter*, aka *Americain Cannibale*, aka *Big Snuff*, dir: Michael and Roberta Findlay/Allan Shackleton, Argentina/U.S. 1973.
The Stepfather, dir: Joseph Rubens, U.S. 1986.
Straitjacket, dir: William Castle, U.S. 1963.
Taboos of the World, dir: Romolo Marcellini, Italy 1963.
The Texas Chainsaw Massacre, dir: Tobe Hooper, U.S. 1974.
The Texas Chainsaw Massacre 2, dir: Tobe Hooper, U.S. 1986.
Theatre of Blood, dir: Douglas Hickox, U.K. 1973.
Thirteen Frightened Girls, aka *The Candy Web*, dir: William Castle, U.S. 1963.
Thirteen Ghosts, dir: William Castle, U.S. 1960.
The Tingler, dir: William Castle, U.S. 1959.
El Topo, dir: Alexandro Joderowsky, Brazil 1970.
The Touch of Her Flesh, dir: Michael and Roberta Findlay, U.S. 1967.
True Gore, dir: M. Dixon Causey, U.S. 1987.
The Twilight Zone—The Movie, dir: John Landis, Steven Spielberg, Joe Dante, and George Miller, U.S. 1976.
Two Thousand Maniacs, dir: Herschel Gordon Lewis, U.S. 1964.
The Unholy Three, dir: Tod Browning, U.S. 1925.
The Unknown, dir: Tod Browning, U.S. 1927.
A Victim of Sin, dir: anon., 1915.
Video Violence, dir: Gary Cohen, U.S. 1986–1987.
We Were Soldiers, dir: Randall Wallace, 2002.
The Whistler, dir: William Castle, U.S. 1944.
Zotz! dir: William Castle, U.S. 1962.

Bibliography

Adams, Marilyn McCord, and Norman Kretzmann. 1969. Introduction to *Predestination, God's Foreknowledge, and Future Contingents*, by William Ockham, 3–4. New York: Apple-Century-Crofts.
Adrian, Werner. 1976. *Freaks: Cinema of the Bizarre*. London: Lorrimer.
Bakhtin, Mikhail M. 1968. *Rabelais and His World*. Translated by Hélène Iswolsky. Cambridge: MIT Press.
———. 1981a. "Discourse in the Novel." In *The Dialogic Imagination*, translated by Caryl Emerson and Michael Holquist. Austin: University of Texas Press.
———. 1981b. "Forms of Times and Chronotope in the Novel." In *The Dialogic Imagination*, translated by Caryl Emerson and Michael Holquist. Austin: University of Texas Press.
———. 1984. *Problems of Dostoyevsky's Poetics*. Translated by Caryl Emerson. History and the Theory of Literature 8. Minneapolis: University of Minnesota Press.
———. 1986. "From Notes Made in 1970–71." In *Speech Genres and Other Late Essays*, translated by Vern W. McGee and edited by Caryl Emerson and Michael Holquist. Austin: University of Texas Press.
Barker, Martin, ed. 1984. *The Video Nasties: Freedom and Censorship in the Media*. London: Pluto Press.
Baudrillard, Jean. 1983. *Simulations*. Foreign Agents Series. Paris: Semiotext(e).
———. 1995. *Simulacra and Simulacrum*. Translated by Sheila Glaser. Ann Arbor: University of Michigan Press.
Bataille, Georges. 1985. *Visions of Excess: Selected Writings 1927–1939*. Minneapolis: University of Minnesota Press.
Bazin, André. 1967. *What is Cinema?* Translated by Hugh Gray. 2 volumes. Berkeley and Los Angeles: University of California Press. Reprinted 1971.
Bettelheim, Bruno. 1976. *The Uses of Enchantment: The Meaning and Importance of Fairy Tales*. New York: Random House, 1988.
Beylie, Claude. 1973. "Freaks." *Ecran*, July/August, 17.
Biette, Jean-Claude. 1978. "Tod Browning et *Freaks*." *Cahiers du Cinéma* 288: 23–26.
Birge, Peter, and Janet Maslin. 1976. "Getting Snuffed in Boston." *Film Comment* 12, no. 3: 35–63.
Blacking, John, ed. 1977. *The Anthropology of the Body*. London: Academic Press.
Bleek, Wolf. 1976. "Witchcraft, Gossip, and Death: A Social Drama." *Man* 11, no. 4 (December): 526–42.

Bloch, Maurice, and Jonathan Parry, eds., 1982. *Death and the Regeneration of Life.* Cambridge: Cambridge University Press.

Bogdan, Robert. 1988. *Freakshow: Presenting Human Oddities for Amusement and Profit.* Chicago: University of Chicago Press.

Bogdan, Robert, and Douglas Biklen. 1977. "Handicapism." *Social Policy* 7, no. 4 (March/April): 14–19.

Boulenger, Gilles. 2003. *John Carpenter: Prince of Darkness.* New York: Silman-James.

Boss, Pete. 1986. "Vile Bodies and Screen Medicine." *Screen* 27: 14–24.

Bradford, Phillips Verner, and Harvey Blume. 1992. *Ota Benga: The Pygmy in the Zoo.* New York: St. Martin's Press.

Briggs, Joe Bob. 2003. *Profoundly Disturbing: Shocking Movies that Changed History!* New York: Rizzoli Books.

Briggs, George William. 1938. *Goraknath and the Kanphata Yogis.* Calcutta: YMCA Publishing House.

Britton, Andrew, et al., eds. 1979. *The American Nightmare: Essays on the Horror Film.* Toronto: Festival of Festivals.

Brophy, Phil. 1986. "Horrality—The Textuality of Contemporary Horror Films." *Screen* 27: 1–7.

Brottman, Mikita. 1999. *Meat is Murder! An Illustrated Guide to Cannibal Culture.* London: Creation Books. Reissued 2002.

Brunas, John. 1979. "William Castle: Five Portraits in Black (1958–61)." *Midnight Marquee* 28 (September): 4–12.

Buber, Martin. 1957. *Pointing the Way: Collected Essays.* Edited and translated Maurice Freedman. Baltimore: Johns Hopkins University Press.

Burgess, Bill. 1984. "William Castle." *Classic Images* 111 (September): 42–44.

Butler, Ivan. 1967. *The Horror Film.* New York: Zwemmer.

Buxton, Jean. 1968. "Animal Identity and Human Peril: Some Mandari Images." *Man* 3, no. 1 (March): 35–50.

Calhoun, John B. 1972. "Plight of the Ik and Kaiadilt Is Seen as a Chilling Possible End for Man." *Smithsonian* 3, no. 8: 19–23. Reproduced in *Cultural Anthropology*, edited by Marvin Harris. 3rd ed. New York: HarperCollins, 1991.

"Cannibal Holocaust" (review). 1985. *Variety*, June 19, 74.

Carcassonne, Phillipe. 1978. "Freaks—La Monstreuse Parade." *Cinématographe* 37 (April): 32–33.

Carroll, Noel. 1990. *The Philosophy of Horror, or, Paradoxes of the Heart.* New York: Routledge.

Castle, William. 1976. *Step Right Up! I'm Gonna Scare the Pants off America.* New York: Putnam and Sons.

Chagnon, Napoleon A. 1992. *Yanomamo: The Last Days of Eden.* 4th ed. New York: Harcourt Brace Jovanivch. Reprinted 1996.

Clagett, Thomas D. 2003. *William Friedkin: Films of Aberration, Obsession, and Reality.* New York: Silman-James.

BIBLIOGRAPHY

Clover, Carol J. 1987. "Her Body, Himself: Gender in the Slasher Film." *Representations* 20 (Fall): 187–228. Reprinted in *Fantasy in the Cinema*, edited by James Donald. London: BFI Press, 1989.

———. 1992. *Men, Women, and Chainsaws*. London: BFI Press.

Cluny, Claude Michel. 1978. "Freaks dans l'oeuvre de Tod Browning." *Cinéma 78* (May): 27–31.

Corbey, Raymond. 1993. "Ethnographic Showcases 1870–1930." *Cultural Anthropology* 3: 338–69.

Cowan, Noah. 2002. "The Real France: Gaspar Noé's *Irréversible*." *Cinemascope* (Cannes edition), 49–50.

Crabbe, Anthony. 1988. "Feature-Length Sex Films." In *Perspectives on Pornography*, edited by Gary Day and Clive Bloom. London: Macmillan.

Cranefield, Paul F. 1962. "The Discovery of Cretinism." *Bulletin of the History of Medicine* 5, no. 36 (November/December): 511.

Creed, Barbara. 1993. *The Monstrous-Feminine: Film, Feminism, Psychoanalysis*. London: Routledge.

Cros, Jean-Louis. 1981. "Cannibal Holocaust" (review). *Image et Son: Revue du Cinéma* 361 (May): 39–40.

Dadoun, Roger. 1989. "Fetishism in the Horror Film." In *Fantasy in the Cinema*, edited by James Donald. London: BFI Press. Reprinted in *Movies and Methods*, vol. 2, edited by Bill Nichols. Berkeley and Los Angeles: University of California Press, 1989.

David-Neel, Alexandra. 1958. *Initiation and Initiates in Tibet*. Translated by Fred Rothwell. London: Rider. Reprinted 1986.

———. 1967. *Magic and Mystery in Tibet*. London: Souvenir. Reprinted, London: Unwin, 1984.

Day, Gary, and Clive Bloom, eds. 1988. *Perspectives on Pornography*. London: Macmillan.

Derry, Charles. 1977. *Dark Dreams: A Psychological History of the Horror Film*. London: A. S. Barnes.

Dika, Vera. 1990. *Games of Terror: Halloween, Friday the 13th, and the Films of the Stalker Cycle*. Rutherford, N.J.: Fairleigh Dickenson University Press.

Douglas, Mary. 1966. *Purity and Danger: An Analysis of the Concepts of Pollution and Taboo*. London: Routledge and Kegan Paul. Reprinted, London: Routledge, 1984, 1989.

———. 1978. *Implicit Meanings: Essays in Anthropology*. London and Boston: Routledge and Kegan Paul.

———. 1992. *Risk and Blame: Essays in Cultural Theory*. London: Routledge. Reprinted 1994.

Dostoyevsky, Fyodor. 1864. *Notes from the Underground*. London: Penguin, 1972.

Drimmer, Frederick. 1973. *Very Special People*. New York: Amjohn.

Dunne, J. W. 1927. *An Experiment with Time*, Charlotteville, VA: Hampton Roads Publishing, 2001.

Durgnat, Raymond, 1967. *Films and Feelings*. Cambridge: MIT Press.

Easto, Patrick, and Marcello Truzzi. 1972. "Towards an Ethnography of the Carnival Social System." *Journal of Popular Culture* 2: 551–56.

Ebert, Roger. 1981. "Why Movie Audiences Aren't Safe Any More." *American Film* (March): 54–56.

Eder, Richard. 1976. "Fifty Picket Movie Houses to Protest Violent Film." *New York Times*, February 16, 22.

Ellis, Bill. 1989. "Death by Folklore: Ostention, Contemporary Legend, and Murder." *Western Folklore* 48, no. 3 (July 1989): 201–20.

———. 1990. Introduction to Special Issue. "Contemporary Legends in Emergence." *Western Folklore* 49: 1–7.

Eysenck, Hans. 1964. *Crime and Personality*. New York: HarperCollins.

Fiedler, Leslie. 1978. *Freaks*. New York: Simon and Schuster.

Fraser, John. 1990. "Watching Horror Movies." *Michigan Quarterly Review* 16, no. 1: 39–54.

Frazer, Sir James George. 1910. *Totemism and Exogamy: A Treatise on Certain Early Forms of Superstition*. London: Macmillan.

Freud, Sigmund. 1905. *Jokes and Their Relation to the Unconscious*. In Standard Edition of the *Complete Works of Sigmund Freud*, 8: 9–236, translated by James Strachey. London: Hogarth Press, 1960.

———. 1905. *Three Essays on the Theory of Sexuality*. In Standard Edition of the *Complete Works of Sigmund Freud*, 7: 12–34, translated by James Strachey. London: Hogarth Press, 1962.

———. 1913. *Totem and Taboo*. In Standard Edition of the *Complete Works of Sigmund Freud*, 13: 1–161, translated by James Strachey. London: Hogarth Press, 1955.

———. 1919. "The Uncanny." In Standard Edition of the *Complete Works of Sigmund Freud*, 17: 219–52, translated by James Strachey. London: Hogarth Press, 1962.

———. 1923. *Beyond the Pleasure Principle*. In Standard Edition of the *Complete Works of Sigmund Freud*, 18: 1–64, translated by James Strachey. London: Hogarth Press, 1965.

Frith, Raymond. 1936. *We, the Tikopia: A Sociological Study of Kinship in Primitive Polynesia*. London: George Allan and Unwin.

von Füren-Haimendorf, Christoph. 1967. *Morals and Merit*. London: Weidenfield and Nicholson.

Garel, Alain. 1977. "William Castle" (obituary). *Cahiers du Cinèma* 21: 70–71.

Garsault, Alain, 1981. "Cannibal Holocaust" (review). *Positif* no. 243 (June): 65.

Gensler, Howard. 1993. "Terror of the Tingler." *Premiere* (U.S.), May, 89.

Gere, F. 1981. "Cannibal Holocaust" (review). *Cahiers du Cinèma* 63 (July-August): 32–36.

Gigli, Jean A. 1969. "Freaks." *Ciné 69* (April): 135.

Giles, Dennis. 1984. "Conditions of Pleasure in the Horror Cinema." In *Planks of Reason: Essays on the Horror Film*, edited by Barry Keith Grant. Metuchen, N.J.: Scarecrow Press.

BIBLIOGRAPHY

Gilson, Paul. 1951. "Freaks." In *Cinémagic*, edited by André Bonne. Paris: Editions du Cinéma.

Girard, René. 1977. *Violence and the Sacred*. Baltimore: Johns Hopkins University Press. Reprinted, London: Athlone, 1988.

Grant, Barry Keith, ed., 1984. *Planks of Reason: Essays on the Horror Film*. Metuchen, N.J.: Scarecrow Press.

Grieg, Donald. 1989. "The Sexual Differentiation of the Hitchcock Text." In *Fantasy and the Cinema*, edited by James Donald. London: BFI Press.

Grossberger, Lewis. 1986. "Can We Not Talk?" *Rolling Stone*, December 14, 14–18.

Hägglund, Tor-Björn, and Heikki Phia, 1980. "The Inner Space of the Body Image." *Psychoanalytic Quarterly* 49: 256–83.

Halverson, John. 1976. "Animal Categories and Terms of Abuse." *Man* 11 (December): 4.

Hanser, Richard. 1932. "Freaks" (review). *Buffalo Times*, July.

Haskell, Molly. 1976. "The Night Porno Films Turned Me Off." *New York*, March 29, 56–60.

Hays, Matthew. 2002. "The Friendly Ghost: Gaspar Noé defends *Irréversible*," *Cinemascope* (Cannes edition), 49–50.

Heidegger, Martin. 1977. *The Question Concerning Technology*. Translated by W. Lovitt. New York: Harper and Row.

Hilberg, Raul. 1961. *The Destruction of the European Jews*. New York: Holmes and Meier.

Hogan, David. 1986. *Dark Romance: Sexuality in the Horror Film*. Jefferson, N.C.: McFarland.

Horner, Martin. 1962. "Jivaro Souls." *American Anthropologist* 64: 258–72.

Huizinga, Johan. 1955. *The Waning of the Middle Ages*. London: Harmondsworth, Penguin. Reissued 1974.

Huntingdon, Richard. 1973. "Death and the Social Order: Bara Funeral Customs (Madagascar)." *African Studies* 32, no. 2: 65–84.

Iaccino, James. 1994. *Psychological Reflections on Cinematic Terror: Jungian Archetypes in Horror Films*. Westport, Conn.: Greenwood.

Ives, John. 1998. "Computer Virus Hoaxes: Urban Legends for the Digital Age." *Bad Subjects*, March.

Johnson, Eithne, and Eric Shaeffer. 1993. "Soft Core/Hard Gore: Snuff as a Crisis in Meaning." *Journal of Film and Video* 45, nos. 2–3 (Summer/Fall): 40–59.

Jung, Carl G., 1936. *The Archetypes and the Collective Unconscious*. 2nd ed. London: Routledge. Reprinted 1992.

Kazin, Alfred. 1988. "Awaiting the Crack of Doom," *New York Times Book Review*, May 1.

Kerekes, David, and David Slater. 1993. *Killing for Culture: An Illustrated History of Death Film from Mondo to Snuff*. London: Creation Books.

———. 1996. *Killing for Culture: An Illustrated History of Death Film from Mondo to Snuff*. 2nd ed. London: Creation Books.

Klein, Melanie, et al. 1952. *Developments in Psychoanalysis*. London: Hogarth Press and the Institute for Psychoanalysis.

Koch, Stephen. 1976. "The Texas Chainsaw Massacre" (review). *Harper's*, November, 64.
Krasniewicz, Louise, 1992. "Cinematic Gifts: The Moral and Social Exchange of Bodies in Horror Films." In *Tattoo, Torture, Mutilation, and Adornment: The Denaturalization of the Body in Culture and Text*, edited by Frances E. Mascia- Lees and Patricia Sharpe. Albany: State University of New York Press.
Kristeva, Julia. 1982. *Powers of Horror: An Essay on Abjection*. Translated by Leon S. Roudiez. New York: Columbia University Press.
Kuntzel, Thierry. 1979. "Treatment of Ideology in the Textual Analysis of Film." *Screen* 14, no. 3: 17–25.
Lacan, Jacques. 1970. *Ecrits: A Selection*. Translated by Alan Sheridan. London: Tavistock.
Le Bon, Gustave. 1886. *The Crowd*. New York: Dover, 2002.
Lefèvre, Raymond. 1965. "Freaks" (review). *Image et Son* (April): 227.
Léger, Jean-Marie. 1975. "Ni Fantastique, Ni 'Normale.'" *L'Avant-Scène du Cinéma* (July/September): 160–61.
Lelande, Richard. 1981. "Cannibal Holocaust" (review). *Image et Son*, no. 361 (May): 39–40.
Leonard, John. 1976. "Commentary: Cretin's Delight on Film." *New York Times*, February 27, 21.
Lévi-Strauss, Claude. 1984. "Structure and Form: Reflections of a Work by Vladimir Propp." In *Vladimir Propp, Theory and History of Folklore*, edited by Anatoly Liberman and translated by Ariadna Y. Martin and Richard P. Martin. Minneapolis: University of Minnesota Press.
Lewis, Herschel Gordon. 1988. *Blood Feast*. New York: Epics International.
Lewis, Ioan Myrddin. 1976. *Social Anthropology in Perspective*. London: Penguin.
Loudon, John B. 1977. "On Body Products." In *The Anthropology of the Body*, edited by John Blacking. London: Academic Press.
MacCannell, Daniel. 1990. "Cannibal Tours." *Visual Anthropology Review* 6, no. 2: 14–24.
Magny, Joel. 1990. "Tod Browning Inconnu." *Cahiers du Cinéma* (October): 436–77.
Malinowski, Bronislaw. 1926. *Crime and Custom in Savage Society*. London: Routledge and Kegan Paul.
Mannix, Daniel. 1990. *Freaks: We Who Are Not as Others*. San Francisco: ReSearch Publications.
Mascia-Lees, Frances, and Patricia Sharpe, eds. 1992. *Tattoo, Torture, Mutilation, and Adornment: The Denaturalization of the Body in Culture and Text*. New York: State University of New York Press.
———. 1994. "The Anthropological Unconscious." *American Anthropologist* 96: 661–67.
Maybury-Lewis, David. 1977. "Societies on the Brink." *Harvard Magazine* 6: 264.
McElroy, Damien. 2001. "Beijing Produces Videos Glorifying Terrorist Attacks on 'Arrogant' U.S." *Daily Telegraph* (U.K.), November 4.
Modleski, Tania. 1986. "The Terror of Pleasure: The Contemporary Horror Film and Postmodern Theory." In *Studies in Entertainment*, edited by Tania Modleski. Bloomington: Indiana University Press.

Molyneux, John. 1998. "State of the Art: A Review of the 'Sensation' Exhibition at the Royal Academy of Arts, September–December 1997." *International Socialism*, no. 79 (July): 1–10.
"Morgenthau Finds Film Dismembering Was Indeed a Hoax." 1976. *New York Times*, March 10, 41.
Muensterberger, Warner. 1969. *Man and His Culture: Psychoanalytic Anthropology after "Totem and Taboo."* London: Rapp and Whiting.
Musil, Robert. 1979. *The Man without Qualities*. Translated by Eithne Watkins and Ernst Kaiser. Vol. 2. London: Pan Books.
Neale, Steve. 1981. "Halloween: Suspense, Aggression, and the Look." *Framework* 14: 25–29. Reprinted in *Planks of Reason: Essays on the Horror Film*, edited by Barry Keith Grant. Metuchen, N.J.: Scarecrow Press, 1984.
Newman, Kim. 1989. *Nightmare Movies*. London: Bloomsbury. Reprinted, New York: Harmony Books, 1989.
Nietzsche, Friedrich. 1967. *Ecco Homo*. Translated by Walter Kaufmann and R. J. Hollingdale. New York: Vintage. Reissued, London: Penguin, 1992.
O'Neill, James. 1994. *Terror on Tape*. New York: Billboard.
"An Open Letter to the Movie-Going Public of Southern California." 1976. *AFAA Bulletin*, bonus page.
Panoff, F. 1970. "Food and Faeces: A Melanesian rite." *Man* 5, no. 2: 237–53.
Parfrey, Adam, ed. 1977. *Apocalypse Culture*. 1st edition. Los Angeles: Feral House.
———. 2000. *Apocalypse Culture*. 2nd edition. Los Angeles: Feral House.
Parker, Seymour. 1960. "The Wiitiko Psychosis in the Context of Ojibwa Personality and Culture." *American Anthropologist* 62: 603–23.
Parry, Jonathan, 1982. "Sacrificial Death and the Necrophagus Ascetic." In *Death and the Regeneration of Life*, edited by Maurice Bloch and Jonathan Parry. Cambridge: Cambridge University Press.
Peary, Danny. 1981. *Cult Movies: The Classics, the Sleepers, the Weird, and the Wonderful*. New York: Dell.
———. 1983. *Cult Movies 2*. New York: Dell.
Pinturault, Jacques. 1957. "Freaks." *Ciné 57* (July/August): 20.
Platter, Felix. 1608. *Praxeos . . . seu de cognoscendis*. Vol. 1. Basel: Conrad Waldkirch.
Prince, Stephen. 1988. "Dread, Taboo, and the Thing: Toward a Social History of the Horror Film." *Wide Angle* 10, no. 3: 19–29.
Quandt, James, 2002. "Dix Fois Deux: Notes on Twos and Ten at Cannes," *Cinemascope* (Cannes edition), 46–48.
Rank, Otto, 1952. *The Trauma of Birth*. New York: Robert Brunner.
Rensberger, Boyce. 1981. "Racial Odyssey." *Science Digest* (January/February): 78.
Restak, Richard. 2003. *The New Brain, or, How the Media is Rewiring your Mind*. New York: Rodale Press.
Rieff, Philip. 1966. *The Triumph of the Therapeutic: Uses of Faith after Freud*. Chicago: University of Chicago Press.

Robbins, Todd. 1923. "Spurs." *Munsey's Magazine* 8: 76.
Rodowick, David N. 1984. "The Eyes Within: The Economy of Violence in *The Hills Have Eyes*." In *Planks of Reason: Essays on the Horror Film*, edited by Barry Keith Grant. Metuchen, N.J.: Scarecrow Press.
Roheim, Geza. 1925. *"Fire in the Dragon" and Other Psychoanalytic Essays on Folklore*. Edited by Alan Dundes. Princeton, N.J.: Princeton University Press. Reprinted 1992.
Ross, Jonathan. 1993. *The Incredibly Strange Film Book: An Alternative History of Cinema*. London: Simon and Schuster. Reprinted 1995.
Roy, Jean. 1981. "Cannibal Holocaust" (review). *Cinèma 81*, no. 270 (June): 125–26.
Russo, Mary. 1995. *Female Grotesque: Risk, Excess, and Modernity*. New York: Routledge.
Sabatier, Jean-Marie. 1973. "Freaks." In *Les Classiques du Cinéma Fantastique*, edited by R. G. Ballard. Paris: Editions du Cinéma.
Sáez, Nacuñán. 1992. "Torture: A Discourse on Practice." In *Tattoo, Torture, Mutilation, and Adornment: The Denaturalization of the Body in Culture and Text*, edited by Frances Mascia-Lees and Patricia Sharpe. New York: State University of New York Press.
Sanders, Ed. 1976. *The Family: The Story of Charles Manson's Dune Buggy Attack Battalion*. London: Panther. Reissued, London: Nemesis, 1996.
Savada, Eli. 1973. "The Making of Freaks." *Photon* 23: 25–35.
Schaefer, Eric. 1992. "Of Hygiene and Hollywood: Origins of the Exploitation Film." *Velvet Light Trap* 30: 34–37.
von Schelling, Friedrich W. J. 1848 (1994 reprint). *Zur Geschichte der neveren Philsophie*. London: Cambridge University Press.
Schoell, William. 1985. *Stay Out of the Shower: Twenty-Five Years of Shocker Films Beginning with "Psycho."* New York: Dembner. Reprinted, New York: Robinson, 1988.
Senn, Bryan, and John Johnson. 1992. *Fantastic Cinema Guide*. London: MacFarland.
Sharrett, Christopher. 1984. "The Idea of Apocalypse in *The Texas Chainsaw Massacre*." In *Planks of Reason: Essays on the Horror Film*, edited by Barry Keith Grant. Metuchen, N.J.: Scarecrow Press.
Slade, Joseph W. 1984. "Violence in the Hard-Core Pornographic Film: A Historical Survey." *Journal of Communication* 34, no. 3: 148–63.
"Snuff Biz Goes When Pickets Go." 1976. *Variety*, March 24, 36.
"Snuff Case in St. Paul." 1976. *Variety*, February 25, 22.
"Snuff Film Stirs the Wrath of Feminists." 1976. *New York Post*, February 21, 10.
"Snuff (Sex Murders) Film Now Thought Hoax from Argentina." 1976. *Variety*, December 17, 4.
Sobchack, Vivian. 1987. "Bringing It All Back Home: Family Economy and Generic Exchange." In *American Horrors: Essays on the Modern Horror Film*, edited by Gregory Waller. Urbana: University of Illinois Press.
Sontag, Susan. 1977. *On Photography*. New York: Picador, 2001.
Soren, David. 1977. *The Rise and Fall of the Horror Film: An Art Historical Approach to Fantasy Cinema*. Colombia: Lucas Books.

Stallybrass, Peter, and Allon White. 1986. *The Politics and Poetics of Transgression.* Ithaca, N.Y.: Cornell University Press.
Staples, Amy. 1994. "Mondo Meditations." *American Anthropologist* 96: 667–69.
Starr, Marco. 1984. "J. Hills is Alive: A Defense of 'I Spit on Your Grave.'" In *The Video Nasties: Freedom and Censorship in the Media,* edited by Martin Barker. London: Pluto Press.
Steinbrunner, Chris, and Burt Goldblatt. 1972. *Cinema of the Fantastic.* New York: Saturday Review Press.
Steinem, Gloria. 1977. "Erotica and Pornography: A Clear and Present Difference." *Ms.,* November, 53–78.
Storr, Anthony. 1973. *Jung.* London: Fontana. Reissued 1986.
Strathern, Andrew. 1982. "Witchcraft, Greed, Cannibalism, and Death." In *Death and the Regeneration of Life,* edited by Maurice Bloch and Jonathan Parry. Cambridge: Cambridge University Press.
Sutherland, Anne. 1977. "The Body as Symbol Among the Rom." In *The Anthropology of the Body,* edited by John Blacking. London: Academic Press.
Tannahil, Reay. 1975. *Flesh and Blood: A History of Human Cannibalism.* London: Stein and Day.
Tatar, Marie. 1992. *Off with Their Heads! Fairy Tales and the Culture of Childhood.* Princeton, N.J.: Princeton University Press.
Telotte, J. P. 1984. "Faith and Idolatry in the Horror Film." In *Planks of Reason: Essays on the Horror Film,* edited by Barry Keith Grant. Metuchen, N.J.: Scarecrow Press.
Thomas, Kevin. 1976. "Controversial "Snuff" Opens Run." *Los Angeles Times,* March 19, 22.
Tudor, Andrew. 1989. *Monsters and Mad Scientists: A Cultural History of the Horror Movie.* Oxford: Blackwell.
Turnbull, Colin. 1994. *The Mountain People.* London: Pimlico Press. Reissued, London: Cape.
Turner, Bryan. 1984. *The Body and Society: Explorations in Social Theory.* Oxford: Blackwell.
Twitchell, James. 1989. *Dreadful Pleasures: An Anatomy of Modern Horror.* New York: Oxford University Press.
Uhlmann, Eric, and Jane Swanson. 2004. "Exposure to Violent Video Games Increases Automatic Aggressiveness." *Journal of Adolescence* 27, no. 1.
Urban, Greg. 1988. "Ritual Wailing in Amerindian Brazil." *American Anthropologist* 90: 390–99.
Vale, V., and Andrea Juno, eds. 1986. *RESearch #10: Incredibly Strange Films.* San Francisco: ReSearch Publications.
Victor, Jeffrey S. 1993a. *Satanic Panic: The Creation of a Contemporary Legend.* Chicago: Open Court.
———. 1993b. "The Sociology of Contemporary Legends: A Review of the Use of the Concept by Sociologists." *Contemporary Legend* 3: 63–83.
Virilio, Paul. 2003. *Art and Fear.* Translated by Julie Rose. London: Continuum.

Volosinov, V. N., 1976. *Freudianism: A Marxist Critique*. Translated by I. R. Titunik and edited by Neal Bruss. New York: Academic Press.
Waldron, Robert. 1991. *Oprah!* New York: Warner Books.
Waller, Gregory A., ed. 1987. *American Horrors: Essays on the Modern Horror Film*. Urbana: University of Illinois Press.
Warner, Marina. 1996. *From the Beast to the Blonde: Fairy Tales and Their Tellers*. London: Noonday Press.
Waters, John. 1983. "Whatever Happened to Showmanship?" *American Film* 9 (December): 55–58.
———. 1991. *Shock Value*. New York: Delta.
Watson, James L. 1982. "Of Flesh and Bones: The Management of Death Pollution in Cantonese Society." In *Death and the Regeneration of Life*, edited by Maurice Bloch and Jonathan Parry. Cambridge: Cambridge University Press.
Watts, Richard, Jr. 1932. "Freaks" (review). *New York Herald Tribune*, July 8.
Weldon, Michael. 1983. *The Psychotronic Encyclopedia of Film*. New York: Ballantyne Books.
Will, George. 1976. "Naive Hopes and Real Decadence." *Washington Post*, March 28, C7.
Williams, Linda. 1989. *Hard Core: Power, Pleasure, and the "Frenzy of the Visible."* Berkeley and Los Angeles: University of California Press.
Wojcik, Daniel. 1997. *The End of the World as We Know It: Faith, Fatalism, and Apocalypse in America*, New York: New York University Press.
Wilson, Monica. 1959. *Communal Rituals of the Nyakyusa*. Oxford: Oxford University Press, 1989.
Wood, Robin. 1978. "The Return of the Repressed." *Film Comment* 14: 25–32.
———. 1979. "An Introduction to the American Horror Film." In *American Nightmare: Essays on the Horror Film*, edited by Andrew Britton, et al. Toronto: Festival of Festivals. Reprinted in *Movies and Methods*, vol. 2, edited by Bill Nichols. Berkeley and Los Angeles: University of California Press, 1989.
Worsley, Peter M. 1959. "Cargo Cults." *Scientific American* 42: 236–39.
Zimmer, J. 1981. "Cannibal Holocaust" (review). *Image et Son* (hors serie) 25: 49–50.
Ziolkowski, Fabrice. 1978. "Au Déla de la Dernière Image de Freaks." *Cahiers du Cinéma* 288: 27.
Zipes, Jack. 1955. *Fairy Tales and the Art of Subversion*. Reissued. London: Routledge.

Notes

Introduction

1. In this book, I have deliberately employed terms that in other contexts may be considered offensive, such as "freak," "midget," "half-wit," and so on. These terms are employed as a rhetorical device specifically in order to foreground the vivid and discomforting implications of such language (see Russo 1995, 181).

Chapter 1

1. "Spurs" is hardly alluded to at all in *Freaks* except at the bizarre climax to the wedding feast, when Hercules lifts up the mortified Hans and places him on Cleopatra's shoulders to go "horseyback riding." Cleopatra then cavorts around the dinner table screeching with drunken laughter. She is followed by the dancing Hercules blowing a dissonant melody on a piccolo, borrowed from a dwarf.

2. The repeated emphasis in these warning reviews of the film's unsuitability for children is an unsettling confirmation that its influence had, however unconsciously, been vigorously acknowledged. *Freaks* lights upon the interrelatedness of the lovely and the abysmal in the play it makes upon the word "freaks" and the word "children," notably in Madame Tetralini's defense of her troupe of ungodly charges when they are first exhibited to us. "I am Madame Tetralini. These are my children of the circus," she tells Duval. "When I get the chance, I like to take them into the sunshine and let them play, like children, which is what most of them are—children."

3. Although, as Eli Savada (1973) points out, Watts goes on to note that "in some strange way, the picture is not only exciting, but even occasionally touching."

4. Jean-Claude Biette (1978) noted that Browning himself, to a certain extent, endorsed the opinion that the film was of an injurious character.

5. Note Johnny's mimicked "conducting" of the freaks' eerie chant during the wedding banquet, which might have been intended to support rumors of his musical genius.

6. See also Magny 1990—a much later article that poses many of the same questions.

7. See Russo 1995, chapter 3. Russo also draws attention to the connection between the word "demonstration" and its roots in the word "monster": Literally, the freak is a *demonstrator* of the marvelous power of the divine.

8. The reissued version of *Freaks* was cut dramatically in some countries. It was banned in the U.K. and Australia for nearly forty years, and in New Zealand it was banned until 1976.

9. Adrian (1976) goes on to claim that "the credibility of the picture, so cleverly sustained by Tod Browning because he has made the freaks so normal, is destroyed in the last shot. How, after all, could the freaks put *feathers* into Cleopatra?" (59).

10. Russo (1995) claims that it is hardly surprising "that the violence resulting from the encounter of separate and oppositional bodies would transform the body of the beautiful aerialiste into a baby chick, head and claws mutilated and feathered, hands redesigned prosthetically as claws, and finally exhibited as a freak" (91–92).

11. See also the scene of the wedding banquet, where Roscoe refers tautologously to Koo Coo as "Koo . . . Koo . . . Koo . . . Koo . . . Koo."

12. This idea is suggested by Jean-Claude Biette (1978) in a footnote to his article "Tod Browning et *Freaks*."

13. And yet it could equally be argued that the unity of the circus folk has, at this point, already been broken by a symbolic exchange between Venus and her ex-lover, Hercules:

> *Hercules:* I'm through wasting my time and money on things like you!
> *Venus:* Hah! *Your* time, but *my* money!

14. Biette (1978) points out that "when the storm and violence begin, there is no longer any chance for language to be heard above the tumultuous music, parodying Wagner's patriotic theme from *Tristram and Yseult*, which functions as a warning, but also as an expression of suffering" (26).

15. Benga had filed-down teeth, which were considered evidence of his cannibalistic nature. He was give a bow and some arrows, and encouraged to shoot. He was eventually given pants, a jacket, and shoes. For the whole story of Ota Benga, see Bradford and Bloom 1992.

16. It has been found that the more pigmented the eye, the more sensitive it is to colors at the red end of the spectrum, so in situations lit by reddish light, the northern European can see more than the southern European. Anthropologist Boyce Rensberger (1981) points out that it has been suggested that northern Europeans developed lighter eyes to adapt to the longer twilights of the north and because of their greater reliance on firelight to illuminate caves (78–79).

17. Amy Fisher, age eighteen, began an affair with garage mechanic Joey Buttafuoco in July 1991. Fisher, bent on clearing the way for her life with Joey, rang the Buttafuoco's front doorbell on May 19, 1992, and shot Mrs. Buttafuoco in the head.

18. This notion of the abject as polluted or defiling, incidentally, has nothing to do with dirt and hygiene. Anthropology has often pointed out that, although the discovery of pathogenic organisms is recent, the idea of pollution antedates the idea of pathogenicity and is therefore more likely to have universal application. The fear of the pollutant is the fear of anything likely to confuse or contradict cherished cultural classification. In all cultures, rites of transition treat marginal or ill-defined social states as dangerous. In fact, all margins and the edges of all boundaries that are used in ordering the social experience are treated as dangerous.

NOTES

Chapter 2

1. This interview is cited in Burgess 1984.

2. "Isn't it time for a retrospective? A documentary on his life? Some highfalutin critique in *Cahiers du Cinéma*? ... Forget Ed Wood. Forget George Romero. William Castle was best. William Castle was God," claims Waters (1983).

3. "Even the spectator who remains glued to his seat is nevertheless involved. The effects stopped at nothing" (Garel 1977, 70–71).

4. "I hated them," said Robb White of the series of films he made with Castle. "I mean, they're so dumb! God, there's not a worm in your backbone when you get scared!" (cited in Senn and Johnson 1992, 345).

5. In fact, the idea of the Tingler was fashioned not by Castle but by his screenwriter, Robb White, who very quickly came to be embarrassed by it (see above).

6. David-Neel is referring here to the *tulpa* produced by a Tibetan painter's depiction of a wrathful deity, witnessed by David-Neel but not by the painter himself.

7. "In order to avoid being influenced by the form of lamaist deities, which I saw daily around me in paintings and images, I chose for my experiment a most insignificant character: a monk, short and fat, of an innocent and jolly type," writes David-Neel. Later, she observed that "the features which I had imagined, when building my phantom, gradually underwent a change. The fat, chubby-cheeked fellow grew leaner, his face assumed a vaguely mocking, sly, malignant look. He became more troublesome and bold. In brief, he escaped my control" (221).

Chapter 3

1. Astrid Olsen, a bunny girl who worked at Miami's Playboy Club, was selected for the part because she had a mouth large enough to accommodate a sheep's tongue, cranberries, gelatin, and Lewis's special blood solution. Lewis recalled that the sheep's tongue was purchased in Tampa and became so spoiled that on the day of shooting it had to be soaked in Pine-Sol. Olsen's "tongue" scene is perhaps the most notorious episode in *Blood Feast*—critic James O'Neill points out that "the tongue torn from a girl's mouth looks long enough to have come out of a giraffe!" (68). In an interview with John Waters in his book *Shock Value* (1991), Lewis remembers filming the scene. "We pulled out her tongue and her head lolled to one side and she gagged," he recalls. "It worked out very nicely. That was her part. One take. One take only because it messed up her face. Our one big problem with stage blood was that it would *not* come out of clothing. Axion in its original formation was great, but strangely enough they changed it so it wasn't as good" (206–7).

2. Lewis, a former college professor with a Ph.D. in English and the self-styled "Wizard of Gore," lost most of his capital in the courts when he was arrested for his part in a fraudulent car rental agency, along with a series of other mail-fraud convictions, including a fake abortion referral agency and a phony gas-saving device. The arrest brought his filmmaking career to an abrupt end, and he now heads a mail marketing

service in Fort Lauderdale, Florida. According to John Waters (1991), Lewis's exploitation films are "impossible to defend; thus he automatically becomes one of the greatest directors in film history."

3. Capitalizing on the unexpected underground success of the film, Herschel Gordon Lewis published in 1988 the film's story in novel format, extending it into a grim comedy with sardonic overtones. In *Blood Feast* the novel, all references to cannibalism in the screenplay are deliberately embellished and camped up, usually to comic intent.

4. Actually, worldwide, cannibalism is a far more frequent crime than is generally assumed. Seven notable examples of cannibalism, for example, were recorded in the world's press in 1994. In January of that year, Gretchen Steinfurt was jailed for life in Germany for killing and dismembering her husband, Hermann, then serving him up to her boyfriend, Conrad Krueger, in hamburger soup. On April 8, Yuri Lukin, a doorman at the railway hospital in the Russian town of Satarov, was arrested and jailed for raiding the local hospital refrigerator, stealing the body parts, and selling them as cooked meat at a local market to raise money for drink. Also in April, starving slum dwellers in the city of Olinda in the northeast of Brazil were recorded to have been regularly eating human remains taken from murder victims or hospital waste at the city's main open-air rubbish dump. On April 19, in Kazakhstan, five hungry convicts in a prison killed their cellmate, skinned the body, and cut it into pieces, which they boiled in a kettle and ate. On June 2, in Buenos Aires, a pizza delivery boy, Carlos Sanchez, was murdered and eaten by a group of Satanists in an abandoned factory, and on June 9, a drinking binge in the eastern Siberian town of Artyom turned into a night of cannibalism in which one reveler was cooked and eaten by his "companions."

5. Freud (1913) argued that the Oedipus complex is not simply a product of a monogamous patriarchal society, but is in fact universal, a mythic retelling of the "primal horde" theory. It has been suggested—by Darwin, among others—that primitive human societies consisted of bands of males made up of members—brothers—with equal rights, including rights to the sexual possession of the female members of the family, as may be observed in a number of monkey groups today. Adapting Darwin, Freud contended that the brothers who had once been driven out of the primal horde banded together to kill the patriarchal leader ("the father"); and to atone for their crime, they created, out of a "filial sense of guilt," taboos against murder and incest, thereby laying down the foundations for the social organization and moral restrictions of Western culture today.

In many versions of the primal horde story, including that told by Freud, the brothers' killing of their father is followed by their devouring of the father's body—the totem meal. Consequently, the sacramental killing and communal eating of the totem meal, whose consumption is forbidden on all other occasions, is an important feature of totemic religion. In support of this proposal, Freud cites three examples from anthropologist Robertson Smith (the Aztec and Otawa, both of South America, and the Ainu of Japan) and three from Frazer (the Zuni of California, the aborigines of central Australia, and the Bini of West Africa) of the ritualistic devouring of sacred animals. Anthropologist Warner Muensterberger (1969) points out, however, that this list virtually

NOTES   **199**

exhausts the universe of other possible instances and that there are numerous other examples in which the sacramental meal is entirely absent. In fact, when the total ethnographic record is considered, the sacramental totemic meal is a rare phenomenon (63).

6. A brief selection of slasher films directly influenced by the prototype narrative of *Blood Feast* includes Lewis's own *The Gore-Gore Girls* (1972), John Carpenter's *Halloween* (1978), George A. Romero's zombie epic *Dawn of the Dead* (1978), Sean S. Cunningham's *Friday the 13th* (1980), Rick Rosenthal's *Halloween 2* (1981), Tom de Simone's *Hell Night* (1981), Steve Miner's *Friday the 13th Part 2* (1981) and *Friday the 13th Part 3 in 3D* (1982), Tommy Lee Wallace's *Halloween 3—Season of the Witch* (1983), Joseph Zito's *Friday the 13th Part 4—The Final Chapter* (1984), Wes Craven's *Nightmare in Elm Street* (1984), Danny Steinmann's *Friday the 13th Part 5—A New Beginning* (1985), Jack S. Holder's *Nightmare on Elm Street 2—Freddy's Revenge* (1985), Romero's *Day of the Dead* (1985), Tom McLoughlin's *Friday the 13th Part 6—Jason Lives* (1986), Joseph Rubens's *The Stepfather* (1986), Chuck Russell's *Nightmare on Elm Street 3—Dream Warriors* (1987), Renny Harlin's *Nightmare on Elm Street 4—The Dream Master* (1988), John Carl Buechler's *Friday the 13th Part 8—Jason Takes Manhattan* (1989), Stephen Hopkins's *Nightmare on Elm Street 5—The Dream Child* (1989), Mary Lambert's *Pet Sematary* (1989), Ralph S. Singleton's *Graveyard Shift* (1990), Frank Henenlotter's *Frankenhooker* (1990), Rachel Talalay's *Freddy's Dead—The Final Nightmare* (1991), Wes Craven's *Scream* (1996), *Scream 2* (1997), and *Scream 3* (2000). For some of the other significant slasher (and other) films that deal directly with the theme of cannibalism, see Mikita Brottman, *Meat is Murder! An Illustrated History of Cannibal Culture* (London: Creation Books, 1999, 2002).

7. Of course, Lewis himself—however tongue-in-cheek—likens his narrative talent to that of the classical tragedians.

8. See Carol Clover 1992. Willian Schoell (1985) remarks that after Hitchcock's *Psycho*, "other filmmakers figured that the only thing better than one beautiful woman being gruesomely murdered was a whole series of beautiful women being gruesomely murdered" (35).

Chapter 4

1. On August 8, 1969, Sharon Tate Polanski, her houseguests Jay Sebring, Abigail Folger, and Voytek Frykowski, and the caretaker's friend Steven Parent were murdered by Charles Watson, Patricia Krenwinkel, and Susan Atkins, acting on the orders of their cult leader, Charles Manson. The following night, Leno and Rosemary LaBianca were murdered at their home in Los Feliz, also under Manson's orders.

2. Charles Manson and his followers made their home on the Spahn Ranch, an abandoned movie ranch in the California hills, where they were rumored to have experimented with making home movies of real "live" murders, though no such films have ever come to light.

3. With the exception of Patricia Krenwinkel and Susan Atkins (both in low-security women's open prisons), who have been repeatedly denied parole thanks to the tenacious

efforts of Sharon Tate's younger sister, Patti, who, in memory of their mother, founded the Doris Tate Crime Victims' Bureau.

Chapter 5
1. "Young lady, we'll fetch you some supper," says Father to Sally in a macabre parody of Daddy Bear. When Sally later regains consciousness, still tied to the chair, a plate with a knife and fork beside it have been placed in front of her.
2. According to the Polynesian Melpa, bone comes from the father and flesh from the mother. Similarly, for the Bara tribe of Madagascar, it has been observed that life is a precarious balance between the sterile forces of "order," associated with bone derived from the father, and the chaotic forces of "vitality," associated with flesh derived from the mother. In death, the balance is upset: The corpse is reduced to bone, order, and sterility (see Huntingdon 1973, 65–84). Such traditions may help to explain the connection between the preponderance of bone imagery in *The Texas Chainsaw Massacre* and the sterile, wizened family of men, lacking a female principle.

Chapter 6
1. All translations are the author's own.
2. The name is obviously drawn from the Yanomamo Indians of the Brazil–Venezuela border, a primitive race made famous by the anthropologist Napoleon Chagnon (1992).
3. These scenes comprised the lengthiest amount of footage to be edited out of the video version that did make it to the British market—albeit temporarily—on the film's initial release.
4. As opposed to *endophagy*—the eating of one's own family members or tribal group. See chapter 3 for a more lengthy discussion of the symbolic functions of cannibalism.
5. See chapter 3, note 4, for a brief summary of more recent cases.
6. Later on, incidentally, we learn that the Yanomomo have taken from the documentary team a number of their possessions, as well as their lives. Not only do they appropriate the totemic reels of film, but they are also later discovered to be in possession of Faye's cigarette lighter, wrapped around with dried grass, and Yates's compass, worn by one of the tribeswomen as a decorative fetish.
7. Lelande also condemned the film's hauntingly beautiful soundtrack—composed by Riz Ortolani, who won an Academy Award for his "Theme from *Mondo Cane*"—as "syrupy preparatory music."

Chapter 8
1. See, for example, "No Cannes Prize for Rape Movie," *Mercury* (Australia), 18 July 2002, 8; "Cannes Film Causes 'Irreversible' Controversy," Zap2It.com, 17 July 2002, www.zap2it.com/movies/news/story/0,1259—12456.00.html; Kevin Laforest, "*Irréversible,*" *Montreal Film Journal,* 17 July 2002, front page, www.montrealfilmjournal.com.

NOTES

2. See "Cannes Film Sickens Audiencs (26 May 2002, BBC News), http://news.bbc.co.uk/1/hi/entertainment/film/2008796.stm; see also "Cannes VIPs Walk Out of 'Irreversible' Violence," Yahoo! Movie News, 24 May 2002, http://movies.yahoo.com/news/va/20020524/102229780700.html

3. Press Release, Scoop (New Zealand Society for the Protection of Community Standards), www.scoop.co.nz/mason/stories/PO0303/S00182.htm.

4. *Carne* premiered at the Cannes Critics' Week in 1991, at which Noé was hailed as a brilliant new voice in French cinema, and *Seul Contre Tous* played at Cannes in 1998.

5. Quandt continues: "'But,' the press kit, which almost outdoes the film's own portentousness, reminds us, 'Premonitions do not alter the course of events.' Damn" (46).

6. Many thanks for David Sterritt for his assistance and contributions to this chapter.

Index

animal-doubles, 56, 58, 59, 65, 79
animism, 97, 106, 107
anthropology, 13, 32–40, 42, 44, 48, 57, 59, 77, 92, 96, 105–11, 114, 119, 120, 124, 128, 196, 198
apocalypse, apocalypticism, 94, 107, 112, 168–69, 171, 176
archetypes, 7, 87, 89, 97, 104, 105, 106, 131, 154

B-Movies, 9, 50, 55, 87, 94
Bakhtin, Mikhail, 2, 13, 45, 48, 151–56, 158
Baudrillard, Jean, 149, 172
Benga, Ota, 31, 33, 196
Bettelheim, Bruno, 72, 96, 106, 107, 108, 111
Blood Feast. *See* Herschel Gordon Lewis
Briggs, George William, 105, 110
Browning, Tod, 15–49; *Freaks*, 10, 14, 15–49, 195–96; *The Unholy Three*, 15, 16; *The Unknown*, 15

camp, 67
Cannibal Holocaust. *See* Deodato, Ruggero
Cannes Film Festival, 160, 161, 200, 201
cannibals, cannibalism, 31, 36, 68, 71–78, 96, 100, 110, 111, 113–32, 196, 198, 199, 200
cargo cults, 32, 133
carnival, carnivalesque, carnivalization, 13, 15, 24, 35–36, 42, 45–46, 48, 52, 101, 151–56, 158, 159. *See also* Bakhtin, Mikhail
Carroll, Noel, 6, 11, 62
catharsis, 151, 173
Castle, William, 82, 196; *The Chance of a Lifetime*, 52; *Day of the Locust*, 52; *The House on Haunted Hill*, 55; *Rosemary's Baby*, 52; *Shampoo*, 52; *Step Right Up!*,

53; *The Tingler*, 10, 50–66; *The Whistler*, 52
censorship, 8, 128
Chaney, Lon, 15, 20, 23
clowns, 17, 24, 25, 47, 119, 155, 156, 157
Clover, Carol J., 5–7, 11, 68, 75–78, 88, 89, 158, 199
Conrad, Joseph, 77, 170, 171
cult movies, 2, 4, 70, 89, 91, 113, 134

Dahmer, Jeffrey, 71, 140
David-Neel, Alexandra, 59–61
defecation, 5, 62, 64, 65, 66, 119, 153. *See also* feces, excrement
Deodato, Ruggero, 117, 127, 128, 129, 130, 131; *Cannibal Holocaust*, 10, 113–32
Death Scenes, 9, 10, 85, 91, 136–38, 140–43, 151, 152, 154, 155–57, 177
Death Scenes 2, 138–43, 146, 147
documentary, 19, 20, 21, 27, 37, 40, 113, 114, 115, 117, 118, 120, 133, 134, 135, 143–45, 150, 177
Dostoyevsky, Fyodor, 153, 178
Douglas, Mary, 13, 48, 92, 129, 132
dreams, 158, 164–66
driver's education films, 139
Dunne, J.W., *An Experiment in Time*, 164–67, 168
Dwyer, R. Budd, 141, 142, 146

Ellis, Bill, 86, 87
ethnography, 30–49, 199
Eysenck, Hans, 173
excrement, 10, 64, 105, 154. *See also* defecation, feces
execution, executions, 120, 130, 131, 137, 139, 141, 147, 151, 154

203

exploitation film, 3, 4, 8–9, 13, 67, 68, 79, 84, 89, 91, 115, 179

Faces of Death, 85, 133, 143–49, 151, 152, 154, 156, 157, 177. *See also* Le Cilaire, Conan
fairy tales, 10, 72, 78, 96–112
feces, fecal, 61, 62, 64, 65, 66. See alse excrement, defecation
fetish, fetishism, 5, 93, 126, 177, 200
Fiedler, Leslie, 21, 34, 35, 44
Findlay, Michael and Roberta, 79, 146; *Slaughter*, 79, 80, 81, 82, 86; *Snuff*, 3, 4, 9, 10, 14, 79–95, 146; *The Touch of Her Flesh*, 9. *See also* Shackleton, Allan
folklore, 7, 13, 72, 78, 86, 87, 100, 101, 153, 154, 155
Friday the 13th, 76, 77, 199
Friedman, David F., 9, 67
Freaks. *See* Tod Browning
freaks, freak shows, 14, 15–49
Freud, Sigmund, 6, 11, 12, 33, 44, 47, 66, 71–74, 97, 108, 153, 159, 164, 198; *Totem and Taboo*, 2, "The Uncanny," 11, 12, 13, 72, 97

Girard, René, 13, 74
grotesque, the, 4, 9, 45, 48, 152, 154, 157, 158, 159, 172

Halloween, 76, 199
Hitchcock, Alfred, *Psycho*, 75, 199
Hooper, Tobe, *The Texas Chainsaw Massacre*, 10, 76, 96–112, 174, 200

Internet, the, 172, 173, 175, 176, 177
Irréversible. *See* Noé, Gaspar

Jung, Carl, 73, 96, 103, 104, 105

Kennedy (John F.) assassination, 134, 139
Kennedy (Robert) assassination, 135, 139
Kerekes, David, and David Slater, 80, 84, 85, 86, 91, 117, 130, 142, 147, 148
Killing of America, The, 133–35, 137, 146
Kristeva, Julia, 6, 11, 12, 150

LaVey, Anton, 136, 137, 138, 142, 153, 155–56, 157
laughter, 26, 46–49, 101, 155–57, 159
Le Cilaire, Conan, 143, *Faces of Death*, 143–59
Lewis, Herschel Gordon, 197, 199; *Blood Feast*, 3, 8–9, 10, 67–79, 197, 198, 199; *Color Me Blood Red*, 71; *The Gore-Gore Girls*, 71; *The Gruesome Twosome*, 9, 67; *Two Thousand Maniacs*, 71
libel, 129, 132

magic, 26, 32, 59, 60, 61, 62, 93, 95, 111, 122, 126, 127, 131, 176
Manson, Charles, 85, 86, 87, 89–95, 140, 147, 199. *See also* Tate/LaBianca murders
Meyer, Russ, 9
Mondo Cane, 37, 113, 133, 200
Mondo Cane 2, 147
mondo movies, 10, 37 , 85, 113, 133–59, 143–59
myth, 7, 58, 72, 75, 78, 86, 87, 89, 95, 96, 103, 123, 131, 150

New York Times, 18, 31, 83
Nightmare on Elm Street, 75, 76, 77
nightmares, 14, 61, 66, 98
Noé, Gaspar, 161, 162, 163, 201; *Carne*, 161, 201; *Irréversible*, 11, 160–69, 173; *Seul Contre Tous*, 161, 201

occult, the, 60, 136
Oedipus, Oedipal, 72–74, 78, 96
ostention, 87

pathology, pathologist, 100–101, 143, 196
Percepto, 52–53
phobic, phobia, 128, 171
pornography, 4, 5, 9, 11, 39, 49, 80, 85, 86, 88, 89, 149, 173, 176, 178
Polanski, Roman, 52, 90
postmodern, postmodernism, 33.
Price, Vincent, 53, 55, 62
Production Code, The, 8.
Psycho. *See* Hitchcock, Alfred

INDEX

psychoanalysis, 13, 36, 43, 44, 49, 51, 66, 71–78, 87, 159
psychopaths, 62, 92, 175
psychosis, psychotic 122, 123, 136, 137, 157, 159

Rabelais, Rabelaisian, 2, 45, 46, 151, 152. *See also* Bakhtin, Mikhail.

Schaefer, Eric, 8, 85, 88
September 11 2001 (9/11), 171, 174, 175, 176, 177
serial killers, 62, 92, 135, 146
Shackleton, Allan, 10, 80, 81–85, 87, 93, 94, 146; *Snuff*, 3, 4, 9, 10, 14, 79–95, 146. *See also* Findlay, Michael and Roberta
slasher movies, 5–7, 10, 11, 12, 73, 75, 76, 78, 88, 89, 150
Snuff. *See* Findlay, Michael and Roberta
"snuff" movies, 10, 81–95, 117, 130, 175
special effects, 9, 174

Tate-LaBianca murders, 10, 81, 86, 87, 90, 91, 94, 95, 140, 142, 199
Texas Chainsaw Massacre. *See* Tobe Hooper
Tingler, The. *See* William Castle
tulpa, 59–61, 197

urban legends, urban myth, 14, 86, 87

Variety, 52, 70, 74, 84, 114, 127, 128
Victor, Jeffrey, 86, 87
vomit, 10, 105, 115, 119, 124
voyeurism, voyeur, 4, 22, 24, 38, 39, 40, 42, 49, 114, 124, 127, 128, 129, 130, 131, 136, 137, 138, 151, 175, 176

Waters, John, 50, 51, 52, 53, 196, 197, 198
witchcraft, 122
Wood, Robin, 5, 6–7, 13, 50, 110, 111, 112
World Trade Center Bombing, The, 170, 171, 174, 177. *See also* September 11

www.ingramcontent.com/pod-product-compliance
Lightning Source LLC
Chambersburg PA
CBHW030111010526
44116CB00005B/198